Microsoft®
PowerPoint® 2010

Step by Step

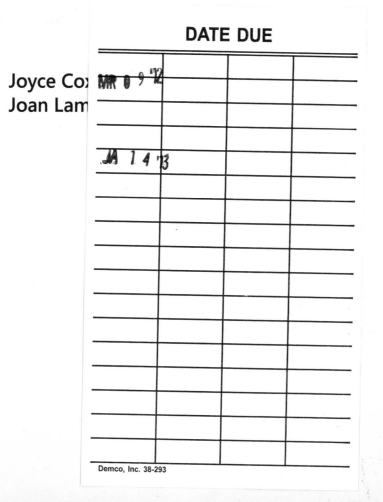
Joyce Cox
Joan Lambert

PUBLISHED BY
Microsoft Press
A Division of Microsoft Corporation
One Microsoft Way
Redmond, Washington 98052-6399

Library of Congress Control Number: 2010928520

Printed and bound in the United States of America.

2 3 4 5 6 7 8 9 10 11 QGT 5 4 3 2 1 0

A CIP catalogue record for this book is available from the British Library.

Microsoft Press books are available through booksellers and distributors worldwide. For further information about international editions, contact your local Microsoft Corporation office or contact Microsoft Press International directly at fax (425) 936-7329. Visit our Web site at www.microsoft.com/mspress. Send comments to mspinput@ microsoft.com.

Native plant photographs courtesy of Rugged Country Plants, Milton-Freewater, OR.

Acquisitions Editor: Juliana Aldous
Developmental Editor: Devon Musgrave
Project Editor: Valerie Woolley
Editorial Production: Online Training Solutions, Inc.
Cover: Girvin

Body Part No. X16-95581

Contents

Part 1   Basic Presentations

What do you think of this book? We want to hear from you!

Microsoft is interested in hearing your feedback so we can continually improve our books and learning resources for you. To participate in a brief online survey, please visit:

microsoft.com/learning/booksurvey

Part 2 Presentation Enhancements

What do you think of this book? We want to hear from you!

Microsoft is interested in hearing your feedback so we can continually improve our books and learning resources for you. To participate in a brief online survey, please visit:

microsoft.com/learning/booksurvey

Introducing Microsoft PowerPoint 2010

Microsoft PowerPoint 2010 is a full-featured presentation program that helps you quickly and efficiently develop dynamic, professional-looking presentations and then deliver them to an audience. You can use PowerPoint to:

- Introduce an idea, proposal, organization, product, or process with professionally designed, high-impact slides.
- Use themes, galleries of styles, and formatting options to achieve the right combination of colors, fonts, and effects.
- Bolster your arguments by easily adding pictures, shapes, and fancy display text.
- Convey numeric data in easy-to-grasp ways with styled tables or visually compelling charts.
- Use the SmartArt Graphics tool to create sophisticated diagrams that reflect processes, hierarchies, and other relationships.
- Create custom themes, designs, and layouts so that your presentations have a unique look and feel.
- Collaborate with colleagues, giving and receiving feedback to ensure the best possible presentation.

PowerPoint 2010 builds on previous versions to provide powerful tools for all your presentation needs. This introduction provides an overview of new features that we explore throughout the book.

New Features

If you're upgrading to PowerPoint 2010 from a previous version, you're probably most interested in the differences between the old and new versions and how they will affect you, as well as how to find out about them in the quickest possible way. The following sections list new features you will want to be aware of, depending on the version of PowerPoint you are upgrading from.

If You Are Upgrading from PowerPoint 2007

If you have been using PowerPoint 2007, you might be wondering how Microsoft could have improved on what seemed like a pretty comprehensive set of features and tools. The list of new features includes the following:

- **The Backstage view** Finally, all the tools you need to work with your files, as opposed to their content, really are accessible from one location. You display the Backstage view by clicking the File tab, which replaces the Microsoft Office Button at the left end of the ribbon.

- **Customizable ribbon** The logical next step in the evolution of the command center introduced with PowerPoint 2007: Create your own tabs and groups to suit the way you work.

- **A window for each presentation** You no longer display all presentations in the same window, so you can arrange open presentations for easy comparison or work on different presentations at the same time.

- **Reading view** This new way to preview presentations makes it easy to quickly check the effect of one or two changes.

- **Presentation videos** Now turning a presentation into a Windows Media Video is a simple matter of saving in that format.

- **Paste preview** No more trial and error when moving items to new locations. Preview what an item will look like in each of the available formats, and then pick the one you want.

- **Animation Painter** If you spend time developing a complex animation for one object, you can now copy the animation settings to another object with a few mouse clicks.

- **New themes and transitions** Adding pizzazz to your presentations is just a matter of applying a professional-looking theme or a snazzy dynamic-content transition.

- **Graphics editing** Found the perfect picture, but its colors or style aren't quite right for your presentation? Now after inserting a picture, you can edit it in new ways. In addition to changing color, brightness, and contrast, you can remove the background and, most exciting of all, apply artistic effects that make it appear like a watercolor, pencil drawing, or pastel sketch.

- **Improved cropping** Not only can you drag crop handles to manually crop a picture but you can also apply a built-in cropping ratio and then move the cropping "window" around over the picture until you get precisely the part you want.

- **Text effects** WordArt has had a makeover. You can still use WordArt to create distinctive headlines, but now you can use its effects on any selected text.

- **Screenshots** You no longer need to go outside of PowerPoint when you want to insert a screenshot into a slide. This capability is now built into PowerPoint.

- **Improved SmartArt Graphics tool** A whole new category has been added to SmartArt so that you can include pictures as well as text in your diagrams.

- **Video tools** Found a perfect video, but it is too long to include in a presentation? Now you can insert the video and then use the video editing tools built into PowerPoint to trim and format it. You can also insert a link to a video on a Web site into a slide.

- **Version merging** You can merge two versions of the same presentation and accept or reject changes.

- **Team collaboration** Team members can now work simultaneously on a presentation stored on a Microsoft SharePoint 2010 server or in Windows Live SkyDrive.

- **Broadcasting** You can review a presentation with colleagues via the Web by working through a free broadcasting service. Your colleagues can view the presentation in their Web browsers and give feedback via a conference call.

- **Language support** If you need to conduct business internationally across language lines, you can easily tailor the language of your working environment. You can also use new translation tools to collaborate with team members in other countries.

- **Unsaved file recovery** How many times have you responded No without thinking to the "save changes" message when closing files, only to find that you have discarded work you wanted to keep? PowerPoint now preserves your unsaved files for a period of time, allowing you to recover them if you need them.

If You Are Upgrading from PowerPoint 2003

In addition to the features listed in the previous section, if you're upgrading from PowerPoint 2003, you'll want to take note of the new features that were introduced in PowerPoint 2007. The 2007 upgrade provided a more efficient working environment and included a long list of new and improved features, including the following:

● **The Microsoft Office Fluent Ribbon** No more hunting through menus, submenus, and dialog boxes. This new interface organizes all the commands most people use most often, making them quickly accessible from tabs at the top of the program window.

● **Live Preview** See the effect of a style, theme, or other option before you apply it.

● **Custom layouts** Easily create your own layouts with placeholders for specific objects, and then save them for use in other presentations.

● **SmartArt Graphics tool** Use this awesome new diagramming tool to create sophisticated diagrams with 3-D shapes, transparency, drop shadows, and other effects.

● **Improved charting** Enter data in a linked Microsoft Excel worksheet and watch as your data is instantly plotted in the chart type of your choosing.

● **Slide libraries** Share slide content with team members in a special SharePoint library for presentations and slides.

● **Presentation cleanup** Have PowerPoint check for and remove comments, hidden text, and personal information stored as properties before you declare a presentation final.

● **New file format** The new Microsoft Office Open XML Formats reduce file size and help avoid loss of data.

Let's Get Started!

We've been working with PowerPoint since its debut, and each version has offered something that made daily presentation creation a little easier. Microsoft PowerPoint 2010 is no exception, and we look forward to showing you around.

Modifying the Display of the Ribbon

The goal of the Microsoft Office 2010 working environment is to make working with Office files—including Microsoft Word documents, Excel workbooks, PowerPoint presentations, Outlook e-mail messages, and Access databases—as intuitive as possible. You work with an Office file and its contents by giving commands to the program in which the document is open. All Office 2010 programs organize commands on a horizontal bar called the *ribbon*, which appears across the top of each program window whether or not there is an active document.

A typical program window ribbon.

Commands are organized on task-specific tabs of the ribbon, and in feature-specific groups on each tab. Commands generally take the form of buttons and lists. Some appear in galleries. Some groups have related dialog boxes or task panes that contain additional commands.

Throughout this book, we discuss the commands and ribbon elements associated with the program feature being discussed. In this topic, we discuss the general appearance of the ribbon, things that affect its appearance, and ways of locating commands that aren't visible on compact views of the ribbon.

See Also For detailed information about the ribbon in Microsoft PowerPoint, see "Working in the User Interface" in Chapter 1, "Explore PowerPoint 2010."

Tip Some older commands no longer appear on the ribbon, but are still available in the program. You can make these commands available by adding them to the Quick Access Toolbar. For more information, see "Customizing the Quick Access Toolbar" in Chapter 15, "Customize PowerPoint."

Dynamic Ribbon Elements

The ribbon is dynamic, meaning that the appearance of commands on the ribbon changes as the width of the ribbon changes. A command might be displayed on the ribbon in the form of a large button, a small button, a small labeled button, or a list entry. As the width of the ribbon decreases, the size, shape, and presence of buttons on the ribbon adapt to the available space.

For example, when sufficient horizontal space is available, the buttons on the Review tab of the Word program window are spread out and you're able to see more of the commands available in each group.

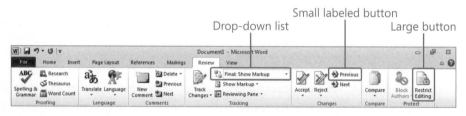

The Review tab of the Word program window at 1024 pixels wide.

If you decrease the width of the ribbon, small button labels disappear and entire groups of buttons hide under one button that represents the group. Click the group button to display a list of the commands available in that group.

The Review tab of the Word program window at 675 pixels wide.

When the window becomes too narrow to display all the groups, a scroll arrow appears at its right end. Click the scroll arrow to display hidden groups.

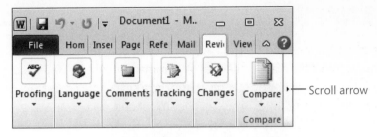

Scroll arrow

The Review tab of the Word program window at 340 pixels wide.

Changing the Width of the Ribbon

The width of the ribbon is dependent on the horizontal space available to it, which depends on these three factors:

● The width of the program window Maximizing the program window provides the most space for ribbon elements. You can resize the program window by clicking the button in its upper-right corner or by dragging the border of a non-maximized window.

Tip On a computer running Windows 7, you can maximize the program window by dragging its title bar to the top of the screen.

● Your screen resolution Screen resolution is the size of your screen display expressed as pixels wide × pixels high. The greater the screen resolution, the greater the amount of information that will fit on one screen. Your screen resolution options are dependent on your monitor. At the time of writing, possible screen resolutions range from 800 × 600 to 2048 × 1152. In the case of the ribbon, the greater the number of pixels wide (the first number), the greater the number of buttons that can be shown on the ribbon, and the larger those buttons can be.

On a computer running Windows 7, you can change your screen resolution from the Screen Resolution window of Control Panel.

You set the resolution by dragging the pointer on the slider.

● **The density of your screen display** You might not be aware that you can change the magnification of everything that appears on your screen by changing the screen magnification setting in Windows. Setting your screen magnification to 125% makes text and user interface elements larger on screen. This increases the legibility of information, but means that less fits onto each screen.

On a computer running Windows 7, you can change the screen magnification from the Display window of Control Panel.

You can choose one of the standard display magnification options, or create another by setting a custom text size.

The screen magnification is directly related to the density of the text elements on screen, which is expressed in dots per inch (dpi) or points per inch (ppi). (The terms are interchangeable, and in fact are both used in the Windows dialog box in which you change the setting.) The greater the dpi, the larger the text and user interface elements appear on screen. By default, Windows displays text and screen elements at 96 dpi. Choosing the Medium - 125% display setting changes the dpi of text and screen elements to 120 dpi. You can choose a custom setting of up to 500% magnification, or 480 dpi, in the Custom DPI Setting dialog box.

You can choose a magnification of up to 200% from the lists, or choose a greater magnification by dragging across the ruler from left to right.

See Also For more information about display settings, refer to *Windows 7 Step by Step* (Microsoft Press, 2009), *Windows Vista Step by Step* (Microsoft Press, 2006), or *Windows XP Step by Step* (Microsoft Press, 2002) by Joan Lambert Preppernau and Joyce Cox.

Adapting Exercise Steps

The screen images shown in the exercises in this book were captured at a screen resolution of 1024 x 768, at 100% magnification, and the default text size (96 dpi). If any of your settings are different, the ribbon on your screen might not look the same as the one shown in the book. For example, you might see more or fewer buttons in each of the groups, the buttons you see might be represented by larger or smaller icons than those shown, or the group might be represented by a button that you click to display the group's commands.

When we instruct you to give a command from the ribbon in an exercise, we do it in this format:

● On the **Insert** tab, in the **Illustrations** group, click the **Chart** button.

If the command is in a list, we give the instruction in this format:

● On the **Page Layout** tab, in the **Page Setup** group, click the **Breaks** button and then, in the list, click **Page**.

The first time we instruct you to click a specific button in each exercise, we display an image of the button in the page margin to the left of the exercise step.

If differences between your display settings and ours cause a button on your screen to look different from the one shown in the book, you can easily adapt the steps to locate the command. First, click the specified tab. Then locate the specified group. If a group has been collapsed into a group list or group button, click the list or button to display the group's commands. Finally, look for a button that features the same icon in a larger or smaller size than that shown in the book. If necessary, point to buttons in the group to display their names in ScreenTips.

If you prefer not to have to adapt the steps, set up your screen to match ours while you read and work through the exercises in the book.

Features and Conventions
of This Book

This book has been designed to lead you step by step through all the tasks you're most likely to want to perform in Microsoft PowerPoint 2010. If you start at the beginning and work your way through all the exercises, you will gain enough proficiency to be able to create and work with most types of PowerPoint presentations. However, each topic is self contained. If you have worked with a previous version of PowerPoint, or if you completed all the exercises and later need help remembering how to perform a procedure, the following features of this book will help you locate specific information:

- **Detailed table of contents** Search the listing of the topics and sidebars within each chapter.

- **Chapter thumb tabs** Easily locate the beginning of the chapter you want.

- **Topic-specific running heads** Within a chapter, quickly locate the topic you want by looking at the running heads at the top of odd-numbered pages.

- **Glossary** Look up the meaning of a word or the definition of a concept.

- **Keyboard Shortcuts** If you prefer to work from the keyboard rather than with a mouse, find all the shortcuts in one place.

- **Detailed index** Look up specific tasks and features in the index, which has been carefully crafted with the reader in mind.

You can save time when reading this book by understanding how the *Step by Step* series shows exercise instructions, keys to press, buttons to click, and other information.

Convention	Meaning
SET UP	This paragraph preceding a step-by-step exercise indicates the practice files that you will use when working through the exercise. It also indicates any requirements you should attend to or actions you should take before beginning the exercise.
CLEAN UP	This paragraph following a step-by-step exercise provides instructions for saving and closing open files or programs before moving on to another topic. It also suggests ways to reverse any changes you made to your computer while working through the exercise.
1 2	Blue numbered steps guide you through hands-on exercises in each topic.
1 2	Black numbered steps guide you through procedures in sidebars and expository text.
See Also	This paragraph directs you to more information about a topic in this book or elsewhere.
Troubleshooting	This paragraph alerts you to a common problem and provides guidance for fixing it.
Tip	This paragraph provides a helpful hint or shortcut that makes working through a task easier.
Important	This paragraph points out information that you need to know to complete a procedure.
Keyboard Shortcut	This paragraph provides information about an available keyboard shortcut for the preceding task.
Ctrl+B	A plus sign (+) between two keys means that you must press those keys at the same time. For example, "Press Ctrl+B" means that you should hold down the Ctrl key while you press the B key.
	Pictures of buttons appear in the margin the first time the button is used in a chapter.
Black bold	In exercises that begin with SET UP information, the names of program elements, such as buttons, commands, windows, and dialog boxes, as well as files, folders, or text that you interact with in the steps, are shown in black, bold type.
Blue bold	In exercises that begin with SET UP information, text that you should type is shown in blue bold type.

Using the Practice Files

Before you can complete the exercises in this book, you need to copy the book's practice files to your computer. These practice files, and other information, can be downloaded from the book's detail page, located at:

go.microsoft.com/fwlink/?LinkId=192149

Display the detail page in your Web browser and follow the instructions for downloading the files.

Important The Microsoft PowerPoint 2010 program is not available from this Web site. You should purchase and install that program before using this book.

The following table lists the practice files for this book.

Chapter	File
Chapter 1: Explore PowerPoint 2010	BuyingTrip_start.pptx
	DesigningColor_start.pptx
	MayMeeting_start.pptx
	SalesMeetingMay_start.pptx
Chapter 2: Work with Slides	Projects.pptx
	ServiceA_start.pptx
	ServiceB_start.pptx
	ServiceC_start.pptx
	ServiceD_start.pptx
	ServiceOrientation.docx
Chapter 3: Work with Slide Text	BuyingTripsB_start.pptx
	BuyingTripsC_start.pptx
	CommunityServiceA_start.pptx
	CommunityServiceB_start.pptx
	CommunityServiceC_start.pptx
Chapter 4: Format Slides	BusinessTravelA_start.pptx
	BusinessTravelB_start.pptx
	ColorDesign_start.pptx
	CompanyMeetingA_start.pptx
	CompanyMeetingB_start.pptx
	Landscaping_start.pptx

Chapter	File
Chapter 5: Add Simple Visual Enhancements	Agastache.jpg
	JournalingA_start.pptx
	JournalingB_start.pptx
	Penstemon.jpg
	WaterConsumption.xlsx
	WaterSavingA_start.pptx
	WaterSavingB_start.pptx
	WaterSavingC_start.pptx
Chapter 6: Review and Deliver Presentations	Harmony_start.pptx
	Meeting_start.pptx
	SavingWater_start.pptx
	ServiceOrientationA_start.pptx
	ServiceOrientationB_start.pptx
	YinYang.png
Chapter 7: Add Tables	FinancialMeeting_start.pptx
	NewEquipment.xlsx
	Temperature_start.pptx
	TemperatureFormatted_start.pptx
Chapter 8: Fine-Tune Visual Elements	GardenResidents_start.pptx
	LandscapingChart_start.pptx
	NativePlant1.jpg through NativePlant8.jpg
	PhotoAlbumTitleSlide.pptx
	ReorganizationMeeting_start.pptx
Chapter 9: Add Other Enhancements	DesertPlants_start.pptx
	MeetingAction_start.pptx
	Organization_start.pptx
	OrganizationLinks_start.pptx
	Procedures.docx
	TemperatureCelsius_start.pptx
Chapter 10: Add Animation	NaturalGardeningA_start.pptx
	NaturalGardeningB_start.pptx

Chapter	File
Chapter 11: Add Sound and Movies	AGKCottage_start.pptx Amanda.wma Bird.jpg Butterfly.wmv HealthyEcosystemsA_start.pptx HealthyEcosystemsB_start.pptx Wildlife.wmv
Chapter 12: Share and Review Presentations	CottageShow_start.pptx HarmonyReview_start.pptx MeetingCompareA_start.pptx MeetingCompareB_start.pptx MeetingThemeA_start.pptx MeetingThemeB.pptx MeetingThemeC.pptx ServiceProjects_start.pptx WaterUse_start.pptx
Chapter 13: Create Custom Presentation Elements	NativePlant1.jpg through NativePlant3.jpg NaturalLayout_start.pptx NaturalMaster_start.pptx NaturalTemplate_start.pptx
Chapter 14: Prepare for Delivery	CottageVideo_start.pptx JournalingTimings_start.pptx OrganizationCD_start.pptx Procedures.docx ServiceShows_start.pptx
Chapter 15: Customize PowerPoint	BuyersSeminar_start.pptx ColorNew_start.pptx

Getting Help

Every effort has been made to ensure the accuracy of this book. If you do run into problems, please contact the sources listed in the following sections.

Getting Help with This Book

If your question or issue concerns the content of this book or its practice files, please first consult the book's errata page, which can be accessed at:

go.microsoft.com/fwlink/?LinkID=192149

This page provides information about known errors and corrections to the book. If you do not find your answer on the errata page, send your question or comment to Microsoft Press Technical Support at:

mspinput@microsoft.com

Getting Help with PowerPoint 2010

If your question is about Microsoft PowerPoint 2010, and not about the content of this book, your first recourse is the PowerPoint Help system. This system is a combination of tools and files stored on your computer when you installed PowerPoint and, if your computer is connected to the Internet, information available from Office.com. You can find general or specific Help information in the following ways:

- To find out about an item on the screen, you can display a ScreenTip. For example, to display a ScreenTip for a button, point to the button without clicking it. The ScreenTip gives the button's name, the associated keyboard shortcut if there is one, and unless you specify otherwise, a description of what the button does when you click it.

- In the PowerPoint program window, you can click the Microsoft PowerPoint Help button (a question mark in a blue circle) at the right end of the ribbon to display the PowerPoint Help window.

- After opening a dialog box, you can click the Help button (also a question mark) at the right end of the dialog box title bar to display the PowerPoint Help window. Sometimes, topics related to the functions of that dialog box are already identified in the window.

To practice getting help, you can work through the following exercise.

 SET UP You don't need any practice files to complete this exercise. Start PowerPoint, and then follow the steps.

1. At the right end of the ribbon, click the **Microsoft PowerPoint Help** button.

    The PowerPoint Help window opens.

Your Help window might look different from this one because the material on the Office.com Web site is constantly being updated.

Tip You can maximize the window or adjust its size by dragging the handle in the lower-right corner. You can change the size of the font by clicking the Change Font Size button on the toolbar.

2. Below the bulleted list under **Browse PowerPoint 2010 support**, click **see all**.

    The window changes to display a list of help topics.

3. In the list of topics, click **Activating PowerPoint**.

    PowerPoint Help displays a list of topics related to activating Microsoft Office programs. You can click any topic to display the corresponding information.

4. On the toolbar, click the **Show Table of Contents** button, and then scroll down the pane that appears on the left.

    Like the table of contents in a book, the Help table of contents is organized in sections. If you're connected to the Internet, PowerPoint displays sections, topics, and training available from the Office Online Web site as well as those stored on your computer.

Clicking any section (represented by a book icon) displays that section's topics (represented by help icons).

5. In the **Table of Contents** pane, click a few sections and topics. Then click the **Back** and **Forward** buttons to move among the topics you have already viewed.

6. At the right end of the **Table of Contents** title bar, click the **Close** button.

7. At the top of the **PowerPoint Help** window, click the **Search** box, type saving, and then press the Enter key.

The PowerPoint Help window displays topics related to the word you typed.

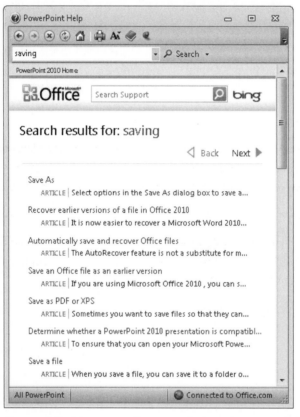

Next and Back buttons appear to make it easier to search for the topic you want.

Tip If you enter a term in the Search box and then click the adjacent Search arrow, you specify the type of help you are looking for or where you want to look for it.

8. In the results list, click the **Recover earlier versions of a file in Office 2010** topic.

   The selected topic appears in the PowerPoint Help window.

9. Below the title at the top of the topic, click **Show All**.

   PowerPoint displays any hidden auxiliary information available in the topic and changes the Show All button to Hide All. You can jump to related information by clicking hyperlinks identified by blue text.

   Tip You can click the Print button on the toolbar to print a topic. Only the displayed information is printed.

 CLEAN UP Click the Close button in the upper-right corner of the PowerPoint Help window.

More Information

If your question is about Microsoft PowerPoint 2010 or another Microsoft software product and you cannot find the answer in the product's Help system, please search the appropriate product solution center or the Microsoft Knowledge Base at:

support.microsoft.com

In the United States, Microsoft software product support issues not covered by the Microsoft Knowledge Base are addressed by Microsoft Product Support Services. Location-specific software support options are available from:

support.microsoft.com/gp/selfoverview/

Part 1
Basic Presentations

Chapter at a Glance

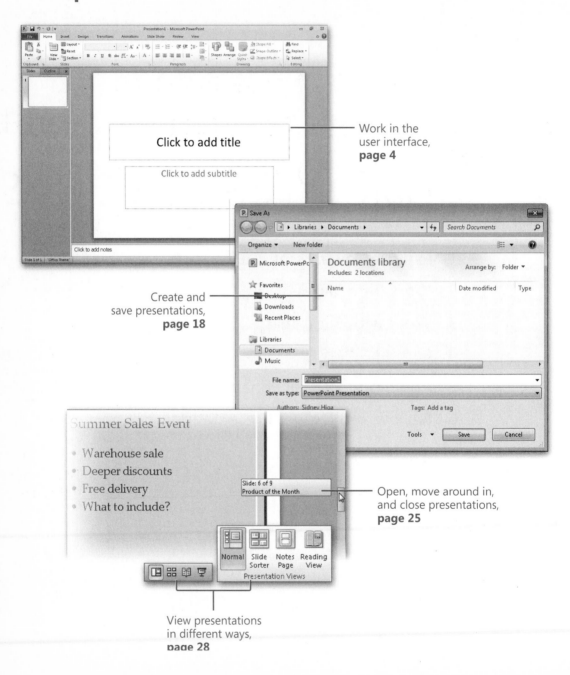

Work in the user interface, **page 4**

Create and save presentations, **page 18**

Open, move around in, and close presentations, **page 25**

View presentations in different ways, **page 28**

1 Explore PowerPoint 2010

In this chapter, you will learn how to

✔ Work in the user interface.

✔ Create and save presentations.

✔ Open, move around in, and close presentations.

✔ View presentations in different ways.

Using Microsoft PowerPoint 2010 is the easiest way to efficiently create effective presentations. Need to convince management to invest in that new piece of equipment? Need to present the new annual budget to the Board of Directors? Need to give a report about a recent research study? PowerPoint can help you get the job done in a professional, visually appealing way.

The PowerPoint 2010 working environment, called the *user interface*, makes sophisticated presentation features accessible. As a result, even novice users will be able to work productively with PowerPoint after only a brief introduction.

In this chapter, you'll first familiarize yourself with the features of the PowerPoint working environment, including the Backstage view, tabs and groups, galleries, and Live Preview. Then after creating and saving several new presentations, you'll open an existing PowerPoint presentation, learn ways to move around in it, and close it. Finally, you'll explore various ways of viewing slides so that you know which view to use and how to tailor the program window for a specific task.

> **Practice Files** Before you can complete the exercises in this chapter, you need to copy the book's practice files to your computer. The practice files you'll use to complete the exercises in this chapter are in the Chapter01 practice file folder. A complete list of practice files is provided in "Using the Practice Files" at the beginning of this book.

Working in the User Interface

As with all Microsoft Office 2010 programs, the most common way to start PowerPoint is from the Start menu displayed when you click the Start button at the left end of the Windows Taskbar. When you start PowerPoint without opening a specific presentation, the program window appears, displaying a new blank presentation.

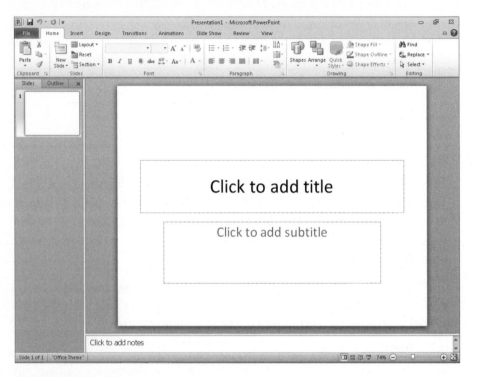

The PowerPoint 2010 program window.

The program window contains the following elements:

● The title bar displays the name of the active presentation. At the left end of the title bar is the PowerPoint icon, which you click to display commands to move, size, and close the program window. At the right end of the title bar are three buttons that control the window. You can temporarily hide the program window by clicking the Minimize button, adjust the size of the window by clicking the Restore Down/ Maximize button, and close the active presentation or exit PowerPoint by clicking the Close button.

These three buttons serve the same function in all Windows programs.

Tip Windows 7 introduced many fun and efficient new window-management techniques. For information about ways to work with the PowerPoint program window on a Windows 7 computer, refer to *Windows 7 Step by Step* by Joan Lambert Preppernau and Joyce Cox (Microsoft Press, 2009).

● By default, the Quick Access Toolbar appears to the right of the PowerPoint icon at the left end of the title bar, and displays the Save, Undo, and Redo buttons. You can change the location of the Quick Access Toolbar and customize it to include any command that you use frequently.

![The default buttons on the Quick Access Toolbar.]

The default buttons on the Quick Access Toolbar.

Tip If you create and work with complicated presentations, you might achieve greater efficiency if you add all the commands you use frequently to the Quick Access Toolbar and display it below the ribbon, directly above the workspace. For information, see "Customizing the Quick Access Toolbar" in Chapter 15, "Customize PowerPoint."

● Below the title bar is the ribbon. All the commands for working with your PowerPoint presentation content are available from this central location so that you can work efficiently with the program.

The ribbon.

Troubleshooting The appearance of buttons and groups on the ribbon changes depending on the width of the program window. For information about changing the appearance of the ribbon to match our screen images, see "Modifying the Display of the Ribbon" at the beginning of this book.

● Across the top of the ribbon is a set of tabs. Clicking a tab displays an associated set of commands.

● Commands related to managing PowerPoint and PowerPoint presentations (rather than slide content) are gathered together in the Backstage view, which you display by clicking the colored File tab located at the left end of the ribbon. (The File tab and Backstage view replace the Microsoft Office Button and Office menu found in Microsoft Office PowerPoint 2007.) Commands available in the Backstage view are organized on pages, which you display by clicking the buttons and page tabs located in the left pane.

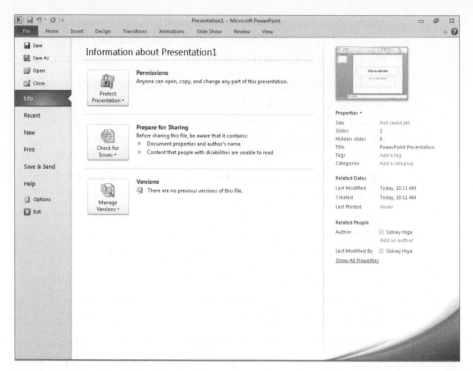

Clicking the File tab displays the Backstage view, where you can manage files and customize the program.

● Commands related to working with slide content are represented as buttons on the remaining tabs of the ribbon. The Home tab is active by default.

Tip Don't be alarmed if your ribbon has tabs not shown in our screens. You might have installed programs that add their own tabs to the PowerPoint ribbon.

● On each tab, buttons are organized into named groups.

● If a button label isn't visible, you can display the command, a description of its function, and its keyboard shortcut (if it has one) in a ScreenTip by pointing to the button.

See Also To see a complete list of keyboard shortcuts, see "Keyboard Shortcuts" at the end of this book.

Tip You can control the display of ScreenTips and of feature descriptions in ScreenTips. Display the Backstage view, click Options to open the PowerPoint Options dialog box, and change settings in the User Interface Options area of the General page. You can also change the language of ScreenTip content on the Language page and control the display of keyboard shortcuts in ScreenTips in the Display area of the Advanced page. For more information, see "Changing Default Program Options" in Chapter 15, "Customize PowerPoint."

- Related but less common commands are not represented as buttons in a group. Instead, they're available in a dialog box or task pane, which you display by clicking the dialog box launcher located in the lower-right corner of the group.

- Some buttons include an integrated or separate arrow. To determine whether a button and arrow are integrated, point to the button or arrow to display its border. If a button and its arrow are integrated within one border, clicking the button will display options for refining the action of the button. If the button and arrow have separate borders, clicking the button will carry out its current default action. You can change the default action of the button by clicking the arrow and then clicking the action you want.

The arrow of the Arrange button is integrated, and the arrow of the New Slide button is separate.

- To the right of the ribbon tab names, below the Minimize/Maximize/Close buttons, is the Minimize The Ribbon button. Clicking this button hides the ribbon commands but leaves the tab names visible. You can then click any tab name to temporarily display its commands. Clicking anywhere other than the ribbon hides the commands again. When the full ribbon is temporarily visible, you can click the button at its right end, shaped like a pushpin, to make the display permanent. When the full ribbon is hidden, you can click the Expand The Ribbon button to redisplay it.

   Keyboard Shortcut Press Ctrl+F1 to minimize or expand the ribbon.

- Clicking the PowerPoint Help button at the right end of the ribbon displays the PowerPoint Help window in which you can use standard techniques to find information.

   Keyboard Shortcut Press F1 to display the PowerPoint Help window.

   See Also For information about the PowerPoint Help system, see "Getting Help" at the beginning of this book.

- Across the bottom of the program window, the status bar displays information about the current presentation and provides access to certain program functions. You can control the contents of the status bar by right-clicking it to display the Customize Status Bar menu, on which you can click any item to display or hide it.

Customize Status Bar		
✓	<u>V</u>iew Indicator	Slide 1 of 1
✓	<u>T</u>heme	"Office Theme"
✓	Number of <u>A</u>uthors Editing	
✓	<u>S</u>pell Check	
✓	<u>L</u>anguage	
✓	Si<u>g</u>natures	Off
✓	<u>I</u>nformation Management Policy	Off
✓	<u>P</u>ermissions	Off
✓	<u>U</u>pload Status	
✓	Document <u>U</u>pdates Available	No
✓	<u>V</u>iew Shortcuts	
✓	<u>Z</u>oom	74%
✓	<u>Z</u>oom Slider	
✓	Zoom to <u>F</u>it	

You can specify which items you want to display on the status bar.

● At the right end of the status bar are the View Shortcuts toolbar, the Zoom Level button, the Zoom Slider, and the Fit Slide To Current Window button. These tools provide you with convenient methods for adjusting the display of presentation content.

*You can switch views and adjust the zoom percentage by using the tools
in the lower-right corner of the program window.*

See Also For information about different views, see "Viewing Presentations in Different Ways" later in this chapter.

The goal of all these features of the PowerPoint environment is to make working on a presentation as intuitive as possible. Commands for tasks you perform often are readily available, and even those you might use infrequently are easy to find.

For example, when a formatting option has several choices available, they are often displayed in a gallery of images, called *thumbnails*. These galleries give you an at-a-glance picture of each choice. If you point to a thumbnail in a gallery, the Live Preview feature shows you what that choice will look like if you apply it to the presentation, slide, or selection.

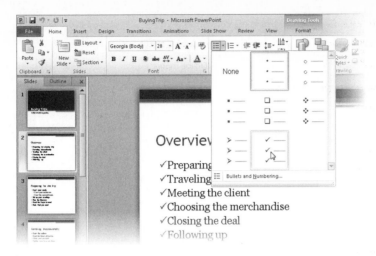

Live Preview shows the effect on the selected text of clicking the thumbnail you are pointing to.

You can display the content of the active presentation in four primary views: Normal view, Slide Sorter view, Reading view, and Slide Show view. You carry out most of the development work on a presentation in Normal view, which is the default.

Normal view consists of the following three panes:

- **Overview** This pane appears by default on the left side of the program window and has two tabs: Slides and Outline. Clicking the Slides tab displays small thumb-nails of all the slides in the active presentation. Clicking the Outline tab shows all the text on the slides displayed as an outline. Clicking the Close button in the pane's upper-right corner closes the pane, and clicking the Normal button in the Presentation Views group of the View tab opens it again.

- **Slide** This pane occupies most of the program window and shows the current slide as it will appear in the presentation.

- **Notes** This pane sits below the Slide pane and provides a place for entering notes about the current slide. These notes might be related to the development of the slide or they might be speaker notes that you will refer to when delivering the presentation.

Overview pane   Notes pane   Slide pane

The three panes of Normal view.

In this exercise, you'll start PowerPoint and explore the Backstage view and ribbon. Along the way, you'll see how to take advantage of galleries and Live Preview.

SET UP You don't need any practice files to complete this exercise. Start your computer, but don't start PowerPoint yet. Then follow the steps.

1. On the taskbar, click the **Start** button, point to **All Programs**, click **Microsoft Office**, and then click **Microsoft PowerPoint 2010**.

   The PowerPoint program window opens, displaying a blank presentation. The Home tab is active.

2. If your program window is not maximized, click the **Maximize** button to maximize it now.

   On the Home tab, buttons related to creating slide content are organized in six groups: Clipboard, Slides, Font, Paragraph, Drawing, and Editing. Only the buttons representing commands that can be performed on the currently selected presentation element are active.

3. Point to the active buttons on this tab to display the ScreenTips that name them and describe their functions.

For example, when you point to the New Slide button, a ScreenTip displays information about the button's function and provides a keyboard shortcut.

This command has a built-in keyboard shortcut.

4. Click the **Insert** tab, and then explore its buttons.

Buttons related to all the items you can insert are organized on this tab in seven groups: Tables, Images, Illustrations, Links, Text, Symbols, and Media.

The Insert tab of the ribbon.

5. Click the **Design** tab, and then explore its buttons.

Buttons related to the appearance of your presentation are organized on this tab in three groups: Page Setup, Themes, and Background.

The Design tab of the ribbon.

6. In the **Background** group, display the ScreenTip for the **Background Styles** button.

The ScreenTip tells you that you can use this command to choose the background graphic that is part of the selected theme.

7. In the lower-right corner of the **Background** group, click the **Background** dialog box launcher.

   The Format Background dialog box opens.

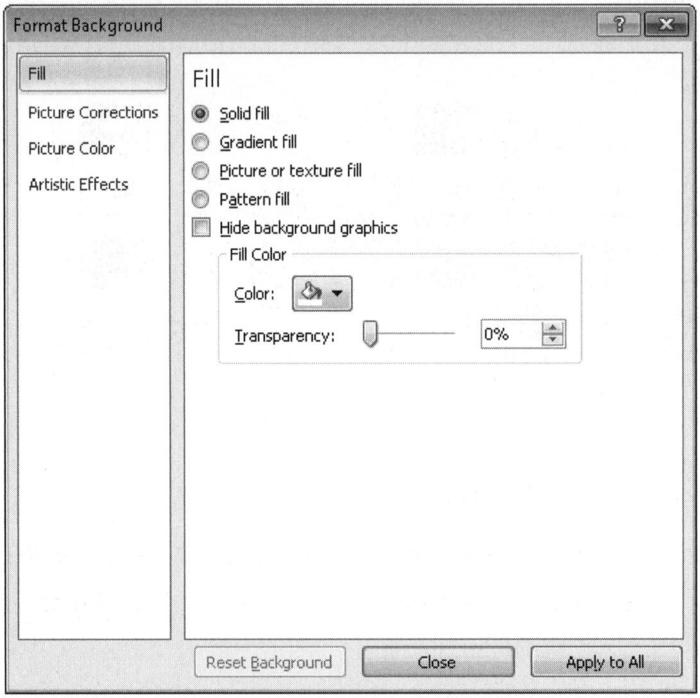

Format Background
Fill
Picture Corrections
Picture Color
Artistic Effects

   Fill

   - Solid fill
   - Gradient fill
   - Picture or texture fill
   - Pattern fill
   - Hide background graphics

   Fill Color

   Color:

   Transparency: ———— 0%

   Reset Background   Close   Apply to All

   In this dialog box, you can set the slide background.

8. In the **Format Background** dialog box, click **Close**.

9. In the **Themes** group, point to (but don't click) each thumbnail in the **Themes** gallery.

   In the Slide pane, PowerPoint displays a live preview of what the slide will look like if you click the thumbnail you're pointing to. You can see the effect of the selection without actually applying the effect.

10. In the scroll bar to the right of the thumbnails in the **Themes** group, click the **Down** button.

    The next row of theme thumbnails scrolls into view.

11. In the **Themes** group, click the **More** button.

    PowerPoint displays the entire Themes gallery.

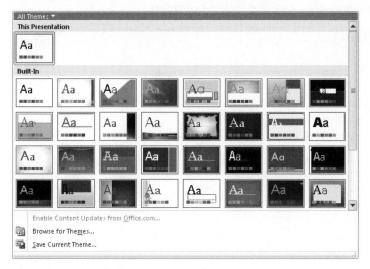

These themes are built into PowerPoint.

12. Point to various themes in the gallery, observing the effect on the slide.

13. Press the Esc key to close the gallery without applying a theme.

14. Click the **Transitions** tab, and then explore its buttons.

    This tab is new in PowerPoint 2010. (Transitions are no longer just another form of animation, but are now a presentation element in their own right.) Buttons related to the transition of slides in your presentation are organized on this tab in three groups: Preview, Transition To This Slide, and Timing.

The Transitions tab of the ribbon.

15. Click the **Animations** tab, and then explore its buttons and gallery.

Buttons related to slide animation are organized on this tab in four groups: Preview, Animation, Advanced Animation, and Timing.

The Animations tab of the ribbon.

16. Click the **Slide Show** tab, and then explore its buttons.

Buttons related to displaying your presentation are organized on this tab in three groups: Start Slide Show, Set Up, and Monitors.

The Slide Show tab of the ribbon.

17. Click the **Review** tab, and then explore its buttons.

Buttons related to editorial tasks are organized on this tab in four groups: Proofing, Language, Comments, and Compare.

The Review tab of the ribbon.

18. Click the **View** tab, and then explore its buttons.

Buttons related to changing the view or the display of the presentation are organized on this tab in seven groups: Presentation Views, Master Views, Show, Zoom, Color/Grayscale, Window, and Macros.

The View tab of the ribbon.

19. Click the **File** tab, which is color-coded to match the color assigned by Microsoft to the PowerPoint program.

    The Backstage view is displayed. Commands related to managing presentations (such as creating, saving, and printing) are available in this view.

20. If the Info page is not already displayed in the Backstage view, click **Info** in the left pane.

    On the Info page of the Backstage view, the middle pane provides a means of controlling who can work on the presentation, of removing properties (associated information), and of accessing versions of the presentation automatically saved by PowerPoint. The right pane displays the associated properties, including dates of modification, creation, and printing, and who created and edited the presentation.

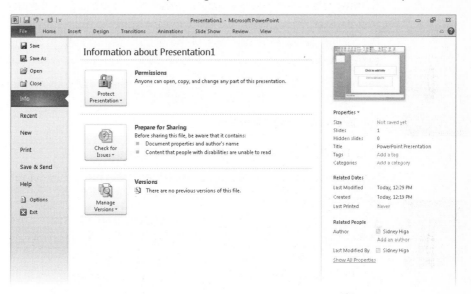

The Info page provides commands for changing the information attached to a presentation.

See Also For information about working with properties, see "Finalizing Presentations" in Chapter 6, "Review and Deliver Presentations."

21. In the left pane, click **Recent**.

    The Recent page displays the names of the presentations you recently worked on. By default, a maximum of 20 names is displayed. You can change this number on the Advanced page of the PowerPoint Options dialog box.

    See Also For information about the PowerPoint Options dialog box, see "Changing Default Program Options" in Chapter 15, "Customize PowerPoint."

22. In the left pane, click **New**.

    The New page displays all the templates on which you can base a new presentation.

    See Also For information about creating presentations, see the next topic, "Creating and Saving Presentations."

23. In the left pane, click **Print**.

    The Print page gathers together all print-related commands and provides a pane for previewing the current slide as it will appear when printed.

    See Also For information about printing, see "Previewing and Printing Presentations" in Chapter 6, "Review and Deliver Presentations."

24. In the left pane, click **Save & Send**.

    The Save & Send page displays all the commands related to making the current presentation available to other people.

    See Also For information about working with other people on presentations, see Chapter 12, "Share and Review Presentations."

25. In the left pane, click **Help**.

    The Help page displays all the ways you can get help and support for PowerPoint.

The right pane of the Help page displays your Office edition, its version number, and your product ID, which you will need if you contact Microsoft Product Support.

26. On the **Help** page, under **Tools for Working With Office**, click **Options**.

    The PowerPoint Options dialog box opens. In this dialog box are program settings that control the way the program looks and behaves.

You can also display this dialog box by clicking Options in the left pane of the Backstage view.

See Also For information about the PowerPoint Options dialog box, see "Changing Default Program Options" in Chapter 15, "Customize PowerPoint."

27. At the bottom of the **PowerPoint Options** dialog box, click **Cancel**.

    You return to the current presentation with the Home tab active on the ribbon.

CLEAN UP Leave the blank presentation you have created in this exercise open for the next exercise.

Creating and Saving Presentations

To work efficiently with PowerPoint 2010, you must be able to decide the best way to start a presentation. The New page of the Backstage view provides several options for creating a new presentation:

- **Blank presentation** If you know what your content and design will be and you want to build the presentation from scratch, you can start with a blank presentation. By the time you finish reading this book and working through its exercises, you'll be able to confidently create powerful presentations of your own. In the meantime, you'll probably want to use the other options available on the New page.

  Tip When you first start PowerPoint, a blank presentation is displayed in the presentation window, ready for you to enter text and design elements. If you're already working in PowerPoint, you can open a new blank presentation by clicking the File tab to display the Backstage view, clicking New, and then double-clicking Blank Presentation.

- **Content template** From the New page of the Backstage view, you can preview and download presentations that are available from the Microsoft Office Online Web site, located at office.microsoft.com, and then customize these templates to meet your needs. When you create a new presentation based on a template, you're not opening the template; instead you're creating a new file that has all the characteristics of the template.

- **Design templates** Creating attractive presentations from scratch is time-consuming and requires quite a bit of skill and knowledge about PowerPoint. You can save time by basing your presentation on one of the design templates that come with PowerPoint. A design template is a blank presentation with a theme, and sometimes graphics already applied to it. PowerPoint supplies a title slide and leaves it to you to add the other slides you need.

- **Existing presentation** If you or a colleague have already created a presentation that is close enough in content and design to be a good starting point, you can use that presentation as the basis for the new one.

Whether you create a new presentation from scratch or base it on a template or existing file, it exists only in your computer's memory until you save it. You save a presentation the first time by clicking the Save button on the Quick Access Toolbar or by displaying the Backstage view and then clicking Save As. Either action opens the Save As dialog box, in which you can assign a name and storage location.

The Save As dialog box.

If you want to save the presentation in a folder other than the one shown in the Address bar, you can use standard Windows techniques in the Address bar or in the Navigation pane on the left to navigate to the folder you want. If you want to create a new folder in which to store the file, you can click the New Folder button on the toolbar.

After you save a presentation for the first time, you can save changes simply by clicking the Save button. The new version of the presentation then overwrites the previous version. If you want to keep both the new version and the previous version, click Save As in the Backstage view, and then save a new version with a different name in the same location or with the same name in a different location. (You cannot have two files with the same name in the same folder.)

Tip By default, PowerPoint periodically saves the presentation you are working on in case the program stops responding or you lose electrical power. To adjust the time interval between saves, display the Backstage view, and click Options. In the left pane of the PowerPoint Options dialog box, click Save. Specify the period of time in the box to the right of the Save AutoRecover Information Every check box, and then click OK.

In this exercise, you'll create and save a couple of presentations based on templates. You'll also use an existing presentation as the basis for a new one.

SET UP You need the SalesMeetingMay_start presentation located in your Chapter01 practice file folder to complete this exercise. With only a blank presentation open in PowerPoint, follow the steps.

1. Click the **File** tab to display the Backstage view, and then click **New**.

   The New page is displayed.

2. In the center pane, below **Office.com Templates**, click the **Presentations** thumbnail.

   The center pane displays folders representing categories of presentations that are available from Office.com.

3. In the center pane, click **Business**.

   The center pane displays images of all the ready-made business presentations that are available from Office.com.

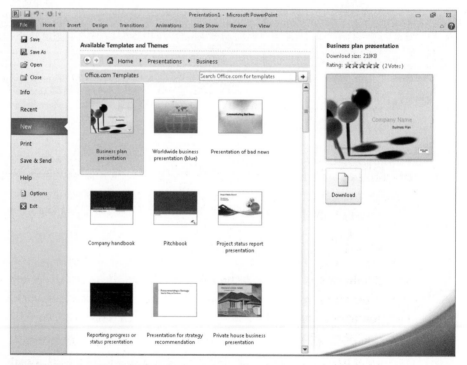

The selected template is indicated by an orange background, and information about that template appears in the right pane.

Troubleshooting Don't be alarmed if your list of presentations is different from ours. New presentations are continually being added. In fact, it is worth checking Office.com frequently, just to see what's new.

4. If necessary, scroll down in the center pane, noticing the wide variety of presentations available.

5. Click the **Project status report presentation** thumbnail, and then in the right pane of the window, click **Download**.

    Tip If a message box appears telling you that you can download templates from Office.com only if you are running a genuine version of PowerPoint, click Continue, and follow any additional instructions.

    A presentation based on the selected template opens in Normal view.

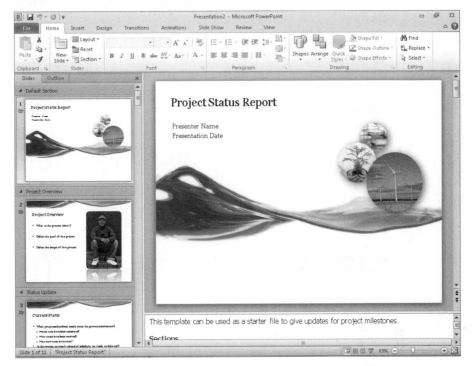

Thumbnails of the presentation's slides are shown on the Slides tab of the Overview pane, and the title slide appears in the Slide pane.

6. On the **Slides** tab of the **Overview** pane, click slide **2**. Then continue clicking slide thumbnails, scrolling down the pane as necessary, to display each slide of the presentation in turn.

    The slides contain generic instructions about the sort of information that you might want to include in a presentation for a project status report. You can replace these instructions with your own text.

7. On the Quick Access Toolbar, click the **Save** button.

    The Save As dialog box opens, displaying the contents of the folder you last used in the Save As or Open dialog box.

8. Use standard Windows techniques to navigate to your **Chapter01** practice file folder.

Tip If the Navigation pane and toolbar are not displayed, you can click Browse Folders in the lower-left corner of the dialog box to display them.

9. On the toolbar, click the **New folder** button.

   A folder named *New folder* appears, with the name selected for editing.

10. Type **My Presentations**, press Enter, and then double-click the new **My Presentations** folder.

    My Presentations is now the current folder in the Save As dialog box.

In the File Name box, PowerPoint suggests Project Status Report, *the first few words in the presentation, as the name of the file.*

11. In the **File name** box, click the existing entry, type **My Presentation**, and then click **Save**.

    Troubleshooting Programs that run on the Windows operating system use file name extensions to identify different types of files. For example, the extension .pptx identifies PowerPoint 2010 as well as PowerPoint 2007 presentations. Windows 7 programs do not display these extensions by default, and you shouldn't type them in the Save As dialog box. When you save a file, PowerPoint automatically adds whatever extension is associated with the type of file selected in the Save As Type box.

12. Display the Backstage view, click **New**, and then in the **Office.com Templates** area, click **Design slides**.

    The center pane now displays categories of ready-made designs.

13. In the center pane, click each category folder in turn, scroll through the thumbnails of the various design collections, and then click the **Back** button at the top of the center pane to return to the list of categories.

14. In the center pane, click the **Business** folder, click the **World in hand design template** thumbnail, and then in the right pane, click **Download**.

    A new presentation with one title slide opens in Normal view.

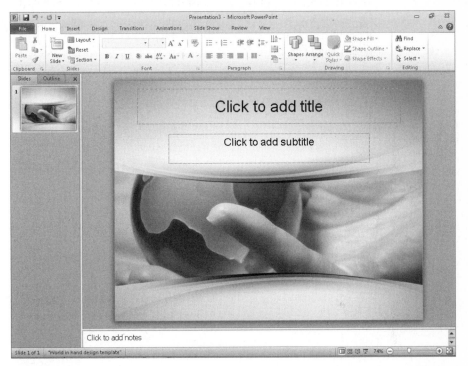

The Slides tab shows a thumbnail of the title slide, and the slide itself appears in the Slide pane.

15. Display the Backstage view, and click **Save As**.

    The Save As dialog box opens, displaying the contents of the My Presentations folder.

16. In the **Address** bar, click **Chapter01** to display the contents of that folder.

17. In the **File name** box, type **My Presentation**, and then click **Save**.

    PowerPoint saves the My Presentation file in your Chapter01 practice file folder. You have now saved two presentations with the same name, but in different folders.

18. Display the Backstage view, click **New**, and at the right end of the top row, click **New from existing**.

    The New From Existing Presentation dialog box opens, displaying the contents of your Chapter01 practice file folder.

19. Double-click the **SalesMeetingMay_start** presentation.

    A quick glance at the title bar tells you that instead of opening the SalesMeetingMay_start presentation, PowerPoint has opened a new presentation based on that file, effectively using SalesMeetingMay_start as a template.

20. On the Quick Access Toolbar, click the **Save** button.

    Because this presentation is a new file, PowerPoint displays the Save As dialog box so that you can name the presentation.

21. In the **File name** box, type **SalesMeetingMay**, and then click **Save**.

 CLEAN UP Leave the presentations you have created in this exercise open for the next exercise.

Compatibility with Earlier Versions

The Microsoft Office 2010 programs use file formats based on XML, called the *Microsoft Office Open XML Formats*, that were introduced with Microsoft Office 2007. By default, PowerPoint 2010 files are saved in the .pptx format, which is the PowerPoint variation of this file format.

The .pptx format provides the following benefits:

- File size is smaller because files are compressed when saved, decreasing the amount of disk space needed to store the file and the amount of bandwidth needed to send files in e-mail, over a network, or across the Internet.

- Recovering at least some of the content of damaged files is possible because XML files can be opened in a text program such as Notepad.

- Security is greater because .pptx files cannot contain macros, and personal data can be detected and removed from the file. (PowerPoint 2010 and PowerPoint 2007 provide a different file format—.pptm—for presentations that contain macros.)

You can open a .ppt presentation created with earlier PowerPoint versions in PowerPoint 2010, but the new features of PowerPoint 2010 will not be available. The presentation name appears in the title bar with *[Compatibility Mode]* to its right. You can work in Compatibility mode, or you can convert the presentation to the .pptx format by displaying the Info tab of the Backstage view and clicking the Convert button in the Compatibility Mode area. You can also click Save As in the Backstage view to save the presentation as a different file in the .pptx format.

If you work with people who are using a version of PowerPoint earlier than 2007, you can save your presentations in a format that they will be able to open and use by changing the Save As Type setting in the Save As dialog box to PowerPoint 97-2003 Presentation.

Opening, Moving Around in, and Closing Presentations

To open an existing presentation, you click the File tab to display the Backstage view and then click Open to display the Open dialog box. The first time you use this command, the Open dialog box displays the contents of your Documents library. If you display the dialog box again in the same PowerPoint session, it displays the contents of whatever folder you last used. To see the contents of a different folder, you use standard Windows techniques to navigate to that folder. After you locate the file you want to work with, you double-click it to open it.

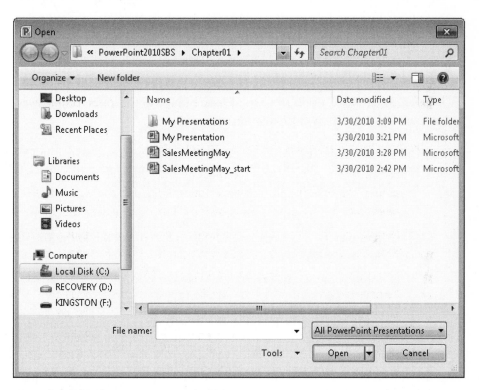

The Open dialog box.

Tip Clicking a file name and then clicking the Open arrow in the lower-right corner of the Open dialog box displays a list of alternative ways to open the selected file. To look through the presentation without making any inadvertent changes, you can open the file as read-only, or you can open an independent copy of the file. You can open a file in a Web browser. In the event of a computer crash or other similar incident, you can tell PowerPoint to open the file and attempt to repair any damage.

When a presentation is open, you can use several techniques to move from slide to slide, including the following:

- By clicking the slide you want to move to on the Slides tab of the Overview pane
- By using the scroll bar on the right side of the Slide pane
- By clicking the Previous Slide or Next Slide button at the bottom of the Slide pane scroll bar
- By pressing the Page Up and Page Down keys on the keyboard

Every time you open a presentation, it opens a new instance of PowerPoint. If you have more than one presentation open, clicking the Close button at the right end of a presentation's title bar closes that presentation and exits that instance of PowerPoint. If you have only one presentation open and you want to close the presentation but leave PowerPoint running, you must click the File tab to display the Backstage view and then click Close in the left pane.

In this exercise, you'll open an existing presentation and explore various ways of moving around in it. Then you'll close the presentation.

SET UP You need the MayMeeting_start presentation located in your Chapter01 practice file folder to complete this exercise. With the presentations from the previous exercise still open on your screen, follow the steps.

1. Click the **File** tab to display the Backstage view, and then click **Open**.

   The Open dialog box opens, showing the contents of the folder you used for your last open or save action.

2. If the contents of the **Chapter01** folder are not displayed, navigate to that folder now.

3. Double-click **MayMeeting_start** to open it, and then save the presentation in your **Chapter01** practice file folder as **MayMeeting**.

   Now you can work with this presentation without fear of overwriting the original.

4. In the **Overview** pane, on the **Slides** tab, click slide **3**.

5. At the bottom of the scroll bar on the right side of the **Slide** pane, click the **Next Slide** button to move to slide **4**.

6. Click the **Previous Slide** button to move back to slide **3**.

7. Drag the scroll box slowly down to the bottom of the scroll bar.

   As you move down the scroll bar, a ScreenTip tells you the number and name of the slide that will be displayed if you release the mouse button at that point.

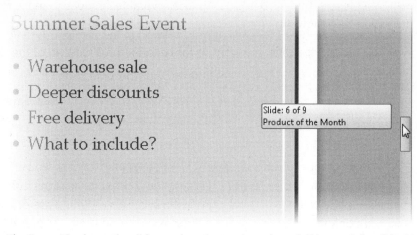

The ScreenTip shows the slide number, the total number of slides, and the slide title.

8. Press the Page Up key until slide **3** is displayed.

9. Press Ctrl+Home to move to slide **1**.

10. At the right end of the title bar, click the **Close** button to close the **MayMeeting** presentation.

11. On the Windows Taskbar, point to the **PowerPoint** button.

    Thumbnails of all the open presentations are displayed.

Pointing to the PowerPoint button on the Windows Taskbar is a quick way of determining which presentations are open. (If your screen is set up to show the Windows Aero theme, your Windows Taskbar will look different.)

12. Point to the **SalesMeetingMay** thumbnail, and then click the **Close** button that appears.

13. Repeat step 12 for all but one of the presentations.

14. Display the Backstage view, and then in the left pane, click **Close**.

PowerPoint closes the last open presentation but remains running.

Troubleshooting If you click the Close button at the right end of the title bar instead of displaying the Backstage view and then clicking Close, you'll close the presentation and exit the PowerPoint program. To continue working, start PowerPoint again.

✖ **CLEAN UP** Leave PowerPoint running for the next exercise.

Viewing Presentations in Different Ways

PowerPoint has four primary views to help you create, organize, and display presentations. There are other views, but these are the ones you'll use most frequently:

- **Normal** As you know, this view includes an Overview pane where you move to a specific slide on the Slides tab or work with the presentation outline on the Outline tab; a Slide pane where you can work on the content of an individual slide; and a Notes pane where you can enter development and delivery notes.

  See Also For information about working with text on the Outline tab and in the Slide pane, see "Entering Text in Placeholders" and "Editing Text" in Chapter 3, "Work with Slide Text."

  See Also For information about working with notes, see "Preparing Speaker Notes and Handouts" in Chapter 6, "Review and Deliver Presentations."

- **Slide Sorter** In this view, the slides of the presentation are displayed as thumbnails so that you can easily reorganize them. You can also apply transitions from one slide to another, as well as specify how long each slide should remain on the screen.

  See Also For information about changing the order of slides, see "Rearranging Slides and Sections" in Chapter 2, "Work with Slides."

  See Also For information about applying transitions, see "Adding Transitions" in Chapter 5, "Add Simple Visual Enhancements."

- **Reading View** In this view, which is ideal for previewing the presentation, each slide fills the screen. You can click buttons on the navigation bar to move through or jump to specific slides.

- **Slide Show** In this view, each slide fills the screen. You use this view to deliver the presentation to an audience.

  See Also For information about delivering a presentation to an audience, see "Delivering Presentations" in Chapter 6, "Review and Deliver Presentations."

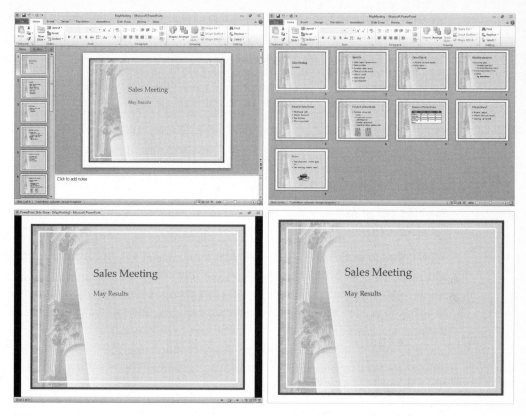

The four primary views: Normal view, Slide Sorter view, Reading view, and Slide Show view.

You can switch among these views by clicking the buttons on the View Shortcuts toolbar at the right end of the status bar. Alternatively, you can click the buttons in the Presentation Views group on the View tab to activate all but Slide Show view, which you activate from the Slide Show tab.

The View Shortcuts toolbar, and the Presentation Views group.

The Presentation Views group also includes a button for Notes Page view. In this view, you can create speaker notes that contain elements other than text. Although you can add speaker notes in the Normal view's Notes pane, you must be in Notes Page view if you want to add graphics to your notes.

See Also For information about creating more elaborate notes, see "Preparing Speaker Notes and Handouts" in Chapter 6, "Review and Deliver Presentations."

Tip Are you wondering what the Master Views group is all about? You can control the default look of a presentation by working with the masters displayed in Slide Master view, Handout Master view, or Notes Master view. For information about masters, see "Viewing and Changing Slide Masters" in Chapter 13, "Create Custom Presentation Elements."

You can use other buttons on the View tab to display rulers and gridlines to help you position and align slide elements, to change the zoom percentage of the current slide, to see how a colored slide will look if rendered in black and white (usually for printing), to arrange and work with windows, and to view macros.

See Also The subject of macros is beyond the scope of this book. For information, see PowerPoint Help.

When you are working in Normal view, you can adjust the relative sizes of the panes to suit your needs by dragging the splitter bar that separates them. When you point to a splitter bar, the pointer changes to a double bar with opposing arrows, and you can drag in either direction. You can hide a pane by dragging the splitter bar to shrink the pane as far as it will go. Simply drag the splitter bar back to widen the pane again. If you adjust the width of the Slides tab in the Overview pane, the size of the slide thumbnails is adjusted accordingly—that is, you can see more small thumbnails in a narrow pane and fewer large thumbnails in a wide pane.

Tip Any changes you make to a view, such as adjusting the sizes of panes, are saved with the presentation that is open at the time and do not affect other presentations.

In this exercise, you'll switch among different PowerPoint views and then return to Normal view, where you'll adjust the size of the panes. You'll see how to display more than one presentation at the same time and experiment with adjusting the zoom percentage.

SET UP You need the BuyingTrip_start and DesigningColor_start presentations located in your Chapter01 practice file folder to complete this exercise. Open both presentations, and save them as *BuyingTrip* and *DesigningColor*, respectively. Then with both presentations open and BuyingTrip displayed on your screen, follow the steps.

1. In the **Overview** pane, click the **Outline** tab.

   The pane switches from showing thumbnails of the slides to showing an outline of the text of the presentation. The pane automatically widens to accommodate the length of the bullet points, and the Slide pane and Notes pane shrink accordingly.

2. On the **Outline** tab, click in the title for slide **3**.

   Slide 3 of the presentation is now shown in the adjacent Slide pane.

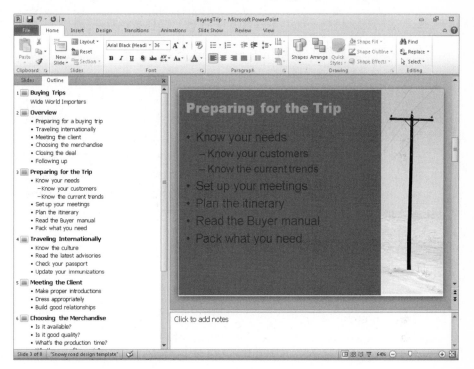

The size of the Outline pane has increased to accommodate the outline.

3. On the **View** tab, in the **Presentation Views** group, click the **Slide Sorter** button.

   All the slides now appear as thumbnails in one large pane. Slide 3 is surrounded by an orange border, indicating that it is selected.

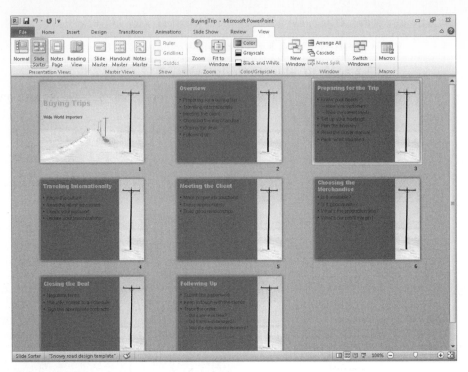

Slide Sorter view.

4. Hold down the Alt key, point to any slide, and then press and hold the mouse button.

   While you hold down the mouse button, only the slide's title is visible against a white background, making it easier to locate the slide you want.

5. Release the Alt key and the mouse button to restore the display of formatting.

6. On the **View Shortcuts** toolbar, click the **Normal** button.

7. On the **Slide Show** tab, in the **Start Slide Show** group, click the **From Beginning** button.

   Keyboard Shortcut Press F5 to start the presentation from the first slide.

   PowerPoint displays a full-screen view of the first slide in the presentation.

8. Without moving your mouse, click its button to advance to the next slide.

   Keyboard Shortcut Press the Esc key to stop a presentation before you reach the end.

9. Continue clicking the mouse button to advance through the presentation one slide at a time.

   After the last slide in the presentation, PowerPoint displays a black slide.

Tip If you don't want a black slide to appear at the end of the presentation, display the Backstage view, and click Options. In the PowerPoint Options dialog box, click Advanced. Then under Slide Show, clear the End With Black Slide check box, and click OK.

10. Click again to return to Normal view.

11. Point to the splitter bar between the **Slide** pane and the **Notes** pane, and when the pointer changes to a double bar with opposing arrows, drag the bar down until the Notes pane is completely closed.

12. Drag the splitter bar at the bottom of the **Slide** pane upward as far as it will go.

    You cannot close the Slide pane completely, but you can make it easier to enter notes about the slide.

You can adjust the size of the Normal view panes to suit your needs.

13. On the **View** tab, in the **Window** group, click the **Switch Windows** button, and then click **DesigningColor**.

    Notice that customizing Normal view for one presentation does not affect Normal view for the other presentation.

14. In the **Window** group, click the **Arrange All** button.

    In the workspace, you can now see both open presentations at the same time.

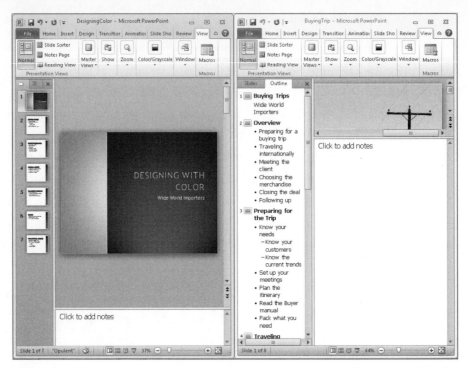

In this view, it is easy to compare two presentations or copy content from one to the other.

15. Experiment with the other commands in the **Window** group, and then at the right end of the **DesigningColor** title bar, click the **Close** button.

16. At the right end of the **BuyingTrip** title bar, click the **Maximize** button, and then reset the size of the Notes pane.

17. Click the slide in the Slide pane, and on the **View** tab, in the **Zoom** group, click the **Zoom** button.

The Zoom dialog box opens.

You can select a zoom percentage or type the percentage you want in the Percent box.

18. In the **Zoom** dialog box, click **100%**, and then click **OK**.

    Notice that the zoom percentage also changes on the View Shortcuts toolbar at the right end of the status bar, and the slider moves to the middle.

19. At the left end of the slider on the status bar, click the **Zoom Out** button until the percentage is **50%**.

    Each time you click the button, the slider moves to the left and the zoom percentage decreases.

    Tip In Normal view, you can set the zoom percentage for each pane independently. For example, clicking the Zoom Out button while the Overview pane is active changes the zoom percentage of the displayed tab.

20. At the right end of the slider, click the **Zoom In** button.

    The zoom percentage increases to 60%.

21. At the right end of the status bar, click the **Fit slide to current window** button.

    The displayed slide expands to fit the available space in the Slide pane

CLEAN UP Close the BuyingTrip presentation.

Key Points

- Because the PowerPoint interface makes commands easily accessible, you can quickly create sophisticated presentations.

- How you create a new presentation depends on whether you need help developing the content, the design, or both.

- Office.com provides many templates that you can customize to meet your needs.

- You can save a presentation in an existing folder or in a new folder. You cannot store two presentations with the same name in the same folder.

- You can move around a presentation in several ways: by clicking thumbnails on the Slides tab; by clicking the Next Slide or Previous Slide button; by scrolling the Slide pane; or by pressing the Page Up or Page Down key.

- PowerPoint has four primary views: Normal, Slide Sorter, Reading View, and Slide Show. You can switch views by clicking buttons on the View Shortcuts toolbar or by clicking buttons in the Presentation Views group on the View tab.

- In Normal view, you can change the zoom percentage of your slides and the size of the panes to suit the way you work.

Chapter at a Glance

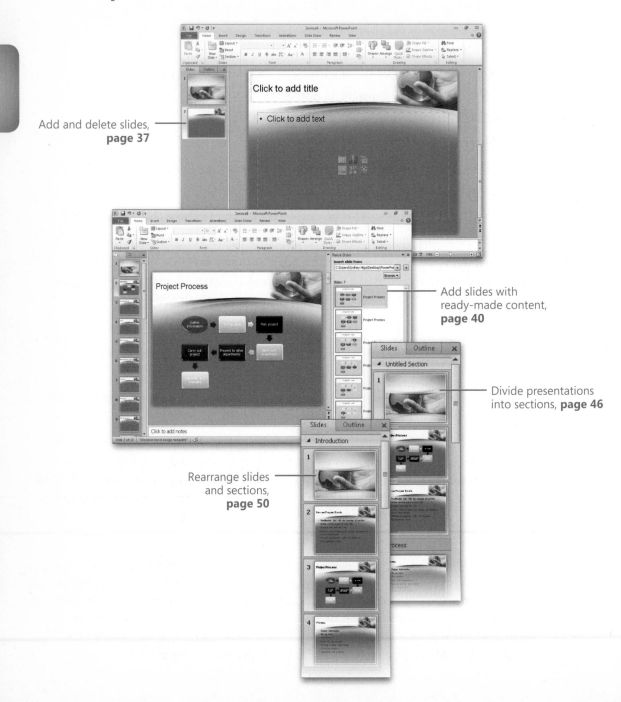

Add and delete slides, **page 37**

Add slides with ready-made content, **page 40**

Divide presentations into sections, **page 46**

Rearrange slides and sections, **page 50**

2 Work with Slides

In this chapter, you will learn how to

✔ Add and delete slides.

✔ Add slides with ready-made content.

✔ Divide presentations into sections.

✔ Rearrange slides and sections.

For each slide to accomplish its purpose, it needs to present its content in the most effective way. The layout of individual slides and the order of slides in the presentation contribute significantly to the logical development of your message.

In this chapter, you'll add slides with different layouts, delete slides, and change the layout of a slide. You'll also divide a presentation into sections and collapse and expand sections. Finally, you'll rearrange slides and sections in a presentation.

> **Practice Files** Before you can complete the exercises in this chapter, you need to copy the book's practice files to your computer. The practice files you'll use to complete the exercises in this chapter are in the Chapter02 practice file folder. A complete list of practice files is provided in "Using the Practice Files" at the beginning of this book.

Adding and Deleting Slides

When you create a presentation, you add a slide by clicking the New Slide button in the Slides group on the Home tab. By default in a new presentation, a slide added after the title slide has the Title And Content layout. Thereafter, each added slide has the layout of the preceding slide. If you want to add a slide with a different layout, you can select the layout you want from the New Slide gallery.

If you change your mind about including a slide, you can easily delete it by selecting it either on the Slides tab of the Overview pane or in Slide Sorter view and then pressing the Delete key. You can also right-click the slide in either the pane or the view and then click Delete Slide. To select a series of slides, click the first slide in the series and hold down the Shift key while you click the last slide. To select noncontiguous slides, click the first one and hold down the Ctrl key as you click additional slides.

If you change your mind about the layout of a slide, you don't have to delete it and then add a new one with the layout you want. Instead, you can change the layout of an existing slide by selecting the new layout from the Layout gallery.

In this exercise, you'll add a slide with the default layout and add slides with other layouts. You'll delete first a single slide and then a series of slides. Then you'll change the layout of a slide.

SET UP You need the ServiceA_start presentation located in your Chapter02 practice file folder to complete this exercise. Open the ServiceA_start presentation, and save it as *ServiceA*. Then follow the steps.

1. With slide **1** displayed, on the **Home** tab, in the **Slides** group, click the **New Slide** button (not its arrow).

   Keyboard Shortcut Press Ctrl+M to add a slide to the presentation.

   See Also For more information about keyboard shortcuts, see "Keyboard Shortcuts" at the end of this book.

   PowerPoint adds slide 2 to the presentation with the default Title And Content layout.

This layout accommodates a title and either text or graphic content—a table, chart, diagram, picture, clip art image, or media clip.

Troubleshooting The appearance of buttons and groups on the ribbon changes depending on the width of the program window. For information about changing the appearance of the ribbon to match our screen images, see "Modifying the Display of the Ribbon" at the beginning of this book.

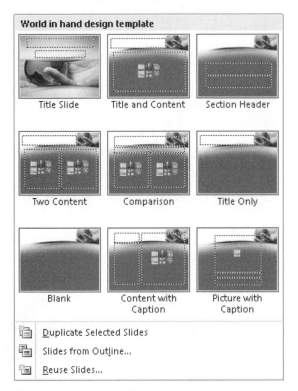

2. In the **Slides** group, click the **New Slide** arrow.

   The New Slide gallery appears.

The World In Hand design template has nine predefined slide layouts.

3. In the gallery, click **Two Content**.

   PowerPoint adds slide 3, which has a placeholder for a title and two placeholders for text or graphic content.

4. In the **Slides** group, click the **New Slide** button.

   PowerPoint adds another slide with the Two Content layout.

   Tip You can also add new slides by pressing keyboard shortcuts while you're entering text on the Outline tab. For more information, see "Entering Text in Placeholders" in Chapter 3, "Work with Slide Text."

5. Continue adding slides from the **New Slide** gallery, selecting a different layout each time so that you can see what each one looks like.

   When you finish, the presentation contains 10 slides.

6. In the **Overview** pane, scroll to the top of the **Slides** tab. Then right-click slide **3**, and click **Delete Slide**.

   PowerPoint removes the slide from the presentation and renumbers all the subsequent slides.

7. On the **Slides** tab, click slide **5**. Then scroll to the bottom of the tab, hold down the Shift key, and click slide **9**.

8. With slides **5** through **9** selected, right-click the selection, and click **Delete Slide**.

   The presentation now has four slides.

9. With slide **4** selected, on the **Home** tab, in the **Slides** group, click the **Layout** button.

   The Layout gallery appears. This gallery is the same as the New Slide gallery, but it applies the layout you choose to an existing slide instead of adding a new one.

10. In the gallery, click the **Title and Content** thumbnail.

✖ **CLEAN UP** Save the ServiceA presentation, and then close it without exiting PowerPoint.

Adding Slides with Ready-Made Content

If your presentation will contain information that already exists in a document created in Microsoft Word or another word processing program, you can edit that information into outline format and then import the outline into a PowerPoint presentation. The outline can be a Word document (.doc or .docx) or a Rich Text Format (RTF) file (.rtf).

For the importing process to work as smoothly as possible, the document must be formatted with heading styles. PowerPoint translates Heading 1 styles into slide titles, Heading 2 styles into bullet points, and Heading 3 styles into second-level bullet points, called *subpoints*.

If you often include a slide that provides the same basic information in your presentations, you don't have to re-create the slide for each presentation. For example, if you create a slide that shows your company's product development cycle for a new product presentation, you might want to use variations of that same slide in all new product presentations. You can easily tell PowerPoint to reuse a slide from one presentation in a different presentation. The slide assumes the formatting of its new presentation.

See Also For information about using a slide library to store slides for reuse, see the sidebar "Working with Slide Libraries" following this topic.

Within a presentation, you can duplicate an existing slide to reuse it as the basis for a new slide. You can then customize the duplicated slide instead of having to create it from scratch.

In this exercise, you'll add slides by importing a Word outline. Then you'll reuse a slide from an existing presentation. Finally, you'll duplicate an existing slide.

SET UP You need the ServiceB_start and Projects presentations and the Service-Orientation document located in your Chapter02 practice file folder to complete this exercise. Open the ServiceB_start presentation, and save it as *ServiceB*. Then follow the steps.

1. On the **Home** tab, in the **Slides** group, click the **New Slide** arrow, and then below the gallery, click **Slides from Outline**.

   The Insert Outline dialog box opens. This dialog box resembles the Open dialog box.

2. Navigate to your **Chapter02** practice file folder, and then double-click the **ServiceOrientation** file.

   PowerPoint converts the outline into 12 slides.

3. In the **Overview** pane, click the **Outline** tab.

   On the Outline tab, each Heading 1 style from the ServiceOrientation document is now a slide title, each Heading 2 style is a bullet point, and each Heading 3 style is a subpoint.

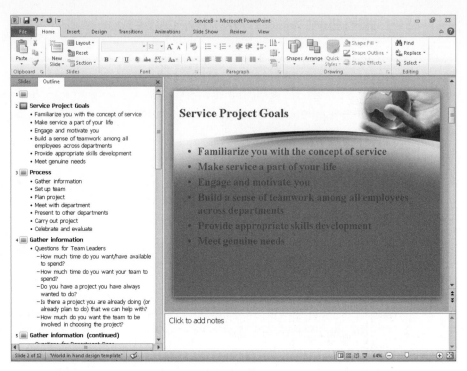

The text from the outline, shown on the Outline tab.

Tip You can start a new presentation from a Word outline. Click the File tab to display the Backstage view, and then click Open. In the Open dialog box, click All PowerPoint Presentations, and in the list of file types, click All Files. Then locate and double-click the outline document you want to use.

4. In the **Overview** pane, click the **Slides** tab, and then click the empty slide **1**.

5. On the **Home** tab, in the **Slides** group, click the **New Slide** arrow, and then below the gallery, click **Reuse Slides**.

   The Reuse Slides task pane opens on the right side of the window.

6. In the **Reuse Slides** task pane, click **Browse**, and then in the list, click **Browse File**.

   PowerPoint displays the Browse dialog box, which resembles the Open dialog box.

7. If the contents of your **Chapter02** practice file folder are not displayed, navigate to that folder now. Then double-click the **Projects** presentation.

   Thumbnails of all the slides in the presentation appear in the Reuse Slides task pane.

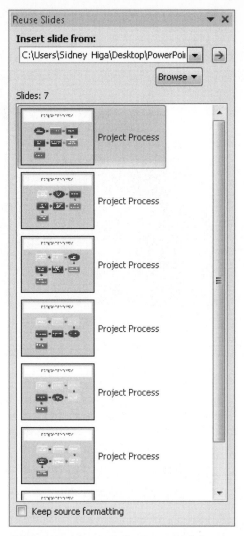

This presentation includes a series of diagrams related to a project workflow.

8. Scroll to the bottom of the task pane to see all the available slides, and then point to the last thumbnail.

   The thumbnail expands so that you can see the slide details, making it easier to select the slide you want.

9. Scroll back to the top of the task pane, and then click the first thumbnail.

   PowerPoint inserts the selected slide from the Projects presentation as slide 2 in the ServiceB presentation. The slide takes on the design of the presentation in which it is inserted.

The presentation now contains a diagram from the Projects *presentation.*

> **Tip** If you want the slide to retain the formatting from the Projects presentation instead of taking on the formatting of the ServiceB presentation, select the Keep Source Formatting check box at the bottom of the Reuse Slides task pane.

 10. Click the task pane's **Close** button.

11. With slide **2** selected on the **Slides** tab, in the **Slides** group of the **Home** tab, click the **New Slide** arrow. Then click **Duplicate Selected Slide**.

> **Tip** You can also right-click the selected slide and then click Duplicate Slide.

PowerPoint inserts a new slide 3 identical to slide 2. You could now modify the existing slide content instead of creating it from scratch.

CLEAN UP Save the ServiceB presentation, and then close it.

Working with Slide Libraries

If your organization is running Microsoft SharePoint Server and has enabled slide libraries, and if PowerPoint Professional Plus is installed on your computer, you and your colleagues can store slides or even entire presentations in a slide library so that they are available for use in any presentation.

For example, suppose a graphically gifted person has developed a slide with a sophisticated chart showing the percentage of income derived from the sale of different categories of merchandise. He or she can store the slide in a slide library so that other people can use it in their presentations without having to take the time to develop a similar chart. Larger organizations might even have people on staff with responsibility for creating this type of slide, so that they can ensure that all presentations convey the same information in the same professional way.

To store slides in a slide library:

1. Display the Backstage view, click Save & Send, and then click Publish Slides.

2. In the right pane, click the Publish Slides button.

   The Publish Slides dialog box opens.

3. In the Publish Slides dialog box, select the check box for the slide you want to store in the library.

4. If the URL of your SharePoint slide library does not appear in the Publish To box, click the box, and type the URL.

5. Click Publish to store the slide in the slide library.

To insert a slide from a slide library:

1. Click the slide after which you want the new slide to appear.

2. On the Home tab, in the Slides group, click the New Slide arrow, and then click Reuse Slides.

3. In the Reuse Slides task pane, in the Insert Slide From box, type the URL of your SharePoint slide library, and then click the Go arrow.

   You can also click Browse, click Browse Slide Library, and then navigate to the URL of the library in the Select A Slide Library dialog box.

4. Double-click the thumbnail of the slide you want to insert in the active presentation.

Exporting Presentations as Outlines

When you want to use the text from a presentation in another program, you can save the presentation outline as an .rtf file. Many programs, including the Windows and Macintosh versions of Word and older versions of PowerPoint, can import outlines saved in .rtf with their formatting intact.

To save a presentation as an .rtf file:

1. Display the Backstage view, and then click Save As.

   The Save As dialog box opens.

2. In the File Name box, specify the name of the file.

3. Display the Save As Type list, and click Outline/RTF.

4. Navigate to the folder in which you want to store the outline, and click Save.

   PowerPoint saves the presentation's outline in .rtf format with the designated name in the designated folder.

Dividing Presentations into Sections

New in PowerPoint 2010 is the ability to divide slides into sections. Sections appear as bars across the Slides tab of the Overview pane in Normal view and across the workspace in Slide Sorter view. They do not appear in other views, and they do not create slides or otherwise interrupt the flow of the presentation.

Dividing a presentation into sections can be a great tool during content development. Because you can hide whole sections of slides, the sections make it easier to focus on one part of a presentation at a time. If you are working on a presentation with other people, you can name one section for each person to delineate who is responsible for which slides.

In this exercise, you'll divide a presentation into two sections, adding one in Normal view and the other in Slide Sorter view. After naming the sections, you'll hide their slides and then display first one section and then both sections.

SET UP You need the ServiceC_start presentation located in your Chapter02 practice file folder to complete this exercise. Open the ServiceC_start presentation, and save it as *ServiceC*. Then follow the steps.

1. With slide **1** displayed, on the **Home** tab, in the **Slides** group, click the **Section** button, and then click **Add Section**.

   On the Slides tab of the Overview pane, PowerPoint adds a section bar before slide 1.

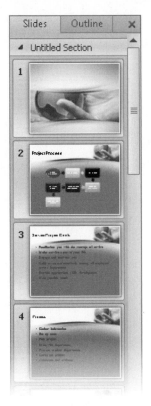

   PowerPoint selects all the slides that are included in the new section.

2. On the **View Shortcuts** toolbar, click the **Slide Sorter** button.

3. Click slide **4**, click the **Section** button, and then click **Add Section**.

   PowerPoint adds a section bar before slide 4.

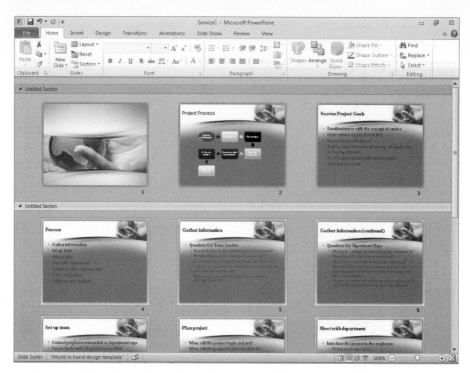

Again, PowerPoint selects the slides in the new section.

4. Right-click the second **Untitled Section** bar, and click **Rename Section**.

   The Rename Section dialog box opens.

Rename Section
Section name:
Untitled Section
Rename   Cancel

The current name is selected, ready to be replaced.

5. In the **Section name** box, type **Process**, and then click **Rename**.

6. On the **View Shortcuts** toolbar, click the **Normal** button.

7. On the **Slides** tab of the **Overview** pane, click the **Untitled Section** bar above slide **1**.

   The section bar and all the slides in the section are selected.

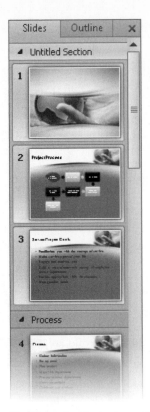

You can select just one section of the presentation.

8. In the **Slides** group, click the **Section** button, and click **Rename Section**. Then in the **Rename Section** dialog box, type **Introduction** as the section name, and click **Rename**.

9. In the **Slides** group, click the **Section** button, and then click **Collapse All**.

   The slides are hidden under their section bars.

Slides	Outline	✕
▷ Introduction (3)		
▷ Process (10)		

You can use sections to provide an "outline" of long presentations.

10. On the **Slides** tab, click the arrow to the left of **Introduction** to display only the slides in that section.

11. In the **Slides** group, click the **Section** button, and then click **Expand All**.

All the slides are now displayed.

✕ CLEAN UP Save the ServiceC presentation, and then close it.

Rearranging Slides and Sections

After you have created several slides, whether by adding them and entering text or by importing them from another presentation, you might want to rearrange the order of the slides so that they effectively communicate your message. You can rearrange a presentation in three ways.

● On the Slides tab, you can drag slides up and down to change their order.

● On the Slides tab, you can move entire sections up or down in a presentation.

● To see more of the presentation at the same time, you can switch to Slide Sorter view. You can then drag slide thumbnails or sections into the correct order.

In this exercise, you'll work on the Slides tab and in Slide Sorter view to logically arrange the slides in a presentation. You'll also delete a section you no longer need.

→ SET UP You need the ServiceD_start presentation located in your Chapter02 practice file folder to complete this exercise. Open the ServiceD_start presentation, and save it as *ServiceD*. Then follow the steps.

1. In the **Overview** pane, on the **Slides** tab, click the slide **2** thumbnail, and then drag it downward to the space above the thumbnail for slide **4**, but don't release the mouse button yet.

The thumbnail itself remains in place, but a bar indicates where the slide will move to when you release the mouse button.

2. Release the mouse button.

PowerPoint moves the slide to its new location in the Process section and switches the numbers of slides 2 and 3.

Tip You can move slides from one open presentation to another in Slide Sorter view. Display both presentations in Slide Sorter view, and then on the View tab, in the Window group, click the Arrange All button. Then drag slides from one presentation window to the other.

3. To the left of **Introduction** in the first section bar, click the black **Collapse Section** button. Then repeat this step for the **Process** section.

   Even with these two sections collapsed, you can't see all the slides.

4. On the **View Shortcuts** toolbar, click the **Slide Sorter** button.

5. Use the **Zoom Slider** at the right end of the status bar to adjust the zoom percentage so that you can see all the slides.

   We set the zoom percentage to 80%.

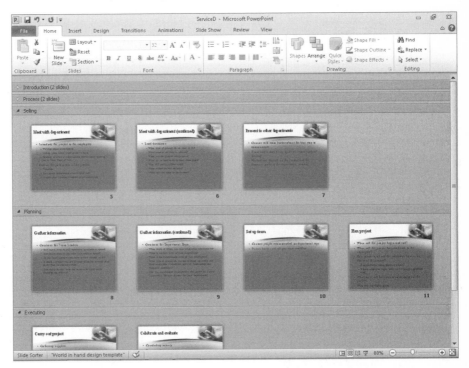

The sections you collapsed in Normal view are still collapsed in Slide Sorter view.

6. In the **Selling** section, click slide **7**, and then drag it to the left until its bar sits to the left of slide **5**.

   PowerPoint renumbers the slides in the section.

7. Point to the **Planning** section bar, right-click it, and then click **Move Section Up**.

   The Planning section bar and all its slides move above the Selling section. PowerPoint renumbers the slides in both sections.

8. Switch to Normal view.

9. Click the white **Expand Section** button to expand the **Introduction** and **Process** sections.

   These two sections could easily be combined into one section.

10. Click the **Process** section bar. Then in the **Slides** group, click the **Section** button, and click **Remove Section**.

    PowerPoint removes the Process section bar.

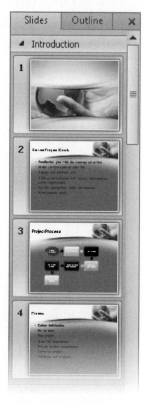

The Introduction section now contains four slides.

✖ **CLEAN UP** Save the ServiceD presentation, and then close it.

Key Points

- You can add as many slides as you want. Most templates provide a variety of ready-made slide layouts to choose from.

- If you change your mind about a slide or its layout, you can delete it or switch to a different layout.

- You can create slides with content already in place by importing an outline or reusing existing slides. Both methods save time and effort.

- Grouping slides into sections makes it easy to focus on specific parts of the presentation.

- If you need to change the order of slides or sections, you can rearrange them on the Slides tab in Normal view or in Slide Sorter view.

Chapter at a Glance

Enter text in placeholders, **page 56**

Add text boxes, **page 59**

Correct and size text while typing, **page 72**

Check spelling and choose the best words, **page 78**

Find and replace text and fonts, **page 84**

3 Work with Slide Text

In this chapter, you will learn how to

- ✔ Enter text in placeholders.
- ✔ Add text boxes.
- ✔ Edit text.
- ✔ Correct and size text while typing.
- ✔ Check spelling and choose the best words.
- ✔ Find and replace text and fonts.

In later chapters of this book, we show you ways to add fancy effects to electronic presentations so that you can really grab the attention of your audience. But no amount of animation, jazzy colors, and supporting pictures will convey your message if the words on the slides are inadequate to the task.

For most of your presentations, text is the foundation on which you build everything else. Even if you follow the current trend of building presentations that consist primarily of pictures, you still need to make sure that titles and any other words on your slides do their job, and do it well. So this chapter shows you various ways to work with text to ensure that the words are accurate, consistent, and appropriately formatted.

In this chapter, you'll learn how to enter and edit text on slides, on the Outline tab, and in text boxes. You'll see how the AutoCorrect feature helps you avoid typographical errors and the AutoFit feature makes the words you type fit in the available space. Then you'll see how the spell-checking feature can help you correct misspellings. Finally, you'll learn how to replace one word with another throughout a presentation by using the Find And Replace feature, which you also use to ensure the consistent use of fonts.

> **Practice Files** Before you can complete the exercises in this chapter, you need to copy the book's practice files to your computer. The practice files you'll use to complete the exercises in this chapter are in the Chapter03 practice file folder. A complete list of practice files is provided in "Using the Practice Files" at the beginning of this book.

Entering Text in Placeholders

When you add a new slide to a presentation, the layout you select indicates with placeholders the type and position of the objects on the slide. For example, a Title And Content slide has placeholders for a title and either a bulleted list with one or more levels of bullet points and subpoints or an illustration such as a table, chart, graphic, or movie clip. You can enter text directly into a placeholder on a slide in the Slide pane, or you can enter text on the Outline tab of the Overview pane, where the entire presentation is displayed in outline form.

When you point to a placeholder on a slide, the pointer changes to an I-beam. When you click the placeholder, a blinking cursor appears where you clicked to indicate where characters will appear when you type. As you type, the text appears both on the slide and on the Outline tab.

In this exercise, you'll enter slide titles, bullet points, and subpoints, both directly in placeholders on a slide and on the Outline tab.

 SET UP You don't need any practice files to complete this exercise. Open a new, blank presentation, and save it as *BuyingTripsA*. Then follow the steps.

1. In the **Slide** pane, click the slide's **Click to add title** placeholder.

   A selection box surrounds the title placeholder, and the cursor appears in the center of the box, indicating that the text you type will be centered in the placeholder.

2. Type **Buying Trips**. (Do not type the period.)

   By tradition, slide titles have no periods.

   Tip If you make a typing error while working through this exercise, press Backspace to delete the mistake, and then type the correct text. For information about more sophisticated ways of checking and correcting spelling, see "Correcting and Sizing Text While Typing" and "Checking Spelling and Choosing the Best Words," both later in this chapter.

3. In the **Overview** pane, click the **Outline** tab.

   Notice that the text you typed also appears there.

On the Outline tab, a slide icon appears adjacent to the slide title.

Troubleshooting The appearance of buttons and groups on the ribbon changes depending on the width of the program window. For information about changing the appearance of the ribbon to match our screen images, see "Modifying the Display of the Ribbon" at the beginning of this book.

4. In the **Slide** pane, click the **Click to add subtitle** placeholder.

5. Type **Ensuring Successful Outcomes**, and then press Enter to move the cursor to a new line in the same placeholder.

6. Type **Judy Lew, Purchasing Manager**.

   As you enter titles and bullet points throughout the exercises, don't type any ending punctuation marks.

7. On the Quick Access Toolbar, click the **Save** button.

   We won't tell you to save your work again in this exercise. Suffice it to say that you should save often.

8. Add a new slide with the **Title and Content** layout.

   See Also For information about adding slides, see "Adding and Deleting Slides" in Chapter 2, "Work with Slides."

   PowerPoint creates a slide with placeholders for a title and either a bulleted list or an illustration. The Outline tab now displays an icon for a second slide, and the status bar displays *Slide 2 of 2*.

9. Without clicking anywhere, type **Overview**.

   If you start typing on an empty slide without first selecting a placeholder, PowerPoint enters the text into the title placeholder.

10. On the **Outline** tab, click to the right of **Overview**, and then press Enter.

    PowerPoint adds a slide to the presentation, and an icon for slide 3 appears in the Outline pane.

11. Press the Tab key.

    The new slide changes to a bullet point on slide 2. The bullet is gray until you enter text for the bullet point.

12. Type **Preparing for a buying trip**, and then press Enter.

    PowerPoint adds a new bullet at the same level.

13. Type **Traveling internationally**, and then press Enter.

14. Type **Meeting the client**, and then press Enter.

15. Press Shift+Tab.

    On the Outline tab, the bullet changes into an icon for slide 3.

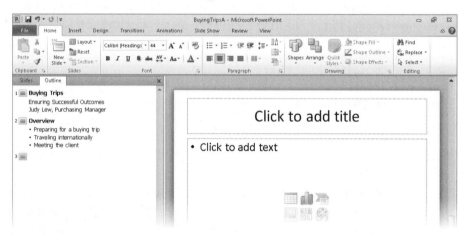

When you create a slide on the Outline tab, the new slide is displayed in the Slide pane.

16. Type **Preparing for a Buying Trip**, press Enter, and then press Tab.

17. Type **Know your needs**, and then press Enter.

18. On the **Home** tab, in the **Paragraph** group, click the **Increase List Level** button.

    PowerPoint creates a subpoint.

    Tip You can use the Increase List Level button to change slide titles to bullet points and bullet points to subpoints, both in the Slide pane and on the Outline tab. You can also use the Decrease List Level button to change subpoints to bullet points and bullet points to slide titles in both places. However, when you're entering text on the Outline tab, it's quicker to use keys—Tab and Shift+Tab—to perform these functions than it is to take your hands off the keyboard to use your mouse.

19. Type **Know your customers**, press Enter, and then type **Know the current trends**.

20. Press Ctrl+Enter.

    Instead of creating another bullet, PowerPoint creates a new slide.

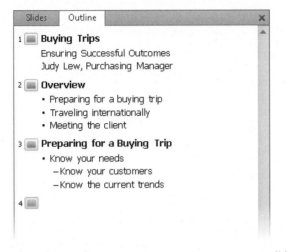

If you know what text you want to appear on your slides, it is often quicker to work on the Outline tab.

✖ **CLEAN UP** Save the BuyingTripsA presentation, and then close it.

Adding Text Boxes

The size and position of the placeholders on a slide are dictated by the slide's design. Every slide you create with a particular layout of a particular design has the same place-holders in the same locations, and the text you type in them has the same format.

If you want to add text that does not belong in a placeholder—for example, if you want to add an annotation to a graphic—you can create an independent text box and enter the text there. You can create a text box in two ways:

● You can click the Text Box button, click the slide where you want the text to appear, and then type. The text box grows to fit what you type on one line, even expanding beyond the border of the slide if necessary.

● You can click the Text Box button, drag a box where you want the text to appear on the slide, and then type. When the text reaches the right boundary of the box, the height of the box expands by one line so that the text can wrap. As you continue typing, the width of the box stays the same, but the height grows as necessary to accommodate all the text.

When you click inside a text box, the box is surrounded by a dashed border. You can then enter new text or edit existing text.

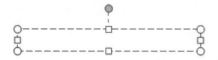

When the border is dashed, you can enter or edit text.

Clicking the dashed border changes it to a solid border. You can then manipulate the text box as a unit.

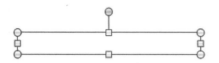

When the border is solid, you can manipulate the box.

You can move a text box by dragging its border, and you can copy it just as easily by holding down the Ctrl key while you drag. You can drag the blue squares and circles around the border of the box, which are called *sizing handles*, to change the size and shape of the text box. If you want the text in the text box to be oriented differently than the rest of the text on the slide, you can drag the green circle, which is called the *rotating handle*, to accomplish this purpose.

If you want to create a text box of a specific size or shape, you can right-click the box's border, click Format Shape, click Size in the Format Shape dialog box, and then change the settings. On the Text Box page of this dialog box, you can change the direction of text by displaying the Text Direction list and clicking one of the Rotate options. You can click Stacked in this list to keep the individual characters horizontal but make them run from top to bottom in the box instead of from left to right.

Tip If you want to change the size, shape, or behavior of a placeholder on an individual slide, you can use the same techniques as those you use with text boxes. If you want to make changes to the same placeholder on every slide, you should make the adjustments on the presentation's master slide. For more information about working with master slides, see "Viewing and Changing Slide Masters" in Chapter 13, "Create Custom Presentation Elements."

The Text Box page of the Format Shape dialog box.

On the Text Box page, you can also specify whether PowerPoint should shrink the text to fit the box if it won't all fit at the default size (18 points), and whether the text should wrap within the box.

To deselect the text box, you click a blank area of the slide. The border then disappears. If you want a text box to have a border when it's not selected, you can display the Format Shape dialog box, and on the Line Color page, select either Solid Line or Gradient Line. You can then fine-tune the border's color or gradient to achieve the effect you want.

In this exercise, you'll select and deselect a placeholder to see the effect on its border. You'll create one text box whose height stays constant while its width increases and another whose width stays constant while its height increases. You'll manipulate these text boxes by rotating and moving one of them and sizing the other.

SET UP You need the BuyingTripsB_start presentation located in your Chapter03 practice file folder to complete this exercise. Open the BuyingTripsB_start presentation, and save it as *BuyingTripsB*. Then follow the steps.

1. Move to slide **2**, and then on the slide, click the slide title.

   The cursor and dashed border indicate that the placeholder is selected for editing.

2. Point to the border of the placeholder, and when the pointer changes to a four-headed arrow, click the mouse button once.

   The placeholder is selected as a unit, as indicated by the solid border. Although you won't usually want to change the size or location of a text placeholder, while the placeholder has a solid border, you can size and move it just like any other text box. Your changes will affect only the placeholder on the current slide, not corresponding placeholders on other slides.

3. To deselect the placeholder, click outside it in a blank area of the slide.

4. Move to slide **5**, and then click anywhere in the bulleted list to display its placeholder.

5. On the **Insert** tab, in the **Text** group, click the **Text Box** button, and then point below and to the left of the placeholder for the bulleted list.

   The pointer shape changes to an upside-down *t*.

6. Click the slide to create a text box.

   A small, empty text box appears with a cursor blinking inside it.

Clicking the slide creates a single-line text box.

7. Type **Critical to get things off to a good start**.

   The width of the text box increases to accommodate the text as you type it.

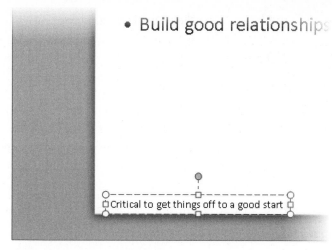

The text box grows horizontally.

8. To rotate the text so that it reads vertically instead of horizontally, point to the green rotating handle that is attached to the upper-middle handle of the text box, and drag it 90 degrees clockwise.

   Tip You can also rotate a text box by selecting the box for manipulation, and then on the Format contextual tab, in the Arrange group, clicking the Rotate button. In the list that appears, you can select an option to rotate the text box by 90 degrees to the left or right or to flip it horizontally or vertically.

9. Point to the border of the box (not to a handle), and then drag the box up and to the right, until it sits at the right edge of the slide.

10. Right-click the border of the box, and then click **Format Shape**.

11. In the **Format Shape** dialog box, click **Line Color**. Then click **Solid Line**.

    The page changes to allow you to pick the line color you want.

The Line Color page of the Format Shape dialog box.

12. Click the **Color** button, and in the top row of the **Theme Colors** palette, click the orange box (**Orange, Accent 6**). Then click **Close**.

13. Click a blank area of the slide to deselect the text box so that you can see the orange border.

14. Move to slide **6**, and then in the **Text** group, click the **Text Box** button. On the left side of the area below the bulleted list, drag approximately **2** inches to the right and **0.5** inch down.

    No matter what height you make the box, it snaps to a standard height when you release the mouse button.

15. Type **The Buyer manual has important information about the minimum requirements**.

    The width of the box does not change, but the height of the box increases to accommodate the complete entry.

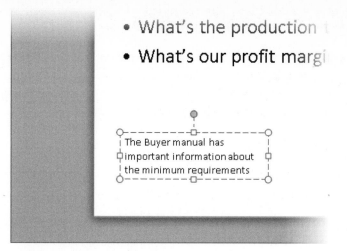

The text box grows vertically.

16. Click the border of the text box to select it as a unit. Then drag the solid border and the white sizing handles until the box is two lines high and the same width as the bullet points.

17. Click a blank area of the slide to deselect the text box.

    The border of the text box is no longer visible.

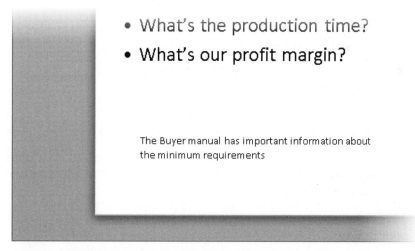

You can manually adjust the size and shape of a text box.

❌ **CLEAN UP** Save the BuyingTripsB presentation, and then close it.

Changing the Default Font for Text Boxes

When you create a text box, PowerPoint applies default settings such as the font, size, and style—regular, bold, and italic—as well as other effects, such as underline, small capitals, and embossing. To save yourself some formatting steps, you can change the default settings for the presentation you are working on.

To save the current settings as the new default:

1. In a new, blank presentation, create a text box and enter some text in it.

2. Select the text, and then on the Home tab, click the Font dialog box launcher.

3. Select the font, font style, size, color, underline style, and effects you want to apply to all the text boxes you create from now on in this presentation, and then click OK.

   You can also add other effects, such as a fill color, outline formatting, or a special effect.

   See Also For information about these other effects, see "Adding WordArt Text" in Chapter 9, "Add Other Enhancements."

4. Select the text box itself, right-click its border, and then click Set As Default Text Box.

5. Create another text box on the same slide, and then enter text in it.

   The text appears with the new default settings.

Editing Text

After you enter text in either a placeholder or a text box, you can change it at any time. You can insert new text by clicking where you want to make the insertion and simply typing. However, before you can change existing text, you have to select it by using the following techniques:

- **Word** Double-click the word to select the word and the space following it. Punctuation following the word is not selected.

- **Adjacent words, lines, or paragraphs** Drag through them. Alternatively, position the cursor at the beginning of the text you want to select, hold down the Shift key, and either press an arrow key to select characters one at a time or click at the end of the text you want to select.

- **Slide title** Click its slide icon on the Outline tab.

- **Bullet point or subpoint** Click its bullet on either the Outline tab or the slide.

- **All the text in a placeholder** Click inside the placeholder, click the Select button in the Editing group on the Home tab, and then click Select All.

  Keyboard Shortcut Press Ctrl+A after clicking inside the placeholder to select all the text.

  See Also For more information about keyboard shortcuts, see "Keyboard Shortcuts" at the end of this book.

- **All the objects on a slide** Select a placeholder (so that it has a solid border), click the Select button, and then click Select All. All the other objects on that slide are added to the selection. You can then work with all the objects as a unit.

  Tip Clicking Select and then Selection Pane displays the Selection And Visibility task pane, where you can specify whether particular objects should be displayed or hidden. You might want to hide an object if you're using the slide in similar presentations for two different audiences, one of which needs more detail than the other.

Selected text appears highlighted in the location where you made the selection—that is, on either the slide or the Outline tab.

To replace a selection, you type the new text. To delete the selection, you press either the Delete key or the Backspace key.

If you want to move or copy the selected text, you have three options:

- **Drag-and-drop editing** Use this feature, which is frequently referred to simply as *dragging*, when you need to move or copy text within the same slide or to a slide that is visible on the Outline tab without scrolling. Start by using any of the methods described previously to select the text. Then point to the selection, hold down the mouse button, drag the text to its new location, and release the mouse button. To copy the selection, hold down the Ctrl key while you drag.

- **Cut, Copy, and Paste buttons** Use this method when you need to move or copy text between two locations that you cannot see at the same time—for example, between slides that are not visible simultaneously on the Outline tab. Select the text, and click the Cut or Copy button in the Clipboard group on the Home tab. (The cut or copied item is stored in an area of your computer's memory called the *Microsoft Office Clipboard*, hence the name of the group.) Then reposition the cursor, and click the Paste button to insert the selection in its new location. If you click the Paste arrow instead of the button, PowerPoint displays a list of different ways to paste the selection.

Under Paste Options, buttons represent the ways in which you can paste the item.

Pointing to a button under Paste Options displays a preview of how the cut or copied item will look when pasted into the text in that format, so you can experiment with different ways of pasting until you find the one you want.

See Also For more information about the Clipboard, see the sidebar "About the Clipboard" later in this chapter.

● **Keyboard shortcuts** It can be more efficient to press key combinations to cut, copy, and paste selections than to click buttons on the ribbon. The main keyboard shortcuts for editing tasks are listed in the following table.

Task	Keyboard shortcuts
Cut	Ctrl+X
Copy	Ctrl+C
Paste	Ctrl+V
Undo	Ctrl+Z
Repeat/Redo	Ctrl+Y

Tip While moving and copying text on the Outline tab, you can collapse bullet points under slide titles so that you can see more of the presentation at one time. Double-click the icon of the slide whose bullet points you want to hide. Double-click again to redisplay the bullet points. To expand or collapse the entire outline at once, right-click the title of a slide, point to Expand or Collapse, and then click Expand All or Collapse All.

If you change your mind about a change you have made, you can reverse it by clicking the Undo button on the Quick Access Toolbar. If you undo an action in error, you can click the Redo button on the Quick Access Toolbar to reverse the change.

To undo multiple actions at the same time, you can click the Undo arrow and then click the earliest action you want to undo in the list. You can undo actions only in the order in which you performed them—that is, you cannot reverse your fourth previous action without first reversing the three actions that followed it.

Tip The number of actions you can undo is set to 20, but you can change that number by clicking the File tab to display the Backstage view, clicking Options to display the PowerPoint Options dialog box, clicking Advanced, and then in the Editing Options area of the Advanced page, changing the Maximum Number Of Undos setting.

In this exercise, you'll delete and replace words, as well as move bullet points and sub-points on the Outline tab and on slides.

SET UP You need the BuyingTripsC_start presentation located in your Chapter03 practice file folder to complete this exercise. Open the BuyingTripsC_start presentation, and save it as *BuyingTripsC*. Then follow the steps.

1. On the **Outline** tab, in the first bullet on slide **2**, double-click the word **buying**.

   When you select text on either the Outline tab or the slide, a small toolbar (called the *Mini Toolbar*) containing options for formatting the text appears. If you ignore the Mini Toolbar, it fades from view.

   See Also For information about using the Mini Toolbar, see "Changing the Alignment, Spacing, Size, and Look of Text" in Chapter 4, "Format Slides."

2. Press the Delete key.

3. In the slide **3** title, double-click **Buying**, and then press the Backspace key.

4. In the third bullet point on slide **5**, double-click **good**, and then type **lasting**, followed by a space.

   What you type replaces the selection. Notice that the text also changes in the Slide pane.

5. On slide **4**, click the bullet to the left of **Know the culture**.

   The entire bullet point is selected, including the invisible paragraph mark at the end.

   Tip When you want to work with a bullet point or subpoint as a whole, you need to ensure that the invisible paragraph mark at its end is included in the selection. If you drag across the text on the slide, you might miss the paragraph mark. As a precaution, hold down the Shift key and press End to be sure that the paragraph mark is part of the selection.

6. On the **Home** tab, in the **Clipboard** group, click the **Cut** button.

   Keyboard Shortcut Press Ctrl+X to cut the selection.

7. Click to the left of the word **Make** in the first bullet point on slide **5**, and then click the **Paste** button.

   Keyboard Shortcut Press Ctrl+V to paste the contents of the Clipboard.

   You have moved the bullet point from slide 4 to slide 5.

8. Display slide **3** in the **Slide** pane, and click the bullet point to the left of **Know your needs** to select the bullet point and its subpoints.

9. Drag the selection down and to the left of **Read the Buyer manual**.

   The bullet point and its subpoints move as a unit.

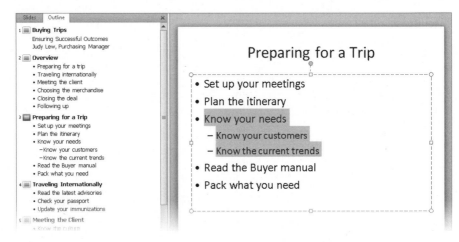

The change is reflected both on the slide and on the Outline tab.

10. On the Quick Access Toolbar, click the **Undo** button to reverse your last editing action.

    Keyboard Shortcut Press Ctrl+Z to undo the last editing action.

    The Redo button appears on the Quick Access Toolbar, to the right of Undo. When you point to the Undo or Redo button, the name in the ScreenTip reflects your last editing action—for example, Redo Drag And Drop.

11. On the Quick Access Toolbar, click the **Redo** button to restore the editing action.

    Keyboard Shortcut Press Ctrl+Y to restore the last editing action.

CLEAN UP Save the BuyingTripsC presentation, and then close it.

About the Clipboard

You can view the items that have been cut or copied to the Clipboard in the Clipboard task pane, which you display by clicking the Clipboard dialog box launcher on the Home tab.

The Clipboard stores items that have been cut or copied from any presentation.

To paste an individual item at the cursor, you simply click the item in the Clipboard task pane. To paste all the items, click the Paste All button. You can point to an item, click the arrow that appears, and then click Delete to remove it from the Clipboard and the task pane, or you can remove all the items by clicking the Clear All button.

You can control the behavior of the Clipboard task pane by clicking Options at the bottom of the pane, and choosing the circumstances under which you want the task pane to appear.

To close the Clipboard task pane, click the Close button at the right end of its title bar.

Correcting and Sizing Text While Typing

We all make mistakes while typing text in a presentation. To help you ensure that these mistakes don't go uncorrected, PowerPoint uses the AutoCorrect feature to catch and automatically correct many common capitalization and spelling errors. For example, if you type *teh* instead of *the* or *WHen* instead of *When*, AutoCorrect immediately corrects the entry.

Tip If you don't want an entry you type to be corrected—for example, if you want to start a new paragraph with a lowercase letter—click the Undo button on the Quick Access Toolbar when AutoCorrect makes the change.

You can customize AutoCorrect to recognize misspellings you routinely type or to ignore text you do not want AutoCorrect to change. You can also create your own AutoCorrect entries to automate the typing of frequently used text. For example, you might customize AutoCorrect to enter the name of your organization when you type only an abbreviation.

In addition to providing the AutoCorrect feature to correct misspellings as you type, PowerPoint provides an AutoFit feature to size text to fit its placeholder. By default, if you type more text than will fit in a placeholder, PowerPoint reduces the size of the text so that all the text fits, and displays the AutoFit Options button to the left of the place-holder. Clicking this button displays a menu that gives you control over automatic sizing. For example, you can stop sizing text for the current placeholder while retaining the AutoFit settings for other placeholders.

Tip You can also change the AutoFit settings for a placeholder on the Text Box page of the Format Shape dialog box. In the Autofit area, you can change the default Shrink Text On Overflow setting to Do Not Autofit. You can also specify that instead of the text being sized to fit the placeholder, the placeholder should be sized to fit the text.

You can change the default AutoFit settings by clicking Control AutoCorrect Options on the AutoFit Options button's menu to display the AutoFormat As You Type page of the AutoCorrect dialog box.

Clear the AutoFit Title Text To Placeholder and AutoFit Body Text To Placeholder check boxes to stop making text fit in the placeholder.

In this exercise, you'll use AutoCorrect to fix a misspelled word and you'll add an AutoCorrect entry. Then you'll use AutoFit to size text so that it fits within its placeholder and to make a long bulleted list fit on one slide by converting its placeholder to a two-column layout.

SET UP You need the CommunityServiceA_start presentation located in your Chapter03 practice file folder to complete this exercise. Open the Community-ServiceA_start presentation, and save it as *CommunityServiceA*. Then follow the steps.

1. Display slide **2**, and click the content placeholder.

2. Being careful for the purposes of this exercise to include the misspellings, type **Set up teh teem**, press the Enter key, and then type **Gather adn analyze data**.

   Almost immediately, AutoCorrect changes *teh* to *the* and *adn* to *and*. Notice that AutoCorrect does not change *teem* to *team*, or even flag it as a misspelling because *teem* is a legitimate word. PowerPoint cannot detect that you have used this homonym for *team* incorrectly. (A homonym is a word that sounds the same as another word but has a different meaning.)

3. Click the **File** tab to display the Backstage view, click **Options**, and then in the left pane of the **PowerPoint Options** dialog box, click **Proofing**.

4. In the **AutoCorrect options** area, click **AutoCorrect Options**.

The AutoCorrect dialog box opens.

The AutoCorrect page of the AutoCorrect dialog box.

Troubleshooting If the AutoCorrect page is not active, click its tab to display its options.

The top part of the dialog box lists general rules for correcting errors such as capitalization mistakes. You can change any of these rules by clearing the associated check box.

5. In the lower part of the dialog box, scroll through the huge table of misspellings.

When you type one of the entries in the first column, PowerPoint automatically substitutes the correct spelling from the second column. For this exercise, suppose you often misspell the word *category* as *catigory*.

6. In the **Replace** box above the table, type **catigory**, and then press the Tab key.

The table below scrolls to show you similar words that are already in the AutoCorrect list.

7. In the **With** box, type **category**, and then click **Add**.

Now if you type *catigory* in any presentation, PowerPoint will replace it with *category*.

8. Click **OK** to close the **AutoCorrect** dialog box, and then click **OK** again to close the **PowerPoint Options** dialog box.

9. On slide **2**, with the cursor to the right of the word **data**, press Enter, type **Assign to a catigory**, and then press Enter.

    PowerPoint changes the word *catigory* to *category*.

10. Display slide **1**, click the subtitle placeholder, and type **Community Service Committee**.

11. Without moving the cursor, hold down the Shift key, and click to the left of **Community** to select the three words you just typed. Then press Ctrl+C to copy the words to the Clipboard.

12. Open the **PowerPoint Options** dialog box, and then open the **AutoCorrect** dialog box.

13. With the cursor in the **Replace** box, type **csc**. Then click the **With** box, press Ctrl+V to paste in the words you copied to the Clipboard, and click **Add**.

14. Close the **AutoCorrect** dialog box, and then close the **PowerPoint Options** dialog box.

15. Display slide **3**, and click to the left of **Responsibilities**. Then type **csc**, and press the Spacebar.

    PowerPoint changes the initials *csc* to *Community Service Committee*.

Set up team

- ## Community Service Committee Responsibilities
  - ### Contact people recommended as department
    reps

AutoCorrect makes the replacement if you follow csc *with a space or a punctuation mark.*

16. Display slide **1**, and click at the right end of the title.

    Notice that the setting in the Font Size box in the Font group on the Home tab is 44.

17. Type **:** (a colon), press Enter, and then type **Planning, Selling, and Executing a Project**.

When you type the word *Project*, AutoFit reduces the size of the title to 40 so that it fits in the title placeholder.

After AutoFit reduces the size of text, the AutoFit Options button appears to the left of the adjusted placeholder.

18. Click the **AutoFit Options** button.

    A menu of options appears.

You can click Stop Fitting Text To This Placeholder to reverse the size adjustment and prevent future adjustments.

19. Press the Esc key to close the menu without making a selection.

20. Display slide **8**, click at the right end of the last subpoint, and notice that the font size is 28. Then press Enter, and type **How do we know if we are successful?**

    The text size changes from 28 to 26.

21. Click the **AutoFit Options** button.

    The menu of options appears.

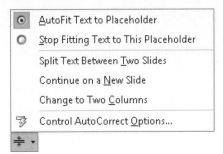

The menu for a bulleted list includes more options than the one for a title placeholder.

22. Click **Change to Two Columns**.

    The placeholder is instantly formatted to accommodate a two-column bulleted list.

23. Click a blank area of the slide.

    When the placeholder is not selected, it is easier to see the results.

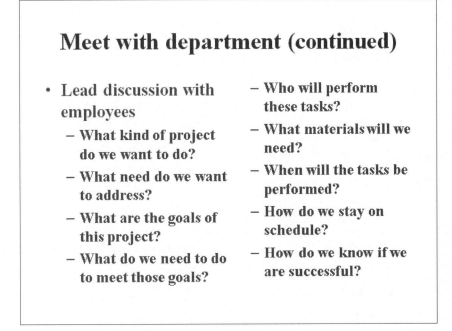

A two-column bulleted list.

 CLEAN UP If you want, display the AutoCorrect dialog box, and remove the *catigory* and *csc* entries from the replacement table. Save the CommunityServiceA presentation, and then close it.

Checking Spelling and Choosing the Best Words

The AutoCorrect feature is very useful if you frequently type the same misspelling. However, most misspellings are the result of erratic finger-positioning errors or memory lapses. You can use two different methods to ensure that the words in your presentations are spelled correctly in spite of these random occurrences.

- By default, PowerPoint's spelling checker checks the spelling of the entire presentation—all slides, outlines, notes pages, and handout pages—against its built-in dictionary. To draw attention to words that are not in its dictionary and that might be misspelled, PowerPoint underlines them with a red wavy underline. You can right-click a word with a red wavy underline to display a menu with a list of possible spellings. You can choose the correct spelling from the menu or tell PowerPoint to ignore the word.

  Tip To turn off this behind-the-scenes spell-checking, display the Backstage view, and click Options to open the PowerPoint Options dialog box. In the left pane, click Proofing, and then clear the Check Spelling As You Type check box.

- Instead of dealing with potential misspellings while you're creating a presentation, you can check the entire presentation in one session by clicking the Spelling button in the Proofing group on the Review tab. PowerPoint then works its way through the presentation, and if it encounters a word that is not in its dictionary, it displays the Spelling dialog box. After you indicate how PowerPoint should deal with the word, it moves on and displays the next word that is not in its dictionary, and so on.

The English-language version of Microsoft Office 2010 includes English, French, and Spanish dictionaries. If you use a word or phrase from a different language, you can mark it so that PowerPoint doesn't flag it as a misspelling.

You cannot make changes to the main dictionary in PowerPoint, but you can add correctly spelled words that are flagged as misspellings to the PowerPoint supplemental dictionary (called *CUSTOM.DIC*). You can also create and use custom dictionaries and use dictionaries from other Microsoft programs.

PowerPoint can check your spelling, but it can't alert you if you're not using the best word. Language is often contextual—the language you use in a presentation to members of a club is different from the language you use in a business presentation. To make sure you're using words that best convey your meaning in any given context, you can use the Thesaurus feature to look up alternative words, called *synonyms*, for a selected word.

Tip For many words, the quickest way to find a suitable synonym is to right-click the word, and point to Synonyms. You can then either click one of the suggested words or click Thesaurus to display the Research task pane.

In this exercise, you'll correct a misspelled word, mark a French phrase so that PowerPoint won't flag it as a misspelling, and check the spelling of an entire presentation. You'll then use the Thesaurus to replace a word on a slide with a more appropriate one.

 SET UP You need the CommunityServiceB_start presentation located in your Chapter03 practice file folder to complete this exercise. Open the Community-ServiceB_start presentation, and save it as *CommunityServiceB*. Then follow the steps.

1. Display slide **2**, and right-click **infermation**, which PowerPoint has flagged as a possible error with a red wavy underline.

   PowerPoint doesn't know whether you want to format the word or correct its spelling, so it displays both a Mini Toolbar and a menu.

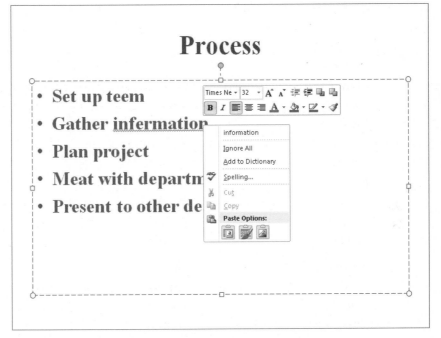

Right-clicking a flagged word displays options to format it or to correct it.

2. On the menu, click **information** to replace the misspelled word.

3. Move to slide **7**.

   The French words *Médecins* and *Frontières* have been flagged as possible errors.

4. Select **Médecins Sans Frontières**, and then on the **Review** tab, in the **Language** group, click the **Language** button, and then click **Set Proofing Language**.

   The Language dialog box opens.

You can choose from a wide selection of languages in this dialog box.

5. Scroll down the list of languages, click **French (France)**, and then click **OK**.

   Behind the scenes, PowerPoint marks *Médecins Sans Frontières* as a French phrase, and the words no longer have red wavy underlines.

6. Click a corner of the slide so that no placeholders are selected, and then press Ctrl+Home.

7. On the **Review** tab, in the **Proofing** group, click the **Spelling** button.

   Keyboard Shortcut Press F7 to begin checking the spelling of a presentation.

   PowerPoint begins checking the spelling in the presentation. The spelling checker stops on the word *Persue* and displays the Spelling dialog box.

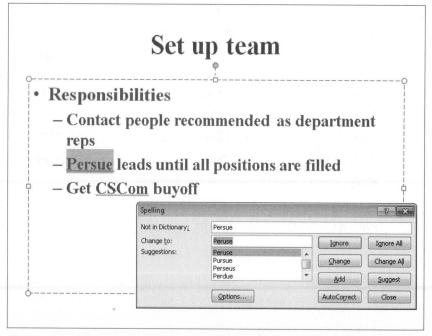

The words in the Suggestions list have the same capitalization as the possible misspelling.

8. In the **Suggestions** list, click **Pursue**, and then click **Change**.

   The spelling checker replaces *Persue* with the suggested *Pursue* and then stops on the word *CSCom*, suggesting *Como* as the correct spelling. For purposes of this exercise, assume that this is a common abbreviation for *Community Service Committee*.

9. Click **Add**.

   The term *CSCom* is added to the CUSTOM.DIC dictionary.

   Tip If you do not want to change a word or add it to the supplemental dictionary, you can click Ignore or Ignore All. The spelling checker then ignores either just that word or all instances of the word in the presentation during subsequent spell checking sessions.

   Next the spelling checker stops on *the* because it is the second of two occurrences of the word.

10. Click **Delete**.

    The duplicated word is deleted. Now the spelling checker identifies *employes* as a misspelling.

11. In the suggestions list, click **employees**, and then click **AutoCorrect**.

    PowerPoint adds the misspelling and the selected spelling to the AutoCorrect substitution table.

12. Click **Change** to change *succesful* to *successful*.

13. When a message box tells you that the spelling check is complete, click **OK**.

    This presentation still has spelling problems—words that are spelled correctly but that aren't correct in context. We'll leave it to you to proof the slides and correct these errors manually. In the meantime, we'll finish the exercise by using the Thesaurus to find a synonym.

14. On slide **1**, select the word **Executing** (but not the space following the word).

15. On the **Review** tab, in the **Proofing** group, click the **Thesaurus** button.

    Keyboard Shortcut Press Shift+F7 to activate the Thesaurus.

    The Research task pane opens on the right side of the screen, displaying a list of synonyms for the selected word.

```
┌────────────────────────────────┐
│ Research              ▼  ✕      │
│ Search for:                    │
│ ┌──────────────────────┐  ┌─┐  │
│ │ Executing            │  │→│  │
│ └──────────────────────┘  └─┘  │
│ ┌──────────────────────┐  ┌─┐  │
│ │ Thesaurus: English (U.S.) │ │▼│ │
│ └──────────────────────┘  └─┘  │
│ ┌─────────┐  ┌─────────┐       │
│ │ ◉ Back ▼│  │ ◉    ▼  │       │
│ └─────────┘  └─────────┘       │
│ ◢ Thesaurus: English (U.S.)  ▲ │
│   ◢ Performing (v.)            │
│     Performing                 │
│     Implementing               │
│     Effecting                  │
│     Completing                 │
│     Accomplishing              │
│     Finishing              ▤   │
│     Achieving                  │
│     Fulfilling                 │
│     Carry out (Dictionary F... │
│     Failing (Antonym)          │
│   ◢ Killing (v.)               │
│     Killing                    │
│     Slaying                    │
│     Murdering                  │
│     Hanging                    │
│     Electrocuting              │
│     Guillotining               │
│     Put to death (Dictionar... │
│                            ▼   │
│ ◉ Get services on Office       │
│   Marketplace                  │
│ 🔍 Research options...         │
└────────────────────────────────┘
```

The synonyms have the same capitalization as the selected word.

16. Below **Performing**, point to **Completing**, click the arrow that appears, and then click **Insert**.

    Tip If you don't see an obvious substitute for the selected word, click a word that is close in the Thesaurus list to display synonyms for that word.

17. At the right end of the **Research** task pane, click the **Close** button.

✖ CLEAN UP If you want, display the AutoCorrect dialog box, and remove the *employes* entry from the replacement table. To remove *CSCom* from the supplemental dictionary, display the Proofing page of the PowerPoint Options dialog box, and click Custom Dictionaries. Then in the Custom Dictionaries dialog box, click Edit Word List. Click CSCom, click Delete, and click OK three times. Then save and close the CommunityServiceB presentation.

Researching Information and Translating Text

In addition to the Thesaurus, the Research task pane provides access to a variety of informational resources. Display the Research task pane by clicking the Research button in the Proofing group and then enter a topic in the Search For box, specifying in the box below which resource PowerPoint should use to look for information about that topic. Clicking Research Options at the bottom of the Research task pane displays the Research Options dialog box, where you can specify which of a predefined set of reference materials and other Internet resources will be available from the list.

PowerPoint also comes with three translation tools with which you can quickly translate words and phrases, or even entire presentations.

- When the Mini Translator is turned on, you can point to a word or selected phrase to display a translation in the specified language. (You turn the Mini Translator on or off by clicking the Translate button in the Language group of the Review tab and then clicking Mini Translator.) When the box containing the translation is displayed, you can click the Expand button to display the Research task pane, where you can change the translation language. You can also copy the translated word or phrase, or hear it spoken for you.

  To change the default language used by the Mini Translator, click Choose Translation Language on the Translate menu. Then in the Translation Language Options dialog box, you can select from a list of languages, including Arabic, Chinese, Greek, Hebrew, Italian, Japanese, Korean, Polish, Portuguese, Russian, Spanish, and Swedish.

- To obtain the translation of a selected word, you can also click Translate Selected Text in the Translate menu to display the Research task pane. In the task pane, you can also type a word in the Search For box, specify the language you want, and then click Start Searching. PowerPoint consults the online bilingual dictionary for the language you chose and displays the result.

Finding and Replacing Text and Fonts

Sometimes a word you use might be correctly spelled but just not be the correct word. You can find and change specific text in a presentation by clicking the buttons in the Editing group on the Home tab to do the following:

- Click the Find button to locate each occurrence of a word, part of a word, or a phrase. In the Find dialog box, you enter the text, and then click Find Next. You can specify whether PowerPoint should locate only matches with the exact capitalization (also known as the *case*); in other words, if you specify *person*, you don't want PowerPoint to locate *Person*. You can also tell PowerPoint whether it should locate only matches for the entire text; in other words, if you specify *person*, you don't want PowerPoint to locate *personal*.

- Click the Replace button to locate each occurrence of a word, part of a word, or a phrase and replace it with something else. In the Replace dialog box, you enter the text you want to find and what you want to replace it with, click Find Next, and then click Replace to replace the found occurrence. You can also click Replace All to replace all occurrences. Again, you can specify whether to match capitalization and whole words.

You can also click the Replace arrow, and in the Replace list, click Replace Fonts to find and replace a font throughout a presentation. In the Replace Font dialog box, you can specify the font you want to change and the font you want PowerPoint to replace it with.

In this exercise, you'll first find and replace a word and then find and replace a font.

SET UP You need the CommunityServiceC_start presentation located in your Chapter03 practice file folder to complete this exercise. Open the Community-ServiceC_start presentation, and save it as *CommunityServiceC*. Then follow the steps.

1. On the **Home** tab, in the **Editing** group, click the **Replace** button.

    Keyboard Shortcut   Press Ctrl+H to open the Replace dialog box.

    The Replace dialog box opens.

If you have already used the Find or Replace command, your previous Find What and Replace With entries carry over to this replace operation.

Tip To move a dialog box so that it doesn't hide the text, drag its title bar.

2. In the **Find what** box, type **department**, and then press Tab.

3. In the **Replace with** box, type **unit**.

4. Select the **Match case** check box to locate text that exactly matches the capitalization you specified and replace it with the capitalization you specified.

5. Click **Find Next**.

PowerPoint finds and selects part of the word *departments* on slide 2.

If you select the Find Whole Words Only check box, PowerPoint does not match this instance of department.

6. Click **Replace**.

   PowerPoint replaces *departments* with *units*, and then locates the next match.

7. Click **Replace All**.

   A message box tells you that PowerPoint has finished searching the presentation and that the replace operation changed nine occurrences of the text.

8. Click **OK**, and then in the **Replace** dialog box, click **Close**.

   Because you selected Match Case for this replace operation, one occurrence of *Department* has not been changed. We'll leave it to you to change it manually.

9. Click a blank area of the current slide so that no placeholder is selected, press Ctrl+Home to move to slide **1**, and then click the title.

   Notice that *Calibri (Headings)* is displayed in the Font box in the Font group.

10. Display slide **2**, and click first the title and then any bullet point.

    Notice that the font used for these elements is Times New Roman. Let's change this font to make it consistent with the title slide.

11. Click a corner of the slide so that no placeholder is selected.

12. In the **Editing** group, click the **Replace** arrow, and then click **Replace Fonts**.

    The Replace Font dialog box opens.

Replace Font	? ✕
Re**p**lace:	**Replace**
Arial ▾	
With:	**Close**
Agency FB ▾	

    The default setting is to replace all instances of the Arial font with the Agency FB font.

13. Display the **Replace** list, and click **Times New Roman**.

    The Replace list includes only Arial and the fonts in the presentation.

14. Display the **With** list, and click **Calibri**.

    The With list includes all the fonts available on your computer.

15. Click **Replace**.

    All the Times New Roman text in the presentation changes to Calibri.

16. Click **Close** to close the **Replace Font** dialog box.

 CLEAN UP Save the CommunityServiceC presentation, and then close it.

Key Points

- You can enter and edit text both on the Outline tab or directly on a slide, depending on which is most efficient.

- You can place text wherever you want it on a slide by using text boxes.

- PowerPoint provides assistance by correcting common spelling errors and adjusting the size of text so that it fits optimally on a slide.

- The spelling checker flags possible misspellings so that you can take care of them as you type. Or you can check the spelling of an entire presentation.

- You can take advantage of the Find and Replace features to ensure consistent use of terms and fonts throughout a presentation.

Chapter at a Glance

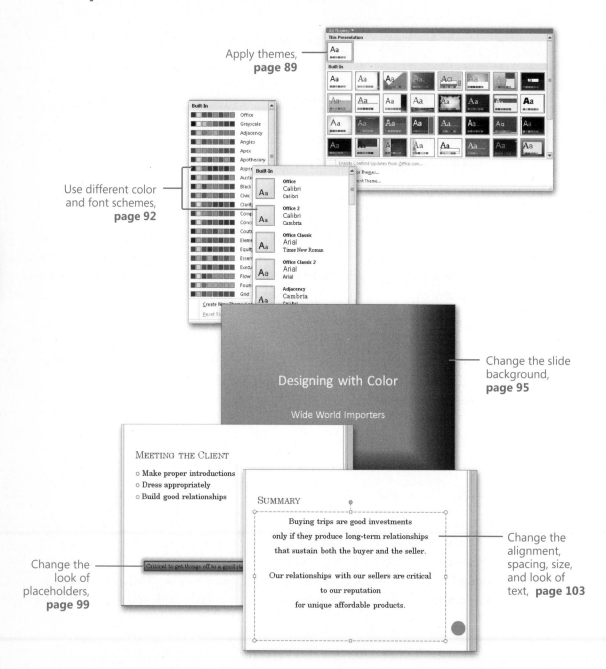

Apply themes, **page 89**

Use different color and font schemes, **page 92**

Change the slide background, **page 95**

Designing with Color

Wide World Importers

MEETING THE CLIENT

o Make proper introductions
o Dress appropriately
o Build good relationships

Critical to get things off to a good st...

SUMMARY

Buying trips are good investments
only if they produce long-term relationships
that sustain both the buyer and the seller.

Our relationships with our sellers are critical
to our reputation
for unique affordable products.

Change the look of placeholders, **page 99**

Change the alignment, spacing, size, and look of text, **page 103**

4 Format Slides

In this chapter, you will learn how to

- ✔ Apply themes.
- ✔ Use different color and font schemes.
- ✔ Change the slide background.
- ✔ Change the look of placeholders.
- ✔ Change the alignment, spacing, size, and look of text.

An overall consistent look, punctuated by variations that add weight exactly where it is needed, can enhance the likelihood that your message will be well received and absorbed by your intended audience. To make your Microsoft PowerPoint 2010 presentations visually appealing, you can add enhancements to the presentation as a whole or to individual slides.

In this chapter, you'll apply a theme to a presentation and then change the theme's color and font schemes. You'll add color and shading to the background of slides and to the background of placeholders. Finally, you'll change the look of specific text elements.

> **Practice Files** Before you can complete the exercises in this chapter, you need to copy the book's practice files to your computer. The practice files you'll use to complete the exercises in this chapter are in the Chapter04 practice file folder. A complete list of practice files is provided in "Using the Practice Files" at the beginning of this book.

Applying Themes

When you create a presentation based on a template or a ready-made design, the presentation includes a theme—a combination of colors, fonts, formatting, graphics, and other elements that gives the presentation a coherent look. Even a presentation developed from scratch has a theme; the Office theme is applied by default. This theme consists of a white background, a very basic set of colors, and the Calibri font.

If you want to change the theme applied to a presentation, you can choose one from the Themes gallery. By using the Live Preview feature, you can easily try different effects until you find the one you want.

See Also For information about creating your own themes, see "Creating Theme Colors and Fonts" in Chapter 13, "Create Custom Presentation Elements."

In this exercise, you'll change the theme applied to one presentation that was created from scratch and to another that was created from a template.

SET UP You need the Landscaping_start and CompanyMeetingA_start presentations located in your Chapter04 practice file folder to complete this exercise. Open the presentations, and save them as *Landscaping* and *CompanyMeetingA*, respectively. Then follow the steps.

1. With the **Landscaping** presentation active, on the **Design** tab, in the **Themes** group, click the **More** button.

   The Themes gallery appears, displaying all the available themes.

   The theme attached to this presentation is identified in the This Presentation area.

2. Point to each theme thumbnail in turn to see a live preview of what the presentation will look like with that theme applied.

   Notice that the themes are organized alphabetically and that their names appear in ScreenTips when you point to them.

3. Click the **Austin** thumbnail to apply that theme to the entire presentation.

4. Click the **Home** tab, and then on slide **1**, click the presentation's title.

   Instead of a white background with black text in the Calibri font, the presentation now has a green background design with title text in the Century Gothic font.

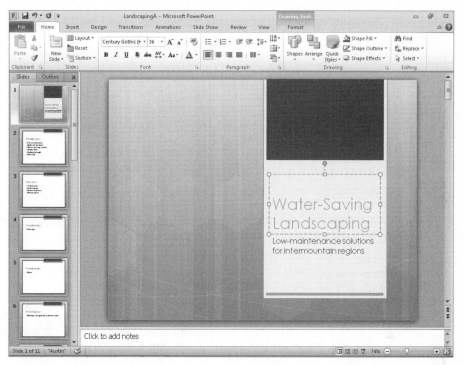

Most built-in themes have a distinctive title slide design that is modified for all the other slide layouts.

Troubleshooting The appearance of buttons and groups on the ribbon changes depending on the width of the program window. For information about changing the appearance of the ribbon to match our screen images, see "Modifying the Display of the Ribbon" at the beginning of this book.

5. On the **View** tab, in the **Window** group, click the **Switch Windows** button, and click **CompanyMeetingA** to switch to that presentation.

   This presentation already has a theme applied to it.

6. Display the **Themes** gallery, and then click the **Urban** thumbnail.

   The background of the presentation now has dark blue and teal accents, and the text is in blue Trebuchet and black Georgia.

 CLEAN UP Save and close the CompanyMeetingA and LandscapingA presentations.

Using Different Color and Font Schemes

Every presentation you create with PowerPoint 2010, even a blank one, has a set of colors, called a *color scheme*, associated with its theme. A color scheme consists of 12 complementary colors designed to be used for the following elements of a slide:

● **Text/Background** Use these four colors for dark text on a light background or light text on a dark background.

● **Accent 1 through Accent 6** Use these six colors for objects other than text.

● **Hyperlink** Use this color to draw attention to hyperlinks.

● **Followed Hyperlink** Use this color to indicate visited hyperlinks.

When you click color buttons such as the Font Color button in the Font group on the Home tab, the color palette displays 10 of the 12 colors with light to dark gradients. (The two background colors are not represented in these palettes.)

Understanding color schemes can help you create professional-looking presentations that use an appealing balance of color. You're not limited to using the colors in a presentation's color scheme, but because they have been selected by professional designers and are based on good design principles, using them ensures that your slides will be pleasing to the eye.

See Also For information about how scheme colors are allocated, see "Creating Theme Colors and Fonts" in Chapter 13, "Create Custom Presentation Elements." For information about using non-scheme colors, see the sidebar "Non–Color Scheme Colors" later in this chapter.

To view the color schemes you can apply to a presentation, you display the Colors gallery, which has Live Preview capabilities. When you find a color scheme you like, you simply click it to change the color scheme of all the slides in the presentation.

Tip To apply a color scheme only to a selected slide, right-click the scheme and then click Apply To Selected Slides

In addition to changing the color scheme, you can change the font scheme, which provides two complementary fonts for each theme. The Fonts gallery lists the combinations in alphabetical order by theme. In each combination, the top font (called the *heading font*) is used for slides titles, and the bottom font (called the *body font*) is used for other slide text.

If none of the color schemes is exactly what you're looking for, you can create your own by clicking Create New Theme Colors at the bottom of the Colors gallery and assembling colors in the Create New Theme Colors dialog box. You can also create a custom font scheme by clicking Create New Theme Fonts at the bottom of the Fonts gallery and then specifying the font combination you want in the Create New Theme Fonts dialog box.

After you save either type of custom scheme, you can apply it to one or all of the slides in a presentation.

When you apply a different color scheme or font scheme to a presentation, your changes are stored with the presentation and do not affect the underlying theme.

Tip Also associated with each theme is an effects scheme. This scheme ensures that the shapes in the presentation have a consistent look. Clicking the Effects button in the Themes group of the Design tab displays a gallery of effect combinations to choose from.

In this exercise, you'll apply a different color scheme to a presentation, create your own scheme, change the color scheme of one slide, and then apply a different font scheme.

SET UP You need the CompanyMeetingB_start presentation located in your Chapter04 practice file folder to complete this exercise. Open the CompanyMeetingB_start presentation, and save it as *CompanyMeetingB*. Then follow the steps.

1. On the **Design** tab, in the **Themes** group, click the **Colors** button.

   The Colors gallery appears.

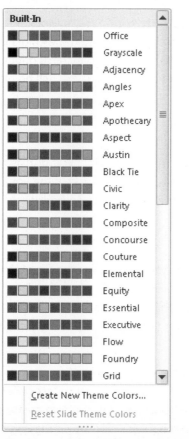

The color schemes show 8 of the 12 available colors.

2. In the gallery, point to a few color schemes, and watch the Live Preview effect on the active slide.

3. Click **Essential** to apply that color scheme to the presentation instead of the default color scheme of the Urban theme.

   Notice that the theme retains all of its other characteristics, such as the fonts and background graphic; only the colors change.

4. With slide **1** displayed, in the **Themes** group, click the **Colors** button.

5. Right-click the **Solstice** color scheme, and then click **Apply to Selected Slides**.

   PowerPoint applies the Solstice color scheme to only the title slide, changing its main background color from red to dark brown, but retaining the gold accent color.

6. On the **Design** tab, in the **Themes** group, click the **Fonts** button.

   The Fonts gallery appears.

| A | Fonts ▾ |

Two fonts are assigned to each theme.

7. In the **Fonts** gallery, point to a few font schemes to display live previews of their effects on the active slide.

8. Click **Newsprint**.

PowerPoint applies that font scheme to the presentation instead of the default font scheme of the Urban theme.

The title slide with the new font scheme.

✖ CLEAN UP Save the CompanyMeetingB presentation, and then close it.

Changing the Slide Background

In PowerPoint, you can customize the background of a slide by adding a solid color, a color gradient, a texture, or even a picture.

A color gradient is a visual effect in which a solid color gradually changes from light to dark or dark to light. PowerPoint offers several gradient patterns, each with variations. You can also choose a preset arrangement of colors from professionally designed backgrounds in which different colors gradually merge.

If you want something fancier than a solid color or a gradient, you can give the slide background a texture. PowerPoint comes with several built-in textures that you can easily apply to the background of slides. If none of these meets your needs, you might want to use a picture of a textured surface. For a dramatic effect, you can also incorporate an image or design of your own, although these are best reserved for small areas of the slide rather than the entire background.

In this exercise, you'll shade the background of one slide. Then you'll apply a textured background to all the slides in the presentation.

SET UP You need the ColorDesign_start presentation located in your Chapter04 practice file folder to complete this exercise. Open the ColorDesign_start presentation, and save it as *ColorDesign*. Then follow the steps.

1. On the **Design** tab, in the **Background** group, click the **Background Styles** button.

    The Background Styles gallery appears.

    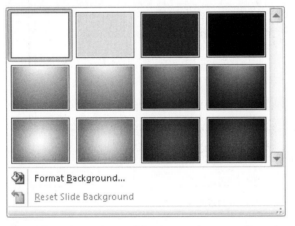

    The gallery shows four solid colors and two gradients in each of four colors taken from the theme's color scheme.

2. In the gallery, point to each thumbnail in turn to see a live preview of its effects.

3. Click the third thumbnail in the second row (**Style 7**).

   Instantly, the background of all the slides in the presentation change to a blue gradient.

4. Click the **Background Styles** button again, and then at the bottom of the gallery, click **Format Background**.

   The Format Background dialog box opens.

The Fill page shows the settings that control the gradient.

5. Click the **Type** arrow to display the list of options, and then click **Rectangular**.

   Behind the dialog box, the active slide changes to reflect this setting.

6. Display the **Direction** list, and click the rightmost thumbnail (**From Top Left Corner**).

7. In the **Gradient stops** area, drag the middle handle on the slider (**Stop 2 of 3**) to the right until the **Position** setting is **80%**.

   Behind the dialog box, you can see that 80 percent of the slide is now a lighter shade, with the gradient to dark occupying only about 20 percent.

8. Display the **Color** list, and then under **Theme Colors**, click the third box in the purple column (**Purple, Accent 4, Lighter 40%**).

9. Click **Close**.

   PowerPoint applies the shaded background to the current slide only.

The title slide has a two-tone gradient that gives a raised effect.

10. Click the **Background Styles** button again, and then click **Format Background**.

11. In the **Format Background** dialog box, click **Picture or texture fill**.

    The active slide shows a live preview of the default texture.

12. Display the **Texture** gallery, and then click **Purple mesh**.

13. Click the **Apply to All** button, and then click **Close**.

    PowerPoint applies the textured background to all the slides in the presentation.

14. In the **Themes** group, click the **More** button.

    The Themes gallery appears.

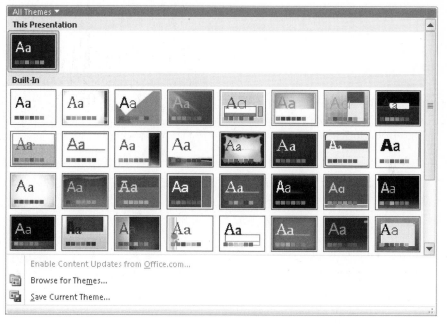

At the top of the gallery is a thumbnail reflecting the formatting you have applied to this presentation.

✖ **CLEAN UP** Save the ColorDesign presentation, and then close it.

Changing the Look of Placeholders

For a consistent look, you won't usually want to change the formatting of a presentation's placeholders. However, when you want to draw attention to an entire slide or an element of a slide, you can do so effectively by making specific placeholders stand out. You might also want to format text boxes that you have drawn manually on a slide.

See Also For information about drawing text boxes, see "Adding Text Boxes" in Chapter 3, "Work with Slide Text."

When you format a placeholder or a text box, you are essentially formatting a shape. You have the following options:

- Fill the background with a color, gradient, texture, pattern, or picture.
- Change the color and style of the shape's outline.
- Apply a style such as a shadow, reflection, or glow.
- Apply a three-dimensional effect.

In this exercise, you'll first apply a color to a text box. Then you'll change its border and give it a glow effect.

SET UP You need the BusinessTravelA_start presentation located in your Chapter04 practice file folder to complete this exercise. Open the BusinessTravelA_start presentation, and save it as *BusinessTravelA*. Then follow the steps.

1. Display slide **5**, click anywhere in the free-standing text at the bottom of the slide, and then click the border of the text box to select the box for manipulation.

2. On the **Format** contextual tab, in the **Shape Styles** group, click the **Shape Fill** arrow.

The Shape Fill palette appears.

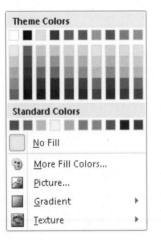

Like other palettes, the Shape Fill palette reflects the theme's colors.

3. In the palette, point to a few colors in turn to see a live preview of its effects on the background of the text box.

4. Click the third shade in the orange column (**Orange, Accent 1, Lighter 40%**).

   The background of the text box is now a medium orange color.

5. Click the **Shape Fill** arrow again, and then below the palette, point to **Gradient**.

   The Gradient gallery appears.

This gallery offers light and dark versions of gradients in different directions.

6. Under **Dark Variations**, click the second thumbnail in the third row (**Linear Up**).

7. In the **Shape Styles** group, click the **Shape Outline** arrow, and under **Standard Colors**, click the **Dark Red** box.

8. Click the **Shape Outline** arrow again. Then below the palette, point to **Weight**, and in the list, click **3 pt**.

   Tip The abbreviation *pt* stands for *point*. A point is a unit of measurement used in the design and publishing industries. There are 72 points to the inch.

9. In the **Shape Styles** group, click the **Shape Effects** button.

   A list of all the types of effects you can apply to the text box appears.

	Preset ▸
	Shadow ▸
	Reflection ▸
	Glow ▸
	Soft Edges ▸
	Bevel ▸
	3-D Rotation ▸

   Many possible effects are available with a couple of mouse clicks.

10. In turn, display the options for each type, and point to a few to see their live previews.

11. When you have finished exploring, point to **Glow**, and then click the first thumbnail in the last row (**Orange, 18 pt glow, Accent color 1**).

12. Click away from the text box to release the selection.

    The text box is less likely to be overlooked now.

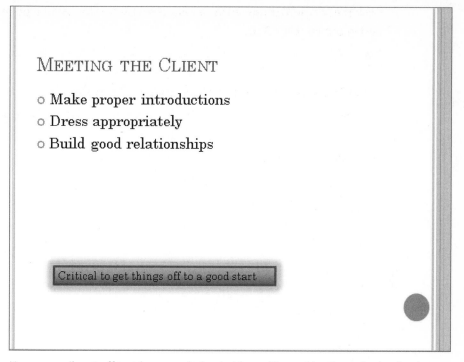

You can easily set off text boxes and placeholders with combinations of color, borders, and effects.

 **CLEAN UP** Save the BusinessTravelA presentation, and then close it.

Changing the Alignment, Spacing, Size, and Look of Text

In most PowerPoint templates, text appears as either a slide title or a bulleted list. The alignment and spacing of the text are controlled by the design built into the template. You can override these settings, which are collectively called *paragraph formatting*. Click anywhere in the paragraph, and then do the following:

● **Lists** Click the Bullets arrow to display a gallery of alternative built-in bullet symbols. You can click None to remove bullet formatting and create an ordinary paragraph. To switch to a numbered list, click the Numbering arrow, and then click the numbering style you want.

- **Alignment** Click one of the following alignment buttons in the Paragraph group on the Home tab:

  ○ Click the Align Text Left button to align text against the placeholder's left edge. Left-alignment is the usual choice for paragraphs.

  Keyboard Shortcut Press Ctrl+L to left-align text.

  See Also For more information about keyboard shortcuts, see "Keyboard Shortcuts" at the end of this book.

  ○ Click the Center button to align text in the middle of the placeholder. Center-alignment is often used for titles and headings.

  Keyboard Shortcut Press Ctrl+E to center text.

  ○ Click the Align Text Right button to align text against the placeholder's right edge. Right-alignment isn't used much for titles and paragraphs, but you might want to use it in text boxes.

  Keyboard Shortcut Press Ctrl+R to right-align text.

  ○ Click the Justify button to align text against both the left and right edges, adding space between words to fill the line. You might justify a single, non-bulleted paragraph on a slide for a neat look.

- **Line spacing** Click the Line Spacing button in the Paragraph group, and make a selection.

- **Paragraph spacing** Open the Paragraph dialog box, either by clicking the Line Spacing button and then clicking Line Spacing Options at the bottom of the menu or by clicking the dialog box launcher in the lower-right corner of the Paragraph group. You can then adjust the Before and After settings for the entire paragraph.

In addition to changing the look of paragraphs, you can manipulate the look of individual words by manually applying settings that are collectively called *character formatting*. After selecting the characters you want to format, you can make changes by using the commands in the Font group on the Home tab, as follows:

- **Font** Override the font specified by the font scheme by making a selection in the Font box.

- **Size** Manually control the size of text either by clicking the Increase Font Size or Decrease Font Size button or by setting a precise size in the Font Size box.

  Keyboard Shortcut Press Ctrl+Shift+> or Ctrl+Shift+< to increase or decrease font size.

Tip If you turn off AutoFit so that you can manually size text, you have two ways to adjust the size of placeholders to fit their text: by manually dragging the handles around a selected placeholder, or by clicking Resize Shape To Fit Text on the Text Box page of the Format Shape dialog box. For information about AutoFit, see "Correcting and Sizing Text While Typing" in Chapter 3, "Work with Slide Text."

- **Style** Apply attributes such as bold, italic, underlining, and shadow and strike-through effects to selected characters.

$$\boxed{\textbf{B} \quad \textit{I} \quad \underline{\textbf{U}} \quad \textbf{S} \quad \text{abc}}$$

The character style buttons.

Keyboard Shortcut Press Ctrl+B to make text bold, Ctrl+I to make it italic, or Ctrl+U to underline it.

- **Color** Change the color of the selected characters by clicking the Font Color arrow and then clicking the color you want in the palette.

- **Case** Change the capitalization of the words—for example, you can change small letters to capital letters—by clicking the Change Case button and then clicking the case you want.

- **Character spacing** Increase or decrease the space between the letters in a selection by clicking the Character Spacing button and then clicking the option you want. You can also click More Spacing to display the Character Spacing page of the Font dialog box, where you can specify spacing more precisely.

Tip You can clear all manually applied character formatting from a selection by clicking the Clear All Formatting button.

To make it quick and easy to apply the most common paragraph and character formatting, PowerPoint displays the Mini Toolbar when you make a text selection. This toolbar contains the same buttons you'll find in the Font and Paragraph groups on the Home tab, but they're all in one place, adjacent to the selection. If you don't want to apply any of the Mini Toolbar formats, you can simply ignore it, and it will disappear.

The Mini Toolbar.

After you have formatted the text on a slide, you might find that you want to adjust the way lines break to achieve a more balanced look. This is often the case with slide titles, but bullet points and regular text can sometimes also benefit from a few manually inserted line breaks. You can simply press Shift+Enter to insert a line break at the cursor.

This fine-tuning should wait until you have taken care of all other formatting of the slide element, because changing the font, size, and attributes of text can affect how it breaks.

In this exercise, you'll experiment with changing various types of character formatting and paragraph formatting to achieve the look you want. You'll also insert a few line breaks to balance the text on a slide.

SET UP You need the BusinessTravelB_start presentation located in your Chapter04 practice file folder to complete this exercise. Open the BusinessTravelB_start presentation, and save it as *BusinessTravelB*. Then follow the steps.

1. Display slide **3**, and in the fourth bullet point, double-click **Buyer**.

   The Mini Toolbar appears.

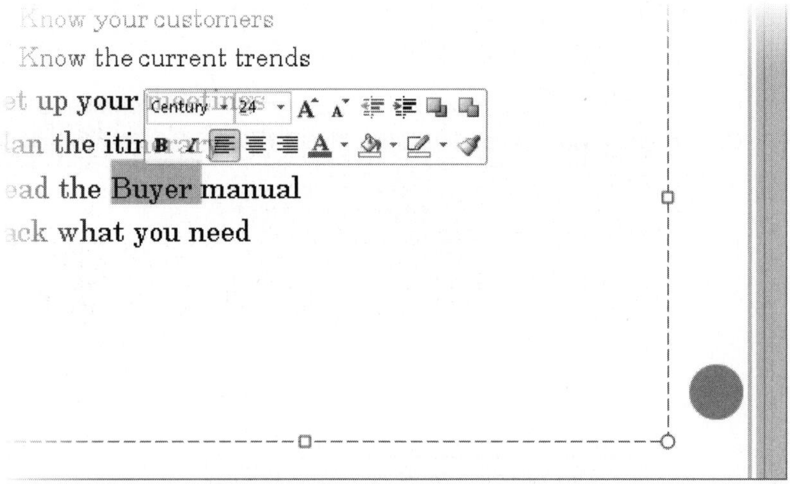

   Know your customers
   Know the current trends
   et up your
   an the itin
   ead the Buyer manual
   ck what you need

   The Mini Toolbar is a shadow until you point to it.

2. Move the pointer over the Mini Toolbar to make it active, and then click the **Italic** button.

3. Display slide **4**, and in the **Slide** pane, drag diagonally across the four bullet points to select them.

4. On the **Home** tab, in the **Font** group, click the **Font Color** arrow. Then under **Standard Colors** in the palette, click the **Red** box.

5. Display slide **5**, and click anywhere in the bulleted list. Then in the **Editing** group, click the **Select** button, and click **Select All**.

   All the text in the placeholder is selected. The text at the bottom is not selected because it is in a separate text box, not in the placeholder.

6. In the **Font** group, click the **Increase Font Size** button until the setting in the **Font Size** box is **44**.

   Keyboard Shortcut Press Ctrl+Shift+> to increase the font size.

   Using the Increase Font Size and Decrease Font Size buttons takes the guesswork out of sizing text.

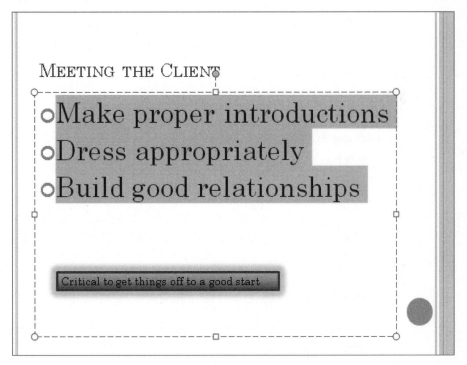

   The first bullet point now spans the width of the placeholder.

7. In the **Font** group, click the **Clear All Formatting** button to return the font size to **24**.

8. Display slide **9**, and select both bullet points.

9. In the **Paragraph** group, click the **Bullets** arrow.

   The Bullets gallery appears.

You can click Bullets And Numbering at the bottom of the gallery to create custom bullets.

10. In the gallery, click **None**.

    The bullet points are converted to regular text paragraphs.

11. With both paragraphs still selected, in the **Paragraph** group, click the **Line Spacing** button, and then click **Line Spacing Options**.

    The Paragraph dialog box opens.

You can set alignment, indentation, line spacing, and paragraph spacing all in one place.

12. In the **General** area, change the **Alignment** setting to **Centered**.

13. In the **Spacing** area, change the **Before** setting to **0 pt** and the **After** settings to **24 pt**. Then change the **Line Spacing** setting to **1.5 lines**.

14. Click **OK**.

15. In the first paragraph, click to the left of the word **only**, and press Shift+Enter to insert a line break.

16. Repeat step 15 to insert another line break before the word **that**.

17. In the second paragraph, insert a line break before the word **to** and another before the word **for**.

The phrases of both paragraphs are now nicely balanced.

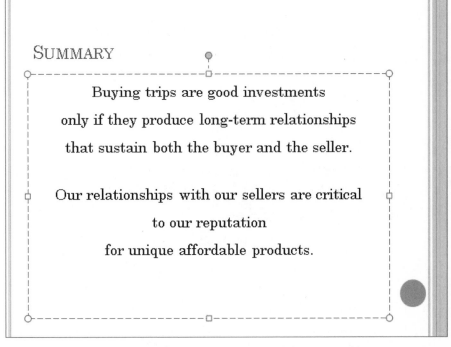

Line breaks can increase readability as well as the look of text on a slide.

✖ **CLEAN UP** Save the BusinessTravelB presentation, and then close it.

Non–Color Scheme Colors

Although working with the 12 colors of a harmonious color scheme enables you to create presentations with a pleasing design impact, you might want to use a broader range of colors. You can add colors that are not part of the color scheme by selecting the element whose color you want to change and then choosing a standard color from the Font Color palette or a custom color from the wide spectrum available in the Colors dialog box.

To apply a custom color:

1. Select text on a slide, and then on the Home tab, in the Font group, click the Font Color arrow.

2. At the bottom of the color palette, click More Colors.

   The Colors dialog box opens.

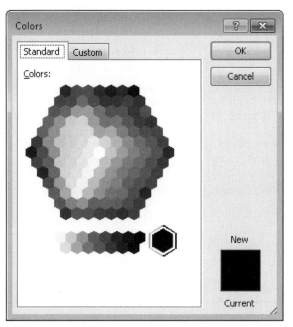

The Standard page of the Colors dialog box.

3. Click a color in the Colors spectrum, and then click OK.

   You can also click the Custom tab to display a color gradient where you can select a color based on precise Red/Green/Blue or Hue/Saturation/Luminescence settings.

After you use a color, it becomes available on all the palettes that appear when you click a button that applies color—for example, the Font Color button in the Font group on the Home tab. The color remains on the palettes even if you change the theme applied to the presentation.

Key Points

- Switching from one predefined theme to another is an easy way of changing the look of an entire presentation.

- You can apply a ready-made color scheme or font scheme to one or all the slides in a presentation, and you can create your own schemes.

- To dress up the background of one slide or of all the slides in a presentation, you can apply a solid color, a color gradient, a texture, or a picture.

- You can change the background, outline, and effect of specific placeholders or of text boxes.

- The formatting of paragraphs and text in a presentation can easily be changed by using the commands in the Font and Paragraph groups on the Home tab.

Chapter at a Glance

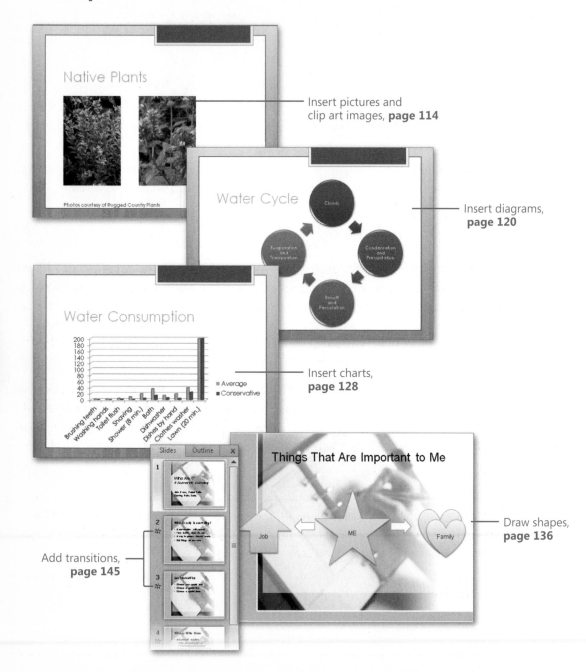

Insert pictures and clip art images, **page 114**

Insert diagrams, **page 120**

Insert charts, **page 128**

Draw shapes, **page 136**

Add transitions, **page 145**

5 Add Simple Visual Enhancements

In this chapter, you will learn how to

✔ Insert pictures and clip art images.

✔ Insert diagrams.

✔ Insert charts.

✔ Draw shapes.

✔ Add transitions.

With the ready availability of professionally designed templates, presentations have become more visually sophisticated and appealing. The words you use on your slides are no longer enough to guarantee the success of a presentation. These days, presentations are likely to have fewer words and more graphic elements. In fact, many successful presenters dispense with words altogether and use their slides only to graphically reinforce what they say when they deliver their presentations.

The general term *graphics* applies to several kinds of visual enhancements, including pictures, clip art images, diagrams, charts, and shapes. All of these types of graphics are inserted as objects on a slide and can then be sized, moved, and copied. For purposes of this chapter, we also consider transitions from one slide to another as a type of visual enhancement.

See Also For information about formatting and otherwise modifying graphics, see Chapter 8, "Fine-Tune Visual Elements."

In this chapter, you'll insert pictures and clip art images. You'll create a diagram and a chart, and you'll draw a simple illustration by using built-in shapes. Finally, you'll change the way slides move on and off the screen during a slide show.

> **Practice Files** Before you can complete the exercises in this chapter, you need to copy the book's practice files to your computer. The practice files you'll use to complete the exercises in this chapter are in the Chapter05 practice file folder. A complete list of practice files is provided in "Using the Practice Files" at the beginning of this book.

Inserting Pictures and Clip Art Images

You can add images created and saved in other programs as well as digital photographs to your Microsoft PowerPoint 2010 presentations. Collectively, these types of graphics are known as *pictures*. You might want to use pictures to make your slides more attractive and visually interesting, but you are more likely to use pictures to convey information in a way that words cannot. For example, you might display photographs of your company's new products in a presentation to salespeople.

If a slide has a content placeholder, you can insert a picture by clicking the Insert Picture From File button in the content placeholder. If the slide has no content placeholder, you can click the Picture button in the Images group on the Insert tab. Either way, the Insert Picture dialog box opens so that you can locate and insert the picture you want.

Tip Pictures you acquire from locations such as Web sites are often copyrighted, meaning that you cannot use them without the permission of the person who created them. Sometimes owners will grant permission if you give them credit. Professional photographers usually charge a fee to use their work. Always assume that pictures are copyrighted unless the source clearly indicates that they are license-free.

In addition to pictures you have acquired from various sources, you can insert clip art images into your slides. PowerPoint provides access to hundreds of license-free clip art items that often take the form of professionally designed cartoons, sketches, or symbolic images, but can also include photographs, animated drawings, and movies. In a PowerPoint presentation, you can use clip art to illustrate a point you are making, as interesting bullet characters, or to mark pauses in a presentation. For example, you might display a question mark image on a slide to signal a time in which you answer questions from the audience.

To add clip art to a slide, you can click the Clip Art button in a content placeholder, or you can click the Clip Art button in the Images group on the Insert tab. Either way, the Clip Art task pane opens. From this task pane, you can locate and insert the clip art image you want. You can search for clip art by keyword, search a specific Microsoft Clip Organizer collection, or search for specific files or media types, such as movies.

If your computer has an Internet connection, by default your search is expanded to include the thousands of free clip art images available on the Office.com Web site.

After you have inserted a picture, you can make it larger or smaller and position it anywhere you want on the slide.

Tip You can save PowerPoint slides as pictures that you can insert in other types of documents. Display the Save & Send page of the Backstage view, and click Change File Type in the center pane. Then click one of the formats listed under Image File Types in the right pane, and click Save As. In the Save As dialog box, specify a name and location, and then click Save. In the message box that appears, click Every Slide to save all the slides as images, or click Current Slide Only to save an image of the current slide.

In this exercise, you'll add pictures and clip art images to slides. After inserting them, you'll move and size them to fit their slides.

 SET UP You need the WaterSavingA_start presentation and the Penstemon and Agastache pictures located in your Chapter05 practice file folder to complete this exercise. Open the WaterSavingA_start presentation, and save it as *WaterSavingA*. Be sure you have an Internet connection so that you can connect to Office.com. Then follow the steps.

1. Press Ctrl+End to move to slide **11**, and delete **<show pictures>**.

   Because you have deleted the text from the content placeholder, PowerPoint redisplays the content buttons.

2. In the content placeholder, click the **Insert Picture from File** button.

   The Insert Picture dialog box opens.

3. Navigate to your **Chapter05** practice file folder, click the **Penstemon** file, and then click **Insert**.

   Tip If a picture might change, you can ensure that the slide is always up to date by clicking the Insert arrow and then clicking Link To File to insert a link to the picture, or by clicking Insert And Link to both insert the picture and link it to its graphic file.

   PowerPoint inserts the picture in the middle of the content pane.

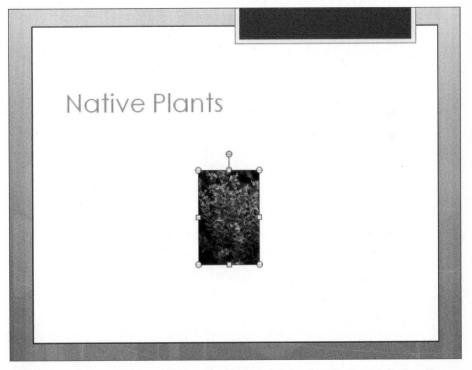

The picture is surrounded by a frame to indicate that it is selected. You use the handles around the frame to size and rotate the picture.

4. On the **View** tab, in the **Show** group, select the **Ruler** check box.

   Horizontal and vertical rulers are displayed across the top and down the left side of the Slide pane. The 0 mark on each ruler indicates the center of the slide. For clarity, we will refer to marks to the left of or above 0 as negative marks.

5. Point to the picture, and when you see a four-headed arrow attached to the pointer, drag to the left and down until its upper-left corner is almost level with the **−4** inch mark on the horizontal ruler and the **0.5** inch mark on the vertical ruler.

6. Point to the handle in the upper-right corner of the photo, and drag up and to the right until that corner sits about level with the **−1.5** inch mark on the horizontal ruler and the **1** inch mark on the vertical ruler.

   The photo increases in size. To make the picture smaller, you would drag in the opposite direction.

When you drag a corner handle, the photograph shrinks or grows proportionally.

Picture

7. On the **Insert** tab, in the **Images** group, click the **Picture** button, and then in the **Insert Picture** dialog box, double-click the **Agastache** file.

You can add pictures or other images to a slide without an available content place-holder, and regardless of the slide layout.

8. Point to the handle in the lower-right corner of the photo, and drag down and to the right until the Agastache photo is about the same size as the Penstemon photo. Then click away from the photo to release the selection.

9. On the **Insert** tab, in the **Text** group, click the **Text Box** button, and then click below the lower-left corner of the Penstemon photo.

Text Box

10. In the text box, type **Photos courtesy of Rugged Country Plants**. Then select the text, make it 14 points and purple, and click a blank area of the slide.

These photographs came from ruggedcountryplants.com and are used with per-mission of the owners.

When you use photos you haven't taken yourself, you should always credit the source.

Clip
Art

11. Move to slide **4**, and on the **Insert** tab, in the **Images** group, click the **Clip Art** button.

The Clip Art task pane opens.

12. In the **Search for** box at the top of the task pane, type **protect**. Then with the **Include Office.com content** check box selected, click **Go**.

Thumbnails of any clip art, movies, and sounds stored on your computer or on the Office.com Web site that have the associated keyword *protect* or *protection* appear in the task pane.

You can find free images of almost any concept by searching in the Clip Art task pane.

> **Tip** If you don't see a suitable image, you can click Find More At Office.com at the bottom of the task pane, and search for additional images there.

13. Scroll down to see all the images that are available, and when you are ready, point to the green and blue drawing of hands protecting a plant.

    A ScreenTip describes the image and gives its dimensions, file size, and format.

This clip art file is in Windows Metafile (WMF) format.

14. Click the thumbnail once.

    PowerPoint inserts the image in the center of the slide.

15. At the right end of the title bar of the **Clip Art** task pane, click the **Close** button.

16. Drag the image to the lower-right corner of the slide, and then drag the upper-left corner handle until the image occupies about half of the slide. Click a blank area to release the selection.

    The image balances the text on the slide.

This image symbolizes people's efforts to protect plants.

✖ CLEAN UP Save the WaterSavingA presentation, and then close it.

Inserting Diagrams

Sometimes the concepts you want to convey to an audience are best presented in diagrams, which depict processes, hierarchies, cycles, or relationships. You can easily create a dynamic, visually appealing diagram for a slide by using SmartArt Graphics, a powerful tool that comes with the Microsoft Office 2010 programs. SmartArt provides predefined sets of formatting for effortlessly putting together any of the following types of diagrams:

- **Process** These visually describe the ordered set of steps required to complete a task—for example, the approval process for the launch of a new book series.

- **Hierarchy** These illustrate the structure of an organization or entity—for example, a company's top-level management structure.

- **Cycle** These represent a circular sequence of steps, tasks, or events; or the relationship of a set of steps, tasks, or events to a central, core element—for example, the looping process for continually improving a product based on customer feedback.

- **Relationship** These show convergent, divergent, overlapping, merging, or containing elements—for example, how organizing your e-mail, calendar, and contacts can converge to improve your productivity.

On a slide that includes a content placeholder, you can click the placeholder's Insert SmartArt Graphic button to start the process of creating a diagram. You can also click the SmartArt button in the Illustrations Group on the Insert tab to add a diagram to any slide. In either case, you then select the type of diagram you want to create and click a specific layout to see a picture and description. When you find the diagram that best conveys your information, you click OK to insert the diagram with placeholder text that you can replace in an adjacent Text pane.

Graphic Formats

You can use picture and clip art files in a variety of formats, including the following:

- **BMP (bitmap)** This format stores graphics as a series of dots, or pixels. There are different qualities of BMP, reflecting the number of bits available per pixel to store information about the graphic—the greater the number of bits, the greater the number of possible colors.

- **GIF (Graphics Interchange Format)** This format is common for images that appear on Web pages because they can be compressed with no loss of information and groups of them can be animated. GIFs store at most 8 bits per pixel, so they are limited to 256 colors.

- **JPEG (Joint Photographic Experts Group)** This compressed format works well for complex graphics such as scanned photographs. Some information is lost in the compression process, but often the loss is imperceptible to the human eye. Color JPEG images store 24 bits per pixel, so they are capable of displaying more than 16 million colors. Grayscale JPEG images store 8 bits per pixel.

- **TIFF (Tag Image File Format)** This format can store compressed images with a flexible number of bits per pixel. Using tags, a single multipage TIFF file can store several images, along with related information such as type of compression and orientation.

- **PNG (Portable Network Graphic)** This format has the advantages of the GIF format but can store colors with 8, 24, or 48 bits per pixel and grayscales with 1, 2, 4, 8, or 16 bits per pixel. A PNG file can also specify whether each pixel blends with its background color and can contain color correction information so that images look accurate on a broad range of display devices. Graphics saved in this format are smaller, so they display faster.

After you create a diagram, you can move and size it to fit the slide, and with a few clicks, you can change the colors and look of its shapes to achieve professional looking results.

In this exercise, you'll add a cycle diagram, enter text, and then move and size it. You'll also format its shapes in simple ways.

SET UP You need the WaterSavingB_start presentation located in your Chapter05 practice file folder to complete this exercise. Open the WaterSavingB_start presentation, and save it as *WaterSavingB*. Display the rulers, and then follow the steps.

1. Display slide **6**, and then click the **Insert SmartArt Graphic** button in the content placeholder.

   The Choose A SmartArt Graphic dialog box opens.

By default, all the available layouts are listed in the center pane, but you can filter them by category. A picture and description of the selected layout appear in the right pane.

2. In the left pane, click each layout type in turn to see all the available layouts of that type in the center pane, and then click **Cycle**.

3. In the center pane, click each layout in turn to view a picture and description in the right pane.

4. When you finish exploring, click the second layout (**Text Cycle**), and then click **OK**.

   PowerPoint inserts a blank cycle diagram into the slide. The Design and Format contextual tabs appear on the ribbon.

5. On the **Design** tab, in the **Create Graphic** group, click the **Text Pane** button. The Text pane opens.

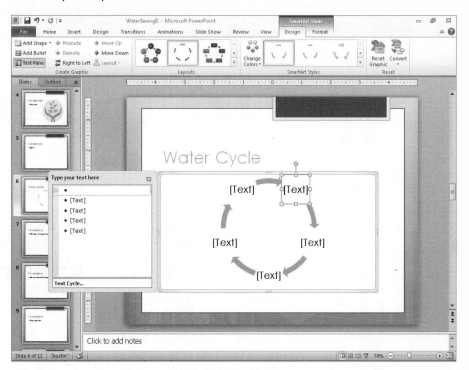

You can use the same techniques to create bullet points and subpoints in the Text pane as you would on the Outline tab of the Overview pane.

Troubleshooting The appearance of buttons and groups on the ribbon changes depending on the width of the program window. For information about changing the appearance of the ribbon to match our screen images, see "Modifying the Display of the Ribbon" at the beginning of this book.

6. With the first bullet in the **Text** pane selected, type **Clouds**, and then press the Down Arrow key to move to the next bullet.

Troubleshooting Be sure to press the Down Arrow key and not the Enter key. Pressing Enter will add a new bullet point (and a new shape).

7. Pressing Shift+Enter after each word, type **Condensation**, **and**, and **Precipitation**. Then press the Down Arrow key.

8. Repeat step 7 to add **Runoff**, **and**, and **Percolation**. Then repeat it again to add **Evaporation**, **and**, and **Transpiration**.

9. You don't need the last bullet point, so on the **Design** tab, in the **Create Graphic** group, click the **Text Pane** button to close the Text pane.

   Tip You can also click the Close button in the upper-right corner of the Text pane.

10. In the diagram, click the **Text** placeholder, and click the border of the empty shape to select it for manipulation. Then press the Delete key.

    The diagram now has four sets of text and arrows.

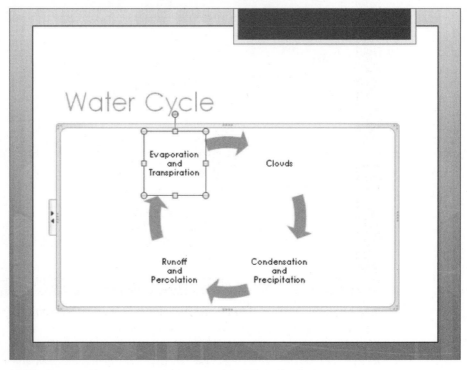

In this diagram, the arrows are more prominent than the text.

Tip You can click the tab with left and right arrows on the left side of the diagram's frame to open the Text pane.

11. In the **Layouts** group, click the **More** button to view the available Cycle diagram layouts, and then click the first thumbnail in the first row (**Basic Cycle**).

The diagram changes to the new layout.

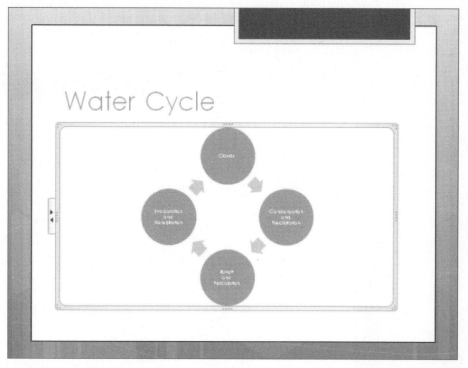

In this diagram, the text is contained in solid-color circles, and the arrows are less prominent.

12. Point to the handle (the four dots) in the middle of the right side of the diagram's frame, and when the pointer changes to a two-headed arrow, drag to the left until the frame is only as wide as the diagram. (Repeat the process as necessary.)

13. Point to a part of the frame where there is no handle, and when a four-headed arrow is attached to the pointer, drag the diagram until it sits in the lower-right corner of the white area of the slide.

14. Point to the handle in the upper-left corner of the frame and drag up and to the left until the frame sits at about the **–2.5** inch mark on both the horizontal and vertical rulers.

   Troubleshooting Remember that the 0 mark on both rulers is centered on the slide. You want the 2.5-inch marks to the left of and above the 0 marks.

   The diagram expands with its frame.

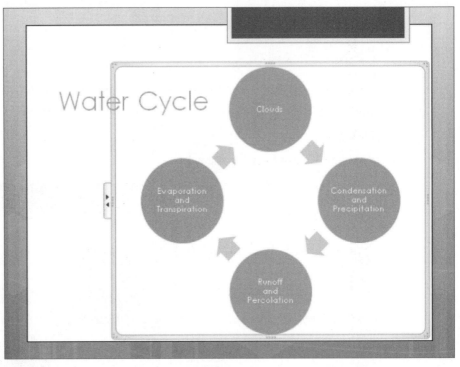

Because the diagram is an independent object, it can sit on top of the empty part of the title placeholder.

15. In the **SmartArt Styles** group, click the **Change Colors** button, and then in the gallery, under **Colorful**, click the second thumbnail (**Colorful Range - Accent Colors 2 and 3**).

   The shapes in the diagram assume the colors of the selected scheme.

16. In the **SmartArt Styles** group, click the **More** button.

   The SmartArt Styles gallery appears.

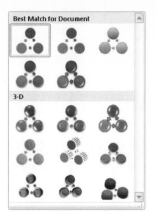

You can apply two-dimensional and three-dimensional styles from this gallery.

17. Under **3-D** in the gallery, click the first thumbnail in the first row (**Polished**).

18. Click outside the frame.

    You can now see the final result.

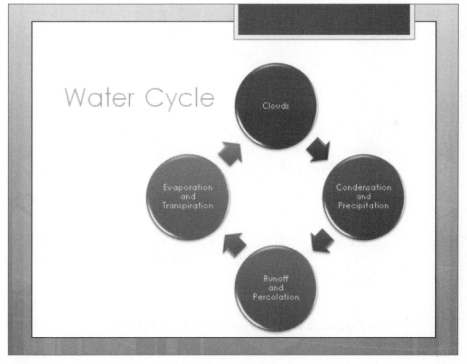

The colors and three-dimensional effect give the diagram pizzazz.

 CLEAN UP Save the WaterSavingB presentation, and then close it.

Converting Existing Bullet Points into Diagrams

You might decide after creating a bulleted list on a slide that a diagram would more clearly convey your point to your audience. You can easily convert a bulleted list to a SmartArt diagram with only a few clicks of the mouse button.

To create a diagram from an existing bulleted list:

1. Click anywhere in the placeholder containing the bulleted list you want to convert.

2. Right-click anywhere in the selected placeholder, and point to Convert To SmartArt.

3. Do one of the following:

    a. If the diagram layout you want appears in the gallery, click its thumbnail.

    b. If you don't see the layout you want, click More SmartArt Graphics. Then in the Choose A SmartArt Graphic dialog box, click the layout you want, and click OK.

4. Adjust the size, position, and look of the diagram in the usual way.

Inserting Charts

For those occasions when you want to display numeric data visually, you can add a chart to a slide. Charts make it easy to see trends that might not be obvious from looking at the numbers themselves.

On a slide that includes a content placeholder, you can click the placeholder's Insert Chart button to start the process of creating a chart. You can also click the Chart button in the Illustrations Group on the Insert tab to add a chart to any slide. In either case, you then select the type of chart you want. If your PowerPoint window is maximized, when you click OK, a sample chart of the type you selected is inserted in the current slide, and the PowerPoint window shrinks so that it occupies half the screen. An associated Microsoft Excel worksheet containing the data plotted in the sample chart is displayed in the other half. You use this worksheet to enter the information you want to plot, following the pattern illustrated by the sample data.

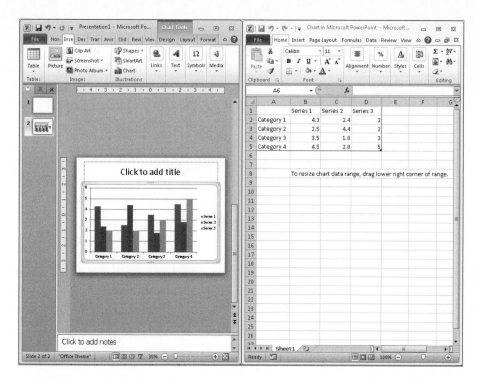

A sample chart and its associated worksheet.

The Excel worksheet is composed of rows and columns of cells that contain values, which in charting terminology are called *data points*. Collectively a set of data points is called a *data series*. Each worksheet cell is identified by an address consisting of its column letter and row number—for example, A2. A range of cells is identified by the address of the cell in the upper-left corner and the address of the cell in the lower-right corner, separated by a colon—for example, A2:D5.

When you replace the sample data in the worksheet, you immediately see the results in the chart in the adjacent PowerPoint window. Each data point in a data series is represented graphically in the chart by a data marker. The data is plotted against an x-axis—also called the *category axis*—and a y-axis—also called the *value axis*. (Three-dimensional charts also have a z-axis—also called the *series axis*.) Tick-mark labels along each axis identify the categories, values, or series in the chart. A legend provides a key for identifying the data series.

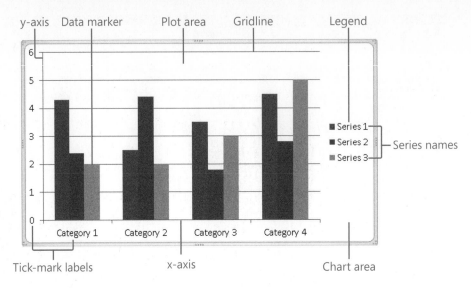

The major elements of a chart.

To enter data in a cell of the Excel worksheet, you first click the cell to select it. You can select an entire column by clicking the column header—the shaded box containing a letter at the top of each column—and an entire row by clicking the row header—the shaded box containing a number to the left of each row. You can select the entire worksheet by clicking the Select All button—the box at the junction of the column and row headers.

Having selected a cell, you can enter your data by typing it directly. However, if your data already exists in an Excel worksheet or a Microsoft Access or Microsoft Word table, you don't have to retype it. You can copy the data from its source program and paste it into the Excel worksheet that is linked to the slide.

After you've plotted your data in the chart, you can move and size the chart to suit the space available on the slide. You can edit the data—both the values and the column and row headings—at any time, and PowerPoint will replot the chart to reflect your changes.

In this exercise, you'll create a chart by pasting existing data into the associated Excel worksheet. You'll then size the chart, and edit its data.

SET UP You need the WaterConsumption workbook and the WaterSavingC_start presentation located in your Chapter05 practice file folder to complete this exercise. From Windows Explorer, open the WaterConsumption workbook in Excel by double-clicking the workbook's file name. Then open the WaterSavingC_start presentation, and save it as *WaterSavingC*. Ensure that the PowerPoint program window is maximized, and then follow the steps.

1. Display slide **7**, and then in the content placeholder, click the **Insert Chart** button.

   The Insert Chart dialog box opens.

You can choose from many types of charts in this dialog box.

2. With **Column** selected in the left pane, click the first thumbnail in the second row (**Clustered Cylinder**), and then click **OK**.

   PowerPoint inserts the chart into the slide and resizes its program window to occupy the left half of your screen. Excel starts and displays the data used to plot the chart in the right half of the screen.

3. From the Windows Taskbar, display the **WaterConsumption** worksheet. Then in the worksheet, point to cell **A3**, and drag down and to the right to cell **C13**.

   Excel selects all the cells in the range A3:C13.

4. On the Excel **Home** tab, in the **Clipboard** group, click the **Copy** button.

5. From the Windows Taskbar, display the **Chart in Microsoft PowerPoint** work-sheet. Then in the worksheet, click cell **A1**.

6. On the Excel **Home** tab, in the **Clipboard** group, click the **Paste** button. Then click **OK** to acknowledge the message that Excel has inserted rows in the worksheet to accommodate the copied data.

   Excel pastes in the data, and PowerPoint immediately replots the chart.

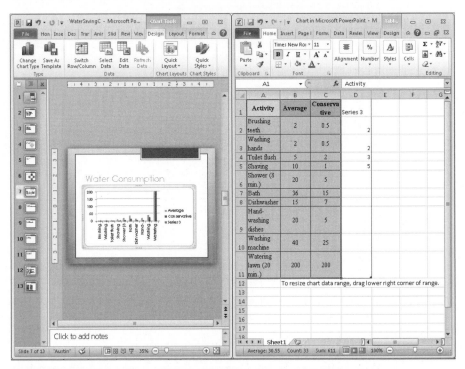

The chart plots all the data within the blue border in the worksheet.

7. To exclude the data in column D from the chart, in the worksheet, drag the handle in the lower-right corner of the blue border to the left, releasing it when cells **D1:D11** are shaded.

   In the PowerPoint window, the chart now reflects the fact that only the Activity, Average, and Conservative columns are plotted.

8. In the upper-right corner of the Excel window, click the **Close** button to close the associated worksheet. Then close the **WaterConsumption** workbook.

   The PowerPoint window expands, giving you a better view of the chart.

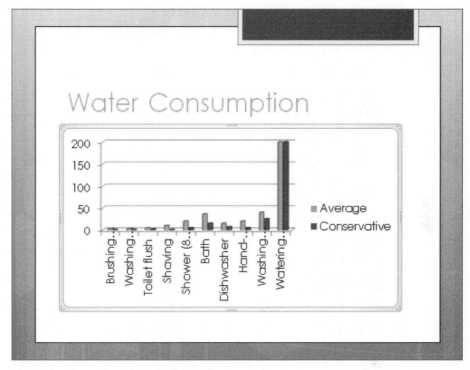

The copied data, plotted as a cylinder chart.

9. Point to the handle (the four dots) in the middle of the bottom of the frame, and drag downward until the frame sits at the bottom of the white area of the slide.

   When you release the mouse button, the chart area expands, but not enough for the category labels to be displayed in their entirety.

10. On the **Design** contextual tab, in the **Data** group, click the **Edit Data** button.

    The associated worksheet opens in Excel so that you can make changes to the plotted data.

11. Click cell **A9**, type **Dishes by hand**, and press Enter. Then in cell **A10**, type **Clothes washer**, and press Enter. Finally in cell **A11**, replace **Watering lawn (20 min.)** with **Lawn (20 min.)**, and press Enter. Then close the Excel worksheet.

Tip If the chart isn't selected (surrounded by a frame) in the PowerPoint window when you make changes to the data in the Excel window, the chart won't automatically update. If this happens, click the chart before proceeding.

PowerPoint replots the chart with the new category labels.

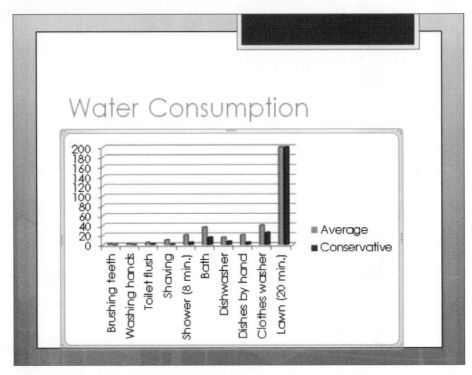

All the category labels now fit in the chart area.

12. Point to the handle in the middle of the right side of the frame, and drag to the right until the frame sits at the edge of the white area on that slide. Then click outside the chart frame.

PowerPoint has rotated the labels so that the chart area can expand even more.

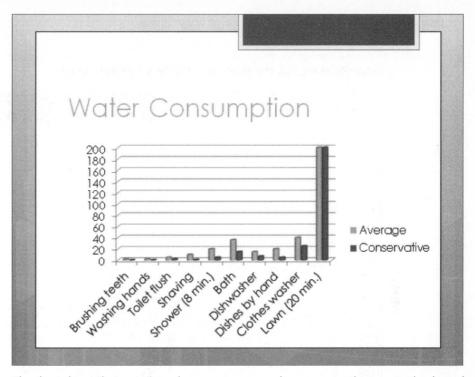

The chart shows that watering a lawn consumes much more water than most other household water usages.

Tip By default, the chart is plotted based on the series in the columns of the worksheet, which are identified in the legend. If you want to base the chart on the series in the rows instead, click the Switch Row/Column button in the Data group on the Design contextual tab. The worksheet must be open for the button to be active. (To open the worksheet, right-click the chart, and then click Edit Data.)

✖ CLEAN UP Save the WaterSavingC presentation, and then close it.

Drawing Shapes

To emphasize the key points in your presentation, you might want to include shapes in addition to text. PowerPoint provides tools for creating several types of shapes, including stars, banners, boxes, lines, circles, and squares. With a little imagination, you'll soon discover ways to create drawings by combining shapes.

To create a shape in PowerPoint, you click the Shapes button in the Illustrations group on the Insert tab, click the shape you want to insert, and then drag the crosshair pointer across the slide.

Tip To draw a circle or a square, click the Oval or a Rectangle shape, and hold down the Shift key while you drag.

After you draw the shape, it is surrounded by a set of handles, indicating that it is selected. (You can select a shape at any time by simply clicking it.) The handles serve the following purposes:

- You can drag the pale blue sizing handles to change the size of a shape.

- If a shape has a yellow diamond-shaped adjustment handle next to one of the sizing handles or elsewhere on the shape, the shape is adjustable. You can use this handle to alter the appearance of the shape without changing its size.

- You can drag the green rotating handle to adjust the angle of rotation of a shape.

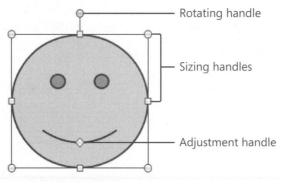

The three types of shape handles.

You can copy or cut a selected shape or multiple shapes and then paste the shapes elsewhere in the same presentation, in another presentation, or in any Office program.

To move a shape from one location to another on the same slide, you simply drag it. You can create a copy of a selected shape by dragging it while holding down the Ctrl key or by clicking the Copy arrow in the Clipboard group on the Home tab and then clicking Duplicate.

After drawing a shape, you can modify it by using the buttons on the Format contextual tab that appears when a shape is selected. For example, you can:

- Add text to a shape. PowerPoint centers the text as you type, and the text becomes part of the shape.
- Change the size and color of the shape and its outline.
- Apply special effects, such as making the shape look three-dimensional.

Having made changes to one shape, you can easily apply the same attributes to another shape by clicking the shape that has the desired attributes, clicking the Format Painter button in the Clipboard group on the Home tab, and then clicking the shape to which you want to copy the attributes. If you want to apply the attributes of a shape to all shapes in the active presentation, right-click the shape and then click Set As Default Shape. From then on, all the shapes you draw in the active presentation will have the new default attributes.

When you have multiple shapes on a slide, you can group them so that you can copy, move, and format them as a unit. You can change the attributes of an individual shape— for example, its color, size, or location—without ungrouping the shapes. If you do un-group the graphics, you can regroup the same shapes by selecting one of them and then clicking Regroup in the Group list.

In this exercise, you'll draw several shapes, add text to them, and change their colors. Then you'll duplicate and copy a shape and switch one shape for another.

SET UP You need the JournalingA_start presentation located in your Chapter05 practice file folder to complete this exercise. Open the JournalingA_start presentation, and save it as *JournalingA*. Display the rulers, and then follow the steps.

1. Display slide **5**, and on the **Insert** tab, in the **Illustrations** group, click the **Shapes** button.

   The Shapes gallery appears.

Many different types of shapes are grouped by category in the Shapes gallery.

2. Under **Stars and Banners** in the gallery, click the **5-Point Star** shape, and then drag the crosshair pointer in the middle of the slide to draw a star shape that spans the shadow of the hand in the background graphic.

   Tip If you click a shape button and then change your mind about drawing the shape, you can release the shape by pressing the Esc key.

   Pale blue handles surround the shape to indicate that it is selected.

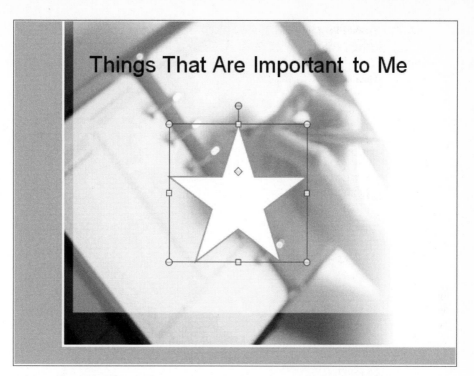

When a shape is selected, the Format contextual tab appears on the ribbon.

3. On the **Format** tab, in the **Insert Shapes** group, click the **More** button to display the **Shapes** gallery. Then under **Block Arrows**, click the **Right Arrow** shape, and draw a small arrow to the right of the star.

4. With the arrow still selected, hold down the Ctrl key, and drag a copy of the arrow to the left of the star.

   Troubleshooting Be sure to release the mouse button before you release the Ctrl key. Otherwise you'll move the shape instead of copying it.

5. With the shape still selected, in the **Arrange** group, click the **Rotate** button, and then click **Flip Horizontal**.

   You could have drawn a Left Arrow shape, but this technique ensures that the two arrows have the same proportions.

   Tip You can rotate or flip any type of image. Rotating turns a shape 90 degrees to the right or left; flipping turns a shape 180 degrees horizontally or vertically. You can also rotate a shape to any degree by dragging the green rotating handle.

6. Adjacent to the left arrow, add a scroll shape, and adjacent to the right arrow, add a heart shape.

All the shapes have the same outline and interior colors.

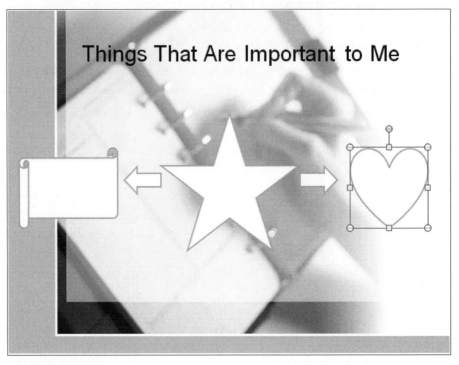

You can build a picture with the shapes available in the Shapes gallery.

7. With the heart selected, on the **Home** tab, in the **Clipboard** group, click the **Copy** arrow, and then in the list, click **Duplicate**.

PowerPoint pastes a copy of the shape on top of the original.

8. Point to the handle in the upper-left corner of the new shape, and drag down and to the right to make the second heart smaller than the first.

9. On the **Format** tab, in the **Insert Shapes** group, click the **Text Box** button, click the center of the star, and then type **ME**.

See Also For information about working with text boxes, see "Adding Text Boxes" in Chapter 3, "Work with Slide Text."

Don't worry that you can barely see the text; you'll fix that in a later step.

10. Repeat step 9 to add the word **Education** to the scroll shape and **Family** to the heart shape.

11. Click the scroll shape (don't click the text), hold down the Shift key, click the star shape, and then click the two hearts.

12. With all four shapes selected, in the **Shape Styles** group, click the **More** button to display the **Shape Styles** gallery.

13. Point to several thumbnails to see live previews of their effects, and then click the last thumbnail in the fourth row (**Subtle Effect – Light Blue, Accent 6**).

    The color of the interior and outline of the shapes changes, as does the color of the text.

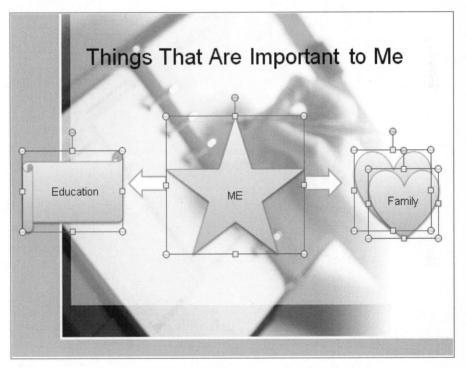

The text stands out after you change the shape style.

14. Click a blank area of the slide to release the selection, and then click the scroll shape (don't click its text).

15. In the **Insert Shapes** group, click the **Edit Shape** button, point to **Change Shape**, and under **Block Arrows**, click the third shape (**Up Arrow**).

    The scroll changes to the selected shape, with all formatting and text intact.

16. Double-click the word **Education**, and type **Job**. Then click outside the shape to release the selection.

    You can now see the results.

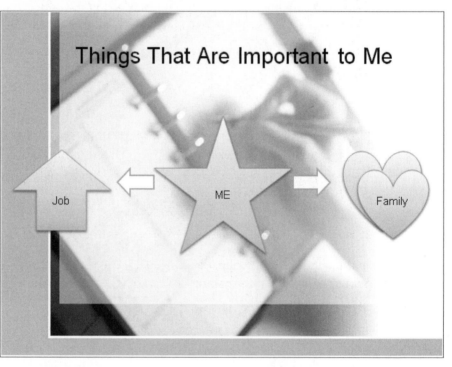

You can tell a story using a combination of shapes and text.

17. Select all the shapes on the slide. Then on the **Format** tab, in the **Arrange** group, click the **Group** button, and in the list, click **Group**.

    The shapes are grouped together as one object.

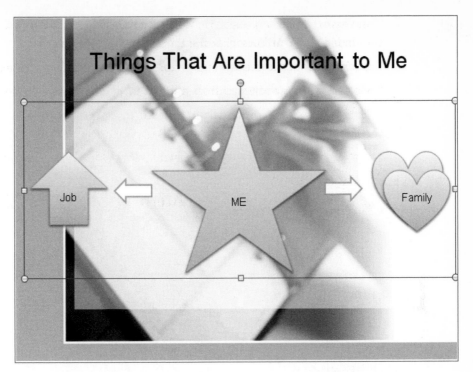

When shapes are grouped, one set of handles surrounds the entire group.

18. In the **Shape Styles** group, click the **Shape Outline** arrow, and then under
Standard Colors in the palette, click the last color (**Purple**).

   The outlines around the shapes change to purple.

19. Point to any shape in the group, and when the pointer has a four-headed arrow
attached to it, drag downward about a half inch.

   The entire group moves.

20. Click the left arrow. In the **Shape Styles** group, click the **Shape Fill** arrow and
change the shape's color to purple.

   Even though the shapes are grouped, you can still change the attributes of one of
the shapes.

21. With the left arrow still selected, on the **Home** tab, in the **Clipboard** group, click the **Format Painter** button, and then click the right arrow.

    Both arrows are now purple.

22. Click away from the selected shape, and then click any shape to select the group.

23. On the **Format** tab, in the **Arrange** group, click the **Group** button, and then click **Ungroup**.

    The group is disbanded, and the individual shapes are now selected.

CLEAN UP Save the JournalingA presentation, and then close it.

Connecting Shapes

If you want to show a relationship between two shapes, you can connect them with a line by joining special handles called *connection points*.

To connect shapes:

1. Click one of the shapes you want to connect. Then on the Format tab, in the Insert Shapes group, display the Shapes gallery, and under Lines, click one of the Connector shapes.

2. Point to the selected shape.

   Red connection points appear, and the pointer changes to a crosshair.

3. Point to a connection point, and then drag over to the other shape (don't release the mouse button).

4. When connection points appear on the other shape, point to a connection point, and release the mouse button.

   Red handles appear at each end of the line, indicating that the shapes are connected.

   Troubleshooting If a blue handle appears instead of a red one, the shapes are not connected. Click the Undo button on the Quick Access Toolbar to remove the connection line, and then redraw it.

Adding Transitions

When you deliver a presentation, you can move from slide to slide by clicking the mouse button or you can have PowerPoint replace one slide with the next at predetermined intervals. You can avoid abrupt breaks between slides by employing transitions that control the way slides move on and off the screen.

PowerPoint comes with the following categories of built-in transition effects:

- **Subtle** This category includes fades, wipes, and a shutter-like effect.

- **Exciting** This category includes more dramatic effects such as checkerboards, ripples, turning, and zooming.

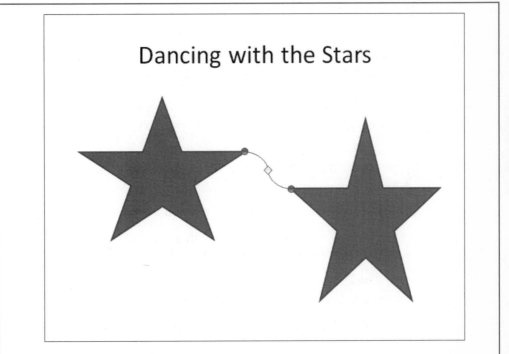

The connector between two connection points.

After you have drawn the connector, you can format it by changing its color and weight. You can then set the formatted line as the default for all future connectors in this drawing. If you move a connected shape, the line moves with it, maintaining the relationship between the shapes.

- **Dynamic Content** This category holds the background of the slides still and applies a dynamic effect to the title and other content, such as rotating or flying onto the slide.

Each slide can have only one transition. You set transitions from the Transitions tab in Normal view or Slide Sorter view, for one slide at a time, for a group of slides, or for an entire presentation. This tab is new in PowerPoint 2010, reflecting the importance of transitions in ensuring a smooth flow for your presentations. (Previously, transitions were included on the Animations tab because they were considered just another form of animation.)

In addition to selecting the type of transition, you can specify the following:

- The sound
- The speed
- When the transition occurs

In this exercise, you'll apply a transition to a single slide, and apply the same transition to all the slides in the presentation. You'll also add sound to the transition and set the transition speed.

SET UP You need the JournalingB_start presentation located in your Chapter05 practice file folder to complete this exercise. Open the JournalingB_start presentation, and save it as *JournalingB*. Then follow the steps.

1. Display slide **2** in Normal view. Then on the **Transitions** tab, in the **Transition to This Slide** group, click each thumbnail in the gallery to see its effects.

2. To the right of the gallery, click the **Down** button, and continue previewing the effects of each transition.

3. When you have finished exploring, click the **More** button to display the entire gallery, and then click the **Cover** thumbnail in the **Subtle** category.

PowerPoint demonstrates the Cover transition effect on slide 2 and indicates that the transition has been applied by placing an animation symbol below the slide number on the Slides tab of the Overview pane. (There is no indication on the slide itself.)

You have applied an animation to one slide.

4. In the **Transition to This Slide** group, click the **Effect Options** button, and then click **From Top-Left**.

5. In the **Timing** group, click the **Apply To All** button.

   An animation symbol appears below each slide number on the Slides tab.

6. On the **Slides** tab in the **Overview** pane, click the animation symbol below slide **3**.

   The Slide pane turns black, and then PowerPoint demonstrates the Cover transition from slide 2 to slide 3.

7. Display slide **1**. In the **Transition to This Slide** group, click the **More** button, and then in the **Transitions** gallery, click the **None** thumbnail.

   PowerPoint removes the animation symbol from below the slide 1 thumbnail.

Because you will usually start a presentation with the title slide displayed, there is no need for a transition on this slide.

8. On the **View Shortcuts** toolbar at the right end of the status bar, click the **Reading View** button.

   PowerPoint switches to Reading view and displays slide 1.

9. At the bottom of the screen, click the **Next** button repeatedly to see the transitions of the first few slides, and then press Esc to return to Normal view.

10. On the **View Shortcuts** toolbar, click the **Slide Sorter** button.

11. In **Slide Sorter** view, click slide **2**, hold down the Shift key, and then click slide **7** to select all the slides that have transitions.

12. In the **Timing** group, click the **Sound** arrow, and then click **Wind**.

   Tip If you want to associate a sound file of your own with a slide transition, click Other Sound at the bottom of the Sound list. Then in the Add Audio dialog box, find and select the sound file you want to use, and click Open.

13. In the **Timing** group, click the **Duration** up arrow until the duration shows as **02.00**.

14. In the **Preview** group, click the **Preview** button to preview the transition effect again. Then if you want, preview it again in Reading view.

PowerPoint demonstrates the transition of each selected slide with the sound specified in step 13.

✖ CLEAN UP Save the JournalingB presentation, and then close it.

Key Points

- When you add pictures or photographs to a slide, keep in mind that using pictures you don't own without permission, especially for business purposes, can breach the copyright of the owner. Limited use for non-commercial purposes is usually allowed as long as you acknowledge the source.

- Thousands of free clip art images are available to help you add visual interest to your slides.

- With SmartArt, you can create a variety of professional-looking diagrams with a few mouse clicks.

- Charts present numeric data in an easy-to-grasp visual format. You can choose from 11 types with many variations.

- Shapes can add interest to a slide and draw attention to key concepts. However, they can become tiresome and produce an amateurish effect if they are overused.

- Avoid abrupt transitions by having one slide smoothly replace another. You can control the transition type, its speed, and when it takes place.

Chapter at a Glance

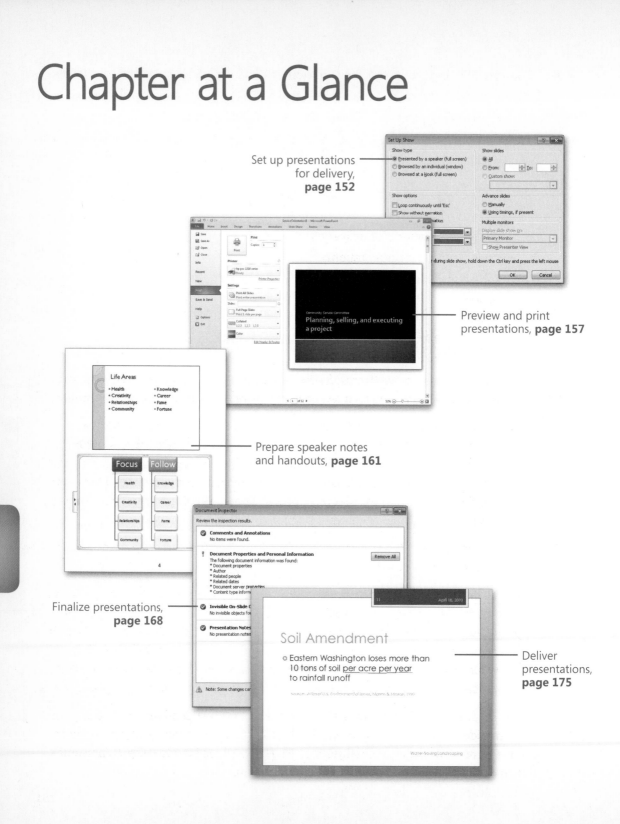

Set up presentations for delivery, **page 152**

Preview and print presentations, **page 157**

Planning, selling, and executing a project

Prepare speaker notes and handouts, **page 161**

Finalize presentations, **page 168**

Deliver presentations, **page 175**

Soil Amendment

o Eastern Washington loses more than 10 tons of soil per acre per year to rainfall runoff

6 Review and Deliver Presentations

In this chapter, you will learn how to

✔ Set up presentations for delivery.

✔ Preview and print presentations.

✔ Prepare speaker notes and handouts.

✔ Finalize presentations.

✔ Deliver presentations.

When it is time to deliver the Microsoft PowerPoint 2010 presentation you have worked so hard to create, taking the time for a few final tasks helps to ensure a successful outcome.

Before exposing a new presentation to the eyes of the world, you should check a few settings and proof the text of the slides, preferably on paper, where typographic errors seem to stand out much better than they do on the screen. When you are satisfied that the presentation is complete, you can prepare for your moment in the spotlight by creating speaker notes. You might also want to create handouts to give to your audience, to remind them later of your presentation's message.

When all these tasks are complete, you should remove extraneous information before declaring the presentation final.

If you will deliver the presentation from your computer as an electronic slide show, it pays to become familiar with the tools available in Slide Show view, where instead of appearing in a window, the slide occupies the entire screen. You navigate through slides by clicking the mouse button or by pressing the Arrow keys, moving forward and backward one slide at a time or jumping to specific slides as the needs of your audience dictate. During the slide show, you can mark slides with an on-screen pen or highlighter to emphasize a point.

In this chapter, you'll set up a slide show for delivery, preview a presentation, and print selected slides. You'll remove the properties attached to a presentation and prevent other people from making further changes to it. Finally, you'll see how to deliver a presentation, including marking up slides while showing them.

> **Practice Files** Before you can complete the exercises in this chapter, you need to copy the book's practice files to your computer. The practice files you'll use to complete the exercises in this chapter are in the Chapter06 practice file folder. A complete list of practice files is provided in "Using the Practice Files" at the beginning of this book.

Setting Up Presentations for Delivery

In the old days, presentations were delivered by speakers with few supporting materials. Little by little, "visual aids" such as white board drawings or flip charts on easels were added, and eventually, savvy speakers began accompanying their presentations with 35mm slides or transparencies projected onto screens. To accommodate these speakers, early versions of PowerPoint included output formats optimized for slides of various sizes, including 35mm slides and the acetate sheets used with overhead projectors.

Although technology has evolved to the point where most presentations are now delivered electronically, PowerPoint 2010 still accommodates those output formats, as well as formats designed for printing on paper. Usually, you'll find the default on-screen format adequate for your needs. If you have a wide-screen monitor, or if you know you'll be using a delivery method other than your computer for your presentation, you should set the format of the presentation before you begin developing your content so that you place elements appropriately for the final size of your slides.

By default, slides are sized for an on-screen slide show with a width-to-height ratio of 4:3 (10 × 7.5 inches). The slides are oriented horizontally, with slide numbers starting at 1. You can change these settings in the Page Setup dialog box, where you can select from the following slide sizes:

- **On-screen Show** For an electronic slide show on screens of various aspects (4:3, 16:9, or 16:10)

- **Letter Paper** For a presentation printed on 8.5 × 11 inch U.S. letter-size paper

- **Ledger Paper** For a presentation printed on 11 × 17 inch legal-size paper

- **A3 Paper, A4 Paper, B4 (ISO) Paper, B5 (ISO) Paper** For a presentation printed on paper of various international sizes

- **35mm Slides** For 35mm slides to be used in a carousel with a projector

- **Overhead** For transparencies for an overhead projector

- **Banner** For a banner for a Web page

- **Custom** For slides that are a nonstandard size

If you want the same identifying information to appear at the bottom of every slide, you can insert it in a footer. You can specify the date and time, the slide number, and custom text in the Header And Footer dialog box, which shows a preview of where the specified items will appear on the slide.

If you are going to deliver a presentation before an audience and will control the progression of slides manually, the default settings will work well. However, provided the slides have been assigned advancement times on the Transitions tab, you can set up the presentation to run automatically, either once or continuously. For example, you might want to set up a product demonstration slide show in a store or at a tradeshow so that it runs automatically, looping until someone stops it. All it takes is a few settings in the Set Up Show dialog box.

In this exercise, you'll explore the Page Setup dialog box and experiment with slide orientation. You'll add footer information to every slide in a presentation, and then turn the presentation into a self-running slide show.

SET UP You need the ServiceOrientationA_start presentation located in your Chapter06 practice file folder to complete this exercise. Open the ServiceOrientationA_start presentation, and save it as *ServiceOrientationA*. Then follow the steps.

Page Setup

1. On the **Design** tab, in the **Page Setup** group, click the **Page Setup** button.

   The Page Setup dialog box opens.

   By default, the slides in a presentation are sized for an on-screen slide show with a width-to-height ratio of 4:3.

2. Display the **Slides sized for** list, and toward the bottom, click **35mm Slides**.

   The Width setting changes to 11.25 inches and the Height setting changes to 7.5 inches.

3. Display the **Slides sized for list** again, and click **Banner**.

The Width setting changes to 8 inches, and the Height setting changes to 1 inch. This format is useful if you want to design a presentation that will display in a frame across the top or bottom of a Web page.

Tip Obviously the current presentation with its long title and many bulleted lists is not suitable for the Banner format. If you want to create a banner, be sure to set the format before you begin developing the content of your presentation so that you choose words and graphics that fit within the space available.

4. Set the size of the slides to **On-screen Show (4:3)**. Then in the **Slides** area, click **Portrait**, and click **OK**.

The slide width changes to 7.5 and its height changes to 10 inches. This orientation is useful if you want to compare two presentations side by side in Reading view.

Slide
Orientation ▾

5. In the **Page Setup** group, click the **Slide Orientation** button, and then click **Landscape**.

Header
& Footer

6. On the **Insert** tab, in the **Text** group, click the **Header & Footer** button.

The Header And Footer dialog box opens with the Slide page displayed.

By default, the slides in this presentation do not display footer information.

7. In the **Include on slide** area, select the **Date and time** check box. Then with **Fixed** selected, type today's date in the text box.

   PowerPoint indicates on the thumbnail in the Preview area that the date will appear in the lower-left corner of the slide. The date will appear in the format in which you typed it.

8. Select the **Slide number** check box.

   The thumbnail in the Preview area shows that the slide number will appear in the lower-right corner.

9. Select the **Footer** check box, and then type your name in the text box.

   Your name will appear in the center of the slide.

10. Select the **Don't show on title slide** check box, and click **Apply to All**. Then display slide **2**.

    The specified footer information appears at the bottom of the slide.

You have entered footer information for all slides except the title slide.

11. On the **Slide Show** tab, in the **Set Up** group, click the **Set Up Slide Show** button.

The Set Up Show dialog box opens.

By default, the presentation is set for presenter delivery and to include all slides.

12. In the **Show type** area, click **Browsed at a kiosk (full screen)**.

When you click this option, the Loop Continuously Until 'Esc' check box in the Show Options area becomes unavailable so that you cannot clear it. Any narration or animation attached to the presentation will play with the presentation unless you select the Show Without Narration or Show Without Animation check box.

See Also For information about narration, see the sidebar "Recording Presentations" in Chapter 14, "Prepare for Delivery." For information about animation, see Chapter 10, "Add Animation."

13. Click **OK**.

14. To test the show, display slide **1**, and on the **View Shortcuts** toolbar, click the **Reading View** button.

The presentation runs continuously, using the transition effect and advancement time applied to all its slides.

See Also For information about transitions, see "Adding Transitions" in Chapter 5, "Add Simple Visual Enhancements."

Tip If the presentation has no advancement time applied to its slides, you should click Manually in the Advance Slides area of the Set Up Show dialog box.

15. When the presentation starts again at slide 1, press Esc to stop the slide show and return to Normal view.

Now when you are ready to run the presentation, you can navigate to the folder where it is stored, and double-click it. When the presentation opens, switch to Slide Show view to start the presentation. You can press Esc to stop the slide show at any time.

✖ CLEAN UP Save the ServiceOrientationA presentation, and then close it.

Previewing and Printing Presentations

Even if you plan to deliver your presentation electronically, you might want to print the presentation to proof it for typographical errors and stylistic inconsistencies. Before you print, you can preview your presentation to see how the slides will look on paper. You preview a presentation on the Print page in the Backstage view, where the presentation appears in the right pane.

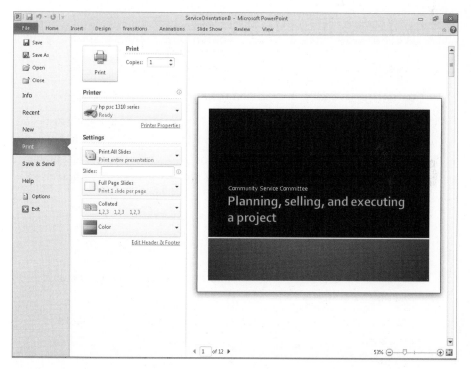

The Print page of the Backstage view.

You can click the Next Page or Previous Page button in the lower-left corner of the pane to move among the slides. To zoom in on part of a slide, click the Zoom In and Zoom Out buttons on the Zoom Slider in the lower-right corner. Click the Zoom To Page button to fit the slide to the pane.

If you will print a color presentation on a monochrome printer, you can preview in grayscale or black and white to verify that the text is legible against the background.

Tip In Normal view, you can see how your slides will look when printed on a monochrome printer by clicking either the Grayscale or the Black And White button in the Color/Grayscale group on the View tab.

When you're ready to print, you don't have to leave the Backstage view. You can simply click the Print button to print one copy of each slide on the default printer. If the default settings aren't what you want, you can make the following changes on the Print page:

● **Number of copies** Click the arrows to adjust the Copies setting.

● **Which printer** If you have more than one printer available, specify the printer you want to use and set its properties (such as paper source and image compression).

● **Which slides to print** You can print all the slides, the selected slides, or the current slide. To print only specific slides, click the Slides box, and enter the slide numbers and ranges separated by commas (no spaces). For example, enter 1,5,10-12 to print slides 1, 5, 10, 11, and 12 .

● **What to print** From the Print Layout gallery, specify whether to print slides (one per page), notes pages (one half-size slide per page with space for notes), or an outline. You can also print handouts, specifying the number of slides that print on each page (1, 2, 3, 4, 6, or 9) and their order.

You select what to print from this gallery.

- **Whether to frame slides** Click this option below the Print Layout and Handouts galleries to put a frame around the slides on the printed page.

- **Whether to scale slides** If you haven't set the size of the slides to match the size of the paper in the printer, click this option to have PowerPoint automatically reduce or increase the size of the slides to fit the paper when you print them.

  See Also For information about setting the size of slides, see "Setting Up Presentations for Delivery" earlier in this chapter.

- **Print quality** Click this option if you want the highest quality printed output.

- **Print comments and ink markup** Click this option if electronic or handwritten notes are attached to the presentation and you want to review them along with the slides.

- **Collate multiple copies** If you're printing multiple copies of a presentation, specify whether complete copies should be printed one at a time.

- **Color range** Specify whether the presentation should be printed in color (color on a color printer and grayscale on a monochrome printer), grayscale (on either a color or a monochrome printer), or pure black and white (no gray on either a color or a monochrome printer).

- **Edit the header or footer** Click this option to display the Header And Footer dialog box.

  See Also For information about adding footers to slides, see "Setting Up Presentations for Delivery" earlier in this chapter.

In this exercise, you'll preview a presentation in grayscale, select a printer, and print a selection of slides.

SET UP You need the ServiceOrientationB_start presentation located in your Chapter06 practice file folder to complete this exercise. Open the ServiceOrientationB_start presentation, and save it as *ServiceOrientationB*. Then follow the steps.

1. Click the **File** tab to display the Backstage view, and then click **Print**.

   The right side of the Print page displays the first slide as it will print with the current settings.

2. Under **Settings**, click **Color**, and then click **Grayscale**.

   The preview shows the slide in black, white, and shades of gray.

3. Click the **Next Page** button to move through the slides, until slide **12** is displayed.

4. On the **Zoom Slider**, click the **Zoom In** button several times, and then use the horizontal scroll bar that appears to scroll all the way to the left.

It's easier to examine the date in the footer of the magnified slide.

You can use the Zoom Slider to zoom in on parts of a slide.

5. Click the **Zoom to Page** button to return to the original zoom percentage.

6. In the middle pane, click the setting for your printer.

A list displays the names of all the printers installed on your computer.

7. In the list, click the printer you want to use.

Tip After choosing a printer, you can customize its settings for this particular print operation by clicking Printer Properties to display the Properties dialog box. For example, if the printer you have selected has duplex capabilities, you might want to specify that it should print slides on both sides of the page.

8. Under **Settings**, in the **Slides** box, type **1-3,5**, and then press Tab.

In the right pane, PowerPoint displays a preview of slide 1. Below the preview, the slide indicator changes to *1 of 4*, and you can now preview only the selected slides.

9. Click **Full Page Slides**, and below the gallery that appears, click **Frame Slides**.

10. At the top of the middle pane, click the **Print** button.

   PowerPoint prints slides 1, 2, 3, and 5 with frames in shades of gray on the selected printer.

✖ CLEAN UP Save the ServiceOrientationB presentation, and then close it.

Preparing Speaker Notes and Handouts

If you will be delivering your presentation before a live audience, you might want some speaker notes to guide you. Each slide in a PowerPoint presentation has a corresponding notes page. As you create each slide, you can enter notes that relate to the slide's content by simply clicking the Notes pane and typing. If you want to include something other than text in your speaker notes, you must switch to Notes Page view by clicking the Notes Page button in the Presentation Views group on the View tab. When your notes are complete, you can print them so that they are readily available to guide the presentation.

Tip In Presenter view, you can see your notes on one monitor while you display the slides to your audience on another monitor. For information about Presenter view, see the sidebar "Setting Up Presenter View" later in this chapter.

As a courtesy for your audience, you might want to supply handouts showing the presentation's slides so that people can take notes. Printing handouts requires a few decisions, such as which of the nine available formats you want to use and whether you want to add headers and footers, but otherwise, you don't need to do anything special to create simple handouts.

Tip The layout of PowerPoint notes pages and handouts is controlled by a special kind of template called a *master*. Usually, you'll find that the default masters are more than adequate, but if you want to make changes, you can. For information about customizing masters, see "Viewing and Changing Slide Masters" in Chapter 13, "Create Custom Presentation Elements."

In this exercise, you'll enter speaker notes for some slides in the Notes pane. Then you'll switch to Notes Page view, and insert a graphic into one note and a diagram into another. Finally, you'll print both speaker notes and handouts.

➡ SET UP You need the Harmony_start presentation and the YinYang graphic located in your Chapter06 practice file folder to complete this exercise. Open the Harmony_start presentation, and save it as *Harmony*. Then follow the steps.

1. With slide **1** displayed, drag the splitter bar between the **Slide** pane and the **Notes** pane upward to enlarge the Notes pane.

2. Click anywhere in the **Notes** pane, type **Welcome and introductions**, and then press Enter.

3. Type **Logistics**, press Enter, and then type **Establish knowledge level**.

4. Display slide **2**, and in the **Notes** pane, type **Talk about the main concepts**.

5. Display slide **3**, and in the **Notes** pane, type **Complementary energies**, and then press Enter twice.

6. On the **View** tab, in the **Presentation Views** group, click the **Notes Page** button.

   Slide 3 is displayed in Notes Page view. The zoom percentage is set so that the entire notes page fits in the window.

7. On the **Insert** tab, in the **Images** group, click the **Picture** button.

8. In the **Insert Picture** dialog box, navigate to your **Chapter06** practice file folder, and then double-click the **YinYang** graphic.

9. Drag the image down below the note you typed in step 5.

   The picture is visible in Notes Page view.

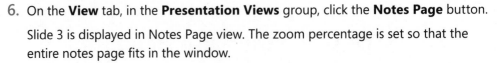

You might want to add images to your speaker notes to remind yourself of concepts you want to cover while the slide is displayed.

10. Below the scroll bar, click the **Next Slide** button to move to slide **4**. Then click the border around the text placeholder to select it, and press Delete.

11. On the **Insert** tab, in the **Illustrations** group, click the **SmartArt** button. In the left pane of the **Choose a SmartArt Graphic** dialog box, click **Hierarchy**, and then in the middle pane, double-click the second thumbnail in the last row (**Hierarchy List**).

    A diagram with six shapes and placeholder text is inserted into the page. Don't worry about its placement for now; you will fix that later.

    See Also For information about how to work with SmartArt diagrams, see "Inserting Diagrams" in Chapter 5, "Add Simple Visual Enhancements," and "Customizing Diagrams" in Chapter 8, "Fine-Tune Visual Elements."

12. Open the **Text** pane, click the first placeholder in the hierarchy, and type the following, pressing the Down Arrow key or the Enter key as indicated:

    Focus (Down Arrow)

    > **Health** (Down Arrow)
    >
    > **Creativity** (Enter)
    >
    > **Relationships** (Enter)
    >
    > **Community** (Down Arrow)

    Follow (Down Arrow)

    > **Knowledge** (Down Arrow)
    >
    > **Career** (Enter)
    >
    > **Fame** (Enter)
    >
    > **Fortune**

    Tip If you have trouble seeing the notes at this zoom percentage, click the Zoom In button on the Zoom Slider in the lower-right corner of the window.

    The speaker notes now include a diagram expressing visually the concepts to be emphasized during the presentation.

13. Use the formatting options available in the **SmartArt Styles** group on the **Design** tab to format the diagram any way you want, and then move and size the diagram to fit in the space below the slide.

    We used the Moderate Effect style and the Gradient Loop – Accent 1 colors.

Diagrams can give you an at-a-glance reminder of important concepts.

14. On the **View** tab, in the **Presentation Views** group, click the **Normal** button.

    The diagram is not visible in Normal view.

15. Display slide **3**.

    The YinYang graphic is not visible in this view either.

Header & Footer

16. Switch to Notes Page view, and then on the **Insert** tab, in the **Text** group, click the **Header & Footer** button.

The Header And Footer dialog box opens with the Notes And Handouts page displayed.

Header and Footer

Slide | Notes and Handouts

Include on page

☐ Date and time

 ◉ Update automatically

 4/17/2010 ▾

  Language: Calendar type:

  English (U.S.) ▾ Western ▾

 ○ Fixed

 4/17/2010

☐ Header

☑ Page number

☐ Footer

Apply to All

Cancel

Preview

On the Notes And Handouts page, you can insert a header and a footer.

17. Select the **Date and Time** check box, and then click **Fixed**.

18. Select the **Header** check box, and then in the text box, type **Harmony in Your Home**.

19. Select the **Footer** check box, and then in the text box, type **Wide World Importers**.

20. Click **Apply to All**.

The notes page reflects your specifications.

21. Switch to Normal view, and then display the **Print** page of the Backstage view.

22. On the **Print** page, under **Settings**, click **Full Page Slides**, and then click **Notes Pages**.

23. Click the **Slides** box, type **1-4**, and then click the **Print** button.

    You now have a copy of the speaker notes to refer to during the presentation.

24. Display the **Print** page of the Backstage view again, and under **Settings**, click **Notes Pages**, and under **Handouts** in the gallery, click **3 slides**.

    The first page of the handouts is previewed in the right pane.

When you print three slides per page, PowerPoint adds lines for notes to the right of each slide image.

25. Change the **Slides** setting to **1-3**, and then click the **Print** button.

✖ CLEAN UP Save the Harmony presentation, and then close it.

Enhanced Handouts

If you want to provide audience handouts that include notes as well as pictures of the slides, you can send the presentation to a Microsoft Word document and then develop the handout content in Word.

To create handouts in Word:

1. Display the Save & Send page of the Backstage view, and under File Types in the middle pane, click Create Handouts.

2. In the right pane, click the Create Handouts button.

    The Send To Microsoft Word dialog box opens.

In two of the five available formats, you can enter notes along with the pictures of the slides.

3. Click the notes format you want.

4. If the slide content might change, under Add Slides To Microsoft Word Document, click Paste Link.

5. Click OK.

    Word starts and opens a document set up to contain the handout format you selected. If you selected Outline Only, the text of the presentation appears in the document as a bulleted list.

Finalizing Presentations

These days, many presentations are delivered electronically, either by e-mail or from a Web site. As you develop a presentation, it can accumulate information that you might not want in the final version, such as the names of people who worked on the presentation, comments that reviewers have added to the file, or hidden text about status and assumptions. If your presentation will never leave your computer, you don't have to worry that it might contain something that you would rather other people did not see. However, if the presentation file is going to be shared with other people, you will want to remove this identifying and tracking information before you distribute the presentation.

To examine some of the information attached to a presentation, you can display the properties on the Info page of the Backstage view. You can change or remove some of the properties in the Properties pane, or you can display the Document Panel or the Properties dialog box by clicking Properties at the top of the pane and clicking the option you want. However, to automate the process of finding and removing all extraneous and potentially confidential information, PowerPoint provides a tool called the *Document Inspector.*

The Document Inspector removes many different types of information.

Tip When rearranging the objects on a slide, you might drag an object to one side while you decide whether to include it. The Off-Slide Content option in the Document Inspector dialog box detects any stray content that you might have overlooked. The Document Inspector also looks for invisible content on the slide. This is content you might have hidden by displaying the Selection And Visibility task pane and then clearing the object's check box. (To display the Selection And Visibility pane, click the Select button in the Editing group on the Home tab, and then click Selection Pane.)

After you run the Document Inspector, you see a summary of its search results, and you have the option of removing all the items found in each category.

PowerPoint also includes two other finalizing tools:

- **Check Accessibility** This tool checks for presentation elements and formatting that might be difficult for people with certain kinds of disabilities to read. It reports its findings in the Accessibility Checker task pane, and offers suggestions for fixing any potential issues.

- **Check Compatibility** This tool checks for the use of features not supported in earlier versions of PowerPoint. It presents a list of features that might be lost or degraded if you save the presentation in an earlier PowerPoint file format.

After you have handled extraneous information and accessibility and compatibility issues, you can mark a presentation as final and make it a read-only file, so that other people know that they should not make changes to this released presentation. This process does not lock the presentation, however; if you want to make additional changes to the presentation, you can easily turn off the final status.

In this exercise, you'll examine the properties attached to a presentation, remove personal information from the file, and then mark the presentation as final.

SET UP You need the Meeting_start presentation located in your Chapter06 practice file folder to complete this exercise. Open the Meeting_start presentation, and save it as *Meeting*. Then follow the steps.

1. Display the **Info** page of the Backstage view.

   The Properties pane on the right side of the window displays the standard properties associated with this presentation.

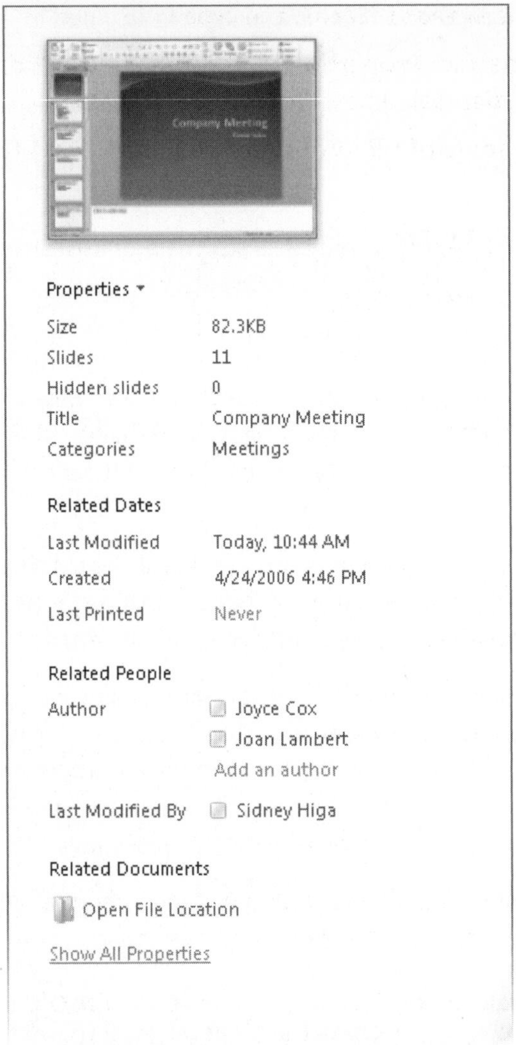

Properties ▾

Size	82.3KB
Slides	11
Hidden slides	0
Title	Company Meeting
Categories	Meetings

Related Dates

Last Modified	Today, 10:44 AM
Created	4/24/2006 4:46 PM
Last Printed	Never

Related People

Author	☐ Joyce Cox
	☐ Joan Lambert
	Add an author
Last Modified By	☐ Sidney Higa

Related Documents

📄 Open File Location

Show All Properties

PowerPoint controls some of the properties, such as the size and dates; you can add and change others, such as the assigned categories and authors.

2. At the bottom on the **Properties** pane, click **Show All Properties**.

The pane expands to show all the properties.

3. Click the property adjacent to **Status**, and type **Done**.

4. At the top of the pane, click **Properties**, and click **Advanced Properties**. Then in the **Meeting Properties** dialog box, click the **Summary** tab.

   This page includes some of the properties you might want to change in a convenient format.

The Summary page of the Properties dialog box.

5. Click in the **Subject** box, type **Morale event**, and then click **OK**.

   The Subject property in the Properties pane reflects your change.

6. Save your changes to the presentation.

7. Display the **Info** page of the Backstage view again. Then in the center pane, click **Check for Issues**, and click **Inspect Document**.

   In the Document Inspector dialog box, you can inspect for six types of content.

8. Clear the **Custom XML Data** check box. Then with the **Comments and Annotations**, **Document Properties and Personal Information**, **Invisible On-Slide Content**, and **Presentation Notes** check boxes selected, click **Inspect**.

   The Document Inspector reports its findings.

This presentation includes properties that you might not want others to be able to view.

9. To the right of **Document Properties and Personal Information**, click **Remove All**.

   PowerPoint removes the presentation's properties.

10. Close the **Document Inspector** dialog box.

   In the Properties pane, all the properties have been cleared.

11. In the center pane of the **Info** page, click **Protect Presentation**, and then click **Mark as Final**.

    A message tells you that the presentation will be marked as final and then saved.

12. Click **OK** in the message box, and then click **OK** in the confirmation box that appears after the document is marked as final.

    The presentation's final status is now indicated on the Info page.

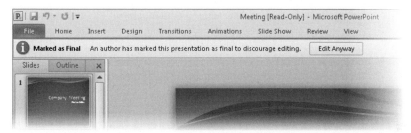

Marking as final discourages but does not prevent editing.

13. Click any tab on the ribbon to return to the presentation.

    The title bar indicates that this is a read-only file, and the ribbon tabs are hidden.

The information bar explains that this presentation has been marked as final.

14. Click the **Home** tab to display its commands, most of which are inactive.

15. On the title slide, double-click the word **Company**, and press the Delete key.

    Nothing happens. You cannot change any of the objects on the slides unless you click the Edit Anyway button in the information bar to remove the final status.

✖ **CLEAN UP** Close the Meeting presentation.

Setting Up Presenter View

If your computer can support two monitors, or if you will be presenting a slide show from your computer through a projector, you might want to check out Presenter view. In this view, you can control the presentation on one monitor while the audience sees the slides in Slide Show view on the delivery monitor or the projector screen.

To deliver a presentation on one monitor and use Presenter view on another:

1. Open the PowerPoint presentation you want to set up.

2. On the Slide Show tab, in the Set Up group, click Set Up Slide Show.

   The Set Up Show dialog box opens. When your computer is set up to use multiple monitors, the settings in the Multiple Monitors area are active.

3. In the Multiple Monitors area, click the Display Slide Show On arrow, and then in the list, click the name of the monitor you want to use to show the slides to your audience.

   The slides will display full-screen on the specified monitor.

4. Select the Show Presenter View check box, and then click OK.

5. With the title slide of the presentation active, switch to Slide Show view.

   The title slide is displayed full screen on the delivery monitor, and Presenter view is displayed on the control monitor. As the presenter, you can see details about what slide or bullet point is coming next, see your speaker notes, jump directly to any slide, black out the screen during a pause in the presentation, and keep track of the time.

6. On the control monitor, use the Presenter view tools to control the presentation.

Delivering Presentations

To deliver a presentation to an audience, you first click the Slide Show button to display the slides full screen. Then depending on how you have set up the presentation, you can either click the mouse button without moving the mouse to display the slides in sequence, or you can allow PowerPoint to display the slides according to the advancement timings you have set on the Transitions tab.

See Also For information about advancement timings, see "Adding Transitions" in Chapter 5, "Add Simple Visual Enhancements."

If you need to move to a slide other than the next one or the previous one, you can move the mouse pointer to display an inconspicuous navigation toolbar in the lower-left corner of the slide. You can use this toolbar in the following ways:

- To move to the next slide, click the Next button.
- To move to the previous slide, click the Previous button.
- To jump to a slide out of sequence, click the Navigation button, click Go To Slide, and then click the slide.

    Tip You can also display the Navigation button's menu by right-clicking the slide.

- To end the presentation, click the Navigation button, and then click End Show.

    Keyboard Shortcuts To display a list of keyboard shortcuts for carrying out presentation tasks, click the Navigation button, and then click Help. For example, you can press the Spacebar, the Down Arrow key, or the Right Arrow key to move to the next slide; press the Page Up key or the Left Arrow key to move to the previous slide; and press the Esc key to end the presentation.

    See Also To see a complete list of keyboard shortcuts, see "Keyboard Shortcuts" at the end of this book.

During a presentation, you can reinforce your message by drawing on the slides with an electronic "pen" or changing the background behind text with a highlighter. You simply click the Pen button on the toolbar that appears when you move the mouse, click the tool you want, and then begin drawing or highlighting. The pen color is determined by the setting in the Set Up Show dialog box, but you can change the pen color during the presentation by clicking the Pen button, clicking Ink Color, and then selecting the color you want.

In this exercise, you'll move around in a presentation in various ways while delivering it. You'll also use a pen tool to mark up one slide, change the color of the markup, and then mark up another.

SET UP You need the SavingWater_start presentation located in your Chapter06 practice file folder to complete this exercise. Open the SavingWater_start presentation, and save it as *SavingWater*. Then follow the steps.

1. With slide **1** selected in Normal view, on the **View Shortcuts** toolbar, click the **Slide Show** button.

   PowerPoint displays the title slide after implementing its applied transition effect.

2. Click the mouse button to advance to slide **2**.

   The slide contents ripple onto the screen.

3. Press the Left Arrow key to move back to the previous slide, and then press the Right Arrow key to display the next slide.

4. Move the mouse.

   The pointer appears on the screen, and barely visible in the lower-left corner, the shadow toolbar appears.

   Troubleshooting If the pop-up navigation toolbar doesn't seem to appear, move the pointer to the lower-left corner of the screen and move it slowly to the right. The four toolbar buttons should become visible in turn. If they don't, press the Esc key to end the slide show. Then display the Backstage view, and click Options. In the PowerPoint Options dialog box, click Advanced, and in the Slide Show area, select the Show Popup Toolbar check box, and click OK.

5. Move the pointer to the bottom of the screen and to the left until the **Next** button appears. Then click the **Next** button to display slide **3**.

6. Right-click anywhere on the screen, and then click **Previous** to redisplay slide **2**.

7. Right-click anywhere on the screen, point to **Go to Slide**, and then in the list of slide names, click **11 Soil Amendment**.

8. Display the toolbar, click the **Navigation** button, and then click **Next** to display slide **12**.

9. Use various navigation methods to display various slides in the presentation until you are comfortable moving around.

10. Right-click anywhere on the screen, and then click **End Show**.

    The active slide appears in Normal view.

    Tip If you click all the way through to the end of the presentation, PowerPoint displays a black screen to indicate that the next click will return you to the previous view. If you do not want the black screen to appear at the end of a presentation, display the PowerPoint Options dialog box, and click Advanced. Then in the Slide Show area, clear the End With Black Slide check box, and click OK. Then clicking while the last slide is displayed will return you to the previous view.

11. Display slide **11**, and switch to Slide Show view.

12. Right-click anywhere on the screen, point to **Pointer Options**, and then click **Highlighter**.

Tip When the pen or highlighter tool is active in Slide Show view, clicking the mouse button does not advance the slide show to the next slide. You need to switch back to the regular pointer to use the mouse to advance the slide.

13. On the slide, highlight the words **10 tons**.

14. Right-click anywhere on the screen, point to **Pointer Options**, and then click **Pen**.

15. On the slide, draw a line below the words **per acre per year**.

PowerPoint draws the line in the color specified in the Set Up Show dialog box as the default for this presentation.

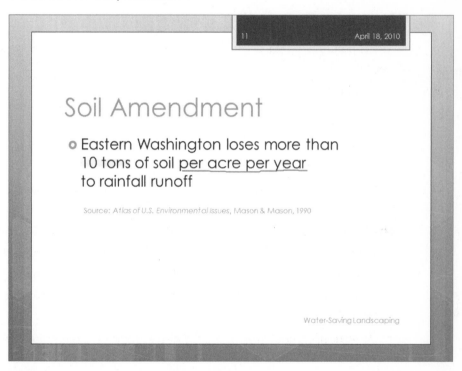

You can emphasize a point with the highlighter or pen.

16. Right-click the screen, point to **Pointer Options**, and then click **Erase All Ink on Slide**.

The highlight and line are erased.

17. Press the Spacebar to move to the next slide.

18. Display the toolbar, click the **Pen** button, point to **Ink Color**, and then under **Standard Colors** in the palette, click the **Dark Red** box.

19. Draw a line below the words **Prevent erosion**.

20. Right-click anywhere on the screen, point to **Pointer Options**, and then click **Arrow**.

   The pen tool changes back to the regular pointer, and you can now click the mouse button to advance to the next slide.

21. Press Esc to stop the presentation.

   A message asks whether you want to keep your ink annotations.

22. Click **Discard**.

   The active slide is displayed in Normal view.

 CLEAN UP Save the SavingWater presentation, and then close it.

Key Points

- It's most efficient to set up your presentation in its intended output format before you begin adding content.

- To proof a presentation on paper, you can print it in color, grayscale, or black and white, depending on the capabilities of your printer.

- You can easily create speaker notes to facilitate a presentation delivery, or print handouts so that your audience can easily follow your presentation.

- Finalizing a presentation ensures that it doesn't contain personal or confidential information and that people are alerted before making further changes.

- Knowing how to use all the navigation toolbar buttons, commands, and keyboard shortcuts to navigate in Slide Show view is important for smooth presentation delivery.

- To emphasize a point, you can mark up slides during a presentation by using a pen in various colors or a highlighter.

Part 2

Presentation Enhancements

Chapter at a Glance

	Winter	Spring	Summer	Fall
Minimum	18	41	73	43
Average	29	57	89	54
Maximum	40	72	105	65

Insert tables,
page 181

	Seasonal Temperatures			
	Winter	Spring	Summer	Fall
Minimum	18	41	73	43
Average	29	57	89	54
Maximum	40	72	105	65

Format tables,
page 185

Equipment Replacement

Insert and update
Excel worksheets,
page 188

Payment Schedule	
Interest Rate	6.0%
Years	10
Loan Amount	$1,550,000
Monthly Payment	$17,208
Cost of Loan	$619,494
10-Year Lease Cost	$1,800,000
Savings	$1,180,506

7 Add Tables

In this chapter, you will learn how to

✔ Insert tables.

✔ Format tables.

✔ Insert and update Excel worksheets.

Often you will want to bolster the argument you are making in a Microsoft PowerPoint 2010 presentation with facts and figures that are best presented in a table. Tables condense information into highly structured row and column grid formats so that identifying categories or individual items and making comparisons is easier. You can place a table on any PowerPoint slide, whether or not it includes a content placeholder.

If the tabular information already exists—for example, as a Microsoft Excel worksheet—you can copy and paste it into a PowerPoint table. If you want to preserve formulas, it's best to embed the worksheet as an object in the PowerPoint slide.

In this chapter, you'll insert and format a table on one PowerPoint slide and then insert and manipulate an Excel worksheet.

> **Practice Files** Before you can complete the exercises in this chapter, you need to copy the book's practice files to your computer. The practice files you'll use to complete the exercises in this chapter are in the Chapter07 practice file folder. A complete list of practice files is provided in "Using the Practice Files" at the beginning of this book.

Inserting Tables

When you want to present a lot of data in an organized and easy-to-read format, a table is often your best choice. On a slide that includes a content placeholder, you can click the placeholder's Insert Table button to start the process of creating a table. On any slide, you can click the Table button in the Tables group on the Insert tab to add a table outside a placeholder.

After you specify the number of columns and rows you want in the table, PowerPoint creates the table structure, which consists of a two-dimensional organization of rows and columns. The box at the intersection of each row and column is called a *cell*. Often the first row is used for column headings, and the leftmost column is used for row headings.

You work with PowerPoint tables in much the same way as you work with tables in Microsoft Word. (If the table you want to use already exists in a Word document, you can copy and paste that table into a PowerPoint slide, rather than re-creating it.)

To enter information in the table, you click a cell and then type the data. You move the cursor from cell to cell by pressing the Tab key. Pressing Tab in the last cell of the last row inserts a new row at the bottom of the table. If you need a new row elsewhere, you can insert a row above or below the row containing the cursor or insert a column to the left or right by clicking the corresponding buttons in the Rows & Columns group of the Layout contextual tab. If you no longer need a column or row, you can remove it by clicking the Delete button in the Rows & Columns group and then clicking Delete Columns or Delete Rows.

You can click the Merge Cells button in the Merge group of the Layout tab to combine (merge) selected cells into one cell that spans two or more columns or rows. Another way to merge cells is by clicking the Eraser button in the Draw Borders group on the Design contextual tab, and then dragging the eraser that appears across the border between two cells.

If you want to split a single cell into two or more cells, you can either select the cell and then click the Split Cells button in the Merge group on the Layout tab, or you can click the Draw Table button in the Draw Borders group on the Design tab, and then draw a cell border with the pencil that appears.

Tip If you don't already have a table on a slide, you can click the Table arrow and then click Draw Table to activate the pencil. You can then drag cells the size and shape you need to create the table.

In this exercise, you'll create a table, enter text in its cells, insert a row, and merge cells.

SET UP You need the Temperature_start document located in your Chapter07 practice file folder to complete this exercise. Open the Temperature_start document, and save it as *Temperature*. Then follow the steps.

1. Display slide **13**, which has the Title And Content layout.

2. In the content placeholder, click the **Insert Table** button.

   The Insert Table dialog box opens.

You specify the number of columns and rows in this dialog box.

3. Leave the **Number of columns** box set at **5**, but change the setting in the **Number of rows** box to **3**.

4. Click **OK**.

A blank table with five columns and three rows is inserted into the slide.

By default, the heading row is shaded and the remaining rows are banded with subtle shades of the same color.

5. In the first cell of the second column, type **Winter**, press Tab, type **Spring**, press Tab, type **Summer**, press Tab, type **Fall**, and then press Tab again.

The cursor moves to the first cell of the second row.

6. Type the following, pressing Tab after each entry:

Minimum	18	41	73	43
Average	29	57	89	54

When you press Tab after the last entry, PowerPoint adds a new row to the table.

7. Type the following, pressing Tab after each entry except the last:

Maximum	40	72	105	65

Here are the results.

	Winter	Spring	Summer	Fall
Minimum	18	41	73	43
Average	29	57	89	54
Maximum	40	72	105	65

The banding in the rows below the heading row makes the information more distinct.

8. Click anywhere in the heading row, and then on the **Layout** tab, in the **Rows & Columns** group, click the **Insert Above** button.

   PowerPoint adds a new row above the headings.

9. Click the second cell in the new row, hold down the Shift key, and then press the Right Arrow key three times.

10. With four cells selected, in the **Merge** group, click the **Merge Cells** button.

11. In the merged cell, type **Seasonal temperatures**.

12. Without moving the cursor, in the **Alignment** group, click the **Center** button.

    Keyboard Shortcut Press Ctrl+E to center text.

    See Also For more information about keyboard shortcuts, see "Keyboard Shortcuts" at the end of this book.

13. Point to the frame of the table (don't point to the sets of dots, which are sizing handles). Then drag the table downward so that it sits in about the center of the slide.

14. Click a blank area of the slide.

    The table is no longer active.

You can see the results when you click outside the table.

CLEAN UP Save the Temperature presentation, and then close it.

Formatting Tables

You can format an entire table as well as individual cells by using the commands on the Design and Format contextual tabs, which appear only when a table is active. For example, you can use buttons on the Design contextual tab to switch to a different table style, instantly changing the look of the text and cells to make key information stand out. If you want, you can also format individual words and individual cells.

In this exercise, you'll apply a different table style, and then format a row and individual cells.

SET UP You need the TemperatureFormatted_start document located in your Chapter07 practice file folder to complete this exercise. Open the TemperatureFormatted_start document, and save it as *TemperatureFormatted*. Then follow the steps.

1. Display slide **13**, and click anywhere in the table to activate it.

2. On the **Design** contextual tab, in the **Table Style Options** group, clear the **Banded Rows** check box.

The banding disappears. All rows except the header row are now the same color.

3. In the **Table Style Options** group, select the **First Column** check box.

The first column is now the same color as the heading, and its text is white.

Seasonal Temperatures				
	Winter	Spring	Summer	Fall
Minimum	18	41	73	43
Average	29	57	89	54
Maximum	40	72	105	65

Two formatting adjustments have completely changed the look of the table.

4. In the **Table Styles** group, click the **More** button.

The Table Styles gallery appears.

An orange selection frame around a thumbnail indicates the applied style.

5. Drag the bottom border of the gallery upward until you can see the table.

6. Point to various styles to preview their effects on the table, and then under **Medium**, click the fifth thumbnail in the second row (**Medium Style 2 - Accent 4**).

7. Drag across the cells containing **Winter**, **Spring**, **Summer**, and **Fall** to select them.

8. On the **Design** contextual tab, in the **Table Styles** group, click the **Shading** arrow, and then under **Theme Colors** in the palette, click the green box at the top of the third column (**Light Green, Background 2**).

9. Click the cell containing **105**, click the **Shading** arrow, and then under **Theme Colors** in the palette, click the orange box at the top of the seventh column (**Orange, Accent 3**).

10. Click the cell containing **18**, click the **Shading** arrow, and below the palette, click **More Fill Colors**. Then on the **Standard** page of the **Colors** dialog box, click a pale blue color near the center of the color wheel, and then click **OK**.

11. Select **Seasonal Temperatures**, and then in the **WordArt Styles** group, display the **Quick Styles** gallery. Then click the fourth thumbnail in the second row (**Fill – Green, Accent 1, Inner Shadow – Accent 1**).

12. Repeat step 10 to format **Minimum**, **Average**, and **Maximum**.

13. On the **Layout** tab, in the **Table** group, click the **Select** button, and then click **Select Table**.

14. In the **Table Styles** group, click the **Borders** arrow, and click **Outside Borders**.

After experimenting, let's try a simpler look.

15. Click anywhere in the table, and display the **Table Styles** gallery. Then, under **Medium**, click the third thumbnail in the second row (**Medium Style 2 – Accent 2**).

The new table style clears the cell formatting but leaves the text effects.

	Seasonal Temperatures			
	Winter	Spring	Summer	Fall
Minimum	18	41	73	43
Average	29	57	89	54
Maximum	40	72	105	65

A simple approach makes the column and row headings stand out.

CLEAN UP Save the TemperatureFormatting presentation, and then close it.

Inserting and Updating Excel Worksheets

The table capabilities of PowerPoint are perfectly adequate for the display of simple information that is unlikely to change during the useful life of the presentation. However, if your data involves calculations or is likely to require updating, you'll probably want to maintain the information in an Excel worksheet. You can then embed the worksheet in a slide as an object, or you can link the slide to the worksheet so that you won't have to worry about keeping the data current in more than one place.

Embedded objects and linked objects differ in the following ways:

- An embedded object is an object that maintains a direct connection to its original program, known as the *source program*. After you insert an embedded object, you can easily edit it by double-clicking it, which opens the program in which it was originally created. Be aware that embedding an object in a presentation increases the presentation's file size, because PowerPoint has to store not only the data itself but also information about how to display the data.

- A linked object is a representation on a slide of information that is still stored in the original document, known as the *source document*. If you edit the source document in the source program after adding a linked object to a slide, PowerPoint updates the representation of the object. Because PowerPoint stores only the data needed to display the information, linking results in a smaller file size than embedding.

  Important Always make modifications to the source document, not the linked object on the slide. Any changes you make to the linked object will be overwritten the next time you open the presentation, because PowerPoint will update the linked object to reflect the version in the source document.

For example, suppose a sales manager stores past sales information and future sales projections in Excel worksheets. On one slide in a presentation, she might embed the past sales information, which won't change, as an object. On another slide, she might link the future sales projections, which she is still in the process of fine-tuning. Then as she updates the projections worksheet, the linked table in the PowerPoint presentation automatically updates as well.

In this exercise, you'll insert an Excel worksheet and then update and format the content of the embedded object.

➡️ **SET UP** You need the FinancialMeeting_start presentation and the NewEquipment workbook located in your Chapter07 practice file folder to complete this exercise. Open the FinancialMeeting_start presentation, and save it as *FinancialMeeting*. Then follow the steps.

Object

1. Display slide **9**, and then on the **Insert** tab, in the **Text** group, click the **Object** button.

   The Insert Object dialog box opens.

   ![Insert Object dialog box showing Create new selected with Object type list including Bitmap Image, Microsoft Equation 3.0, Microsoft Excel 97-2003 Worksheet, Microsoft Excel Binary Worksheet, Microsoft Excel Chart, Microsoft Excel Macro-Enabled Worksheet, Microsoft Excel Worksheet, Microsoft Graph Chart. Result: Inserts a new Bitmap Image object into your presentation.]

   You can create any of the objects in the Object Type list from within PowerPoint.

2. Click **Create from file**, and then click **Browse**.

   The Browse dialog box opens. (It is similar to the Open dialog box.)

3. Navigate to your **Chapter07** practice file folder, click the **NewEquipment** workbook, and then click **OK**.

   The location of the workbook appears in the File box.

   ![Insert Object dialog box showing Create from file selected with File: C:\Users\Sidney Higa\Desktop\PowerPoint2010SBS\Ch, Browse... button, Link check box. Result: Inserts the contents of the file as an object into your presentation so that you can activate it using the application that created it.]

   To link rather than embed the workbook, select the Link check box.

4. Click **OK**.

PowerPoint embeds the data from the specified workbook in the slide.

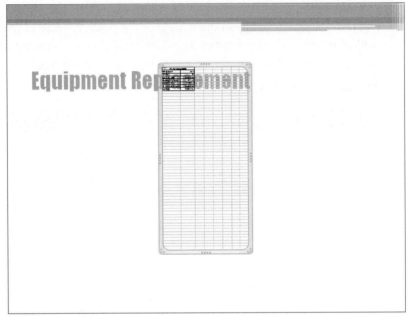

The object is inserted in the center of the slide.

5. Double-click the worksheet object.

The worksheet opens in an Excel window within PowerPoint.

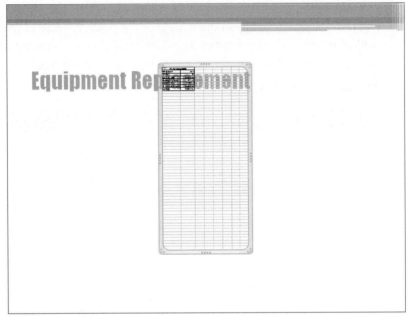

When you double-click an embedded worksheet, the Excel ribbon replaces that of PowerPoint across the top of the program window.

Troubleshooting The appearance of buttons and groups on the ribbon changes depending on the width of the program window. For information about changing the appearance of the ribbon to match our screen images, see "Modifying the Display of the Ribbon" at the beginning of this book.

6. Point to the black handle in the middle of the bottom frame of the Excel window, and when the pointer becomes a double-headed arrow, drag up until the window is just big enough to contain the active part of the worksheet.

   Be careful not to obscure any data.

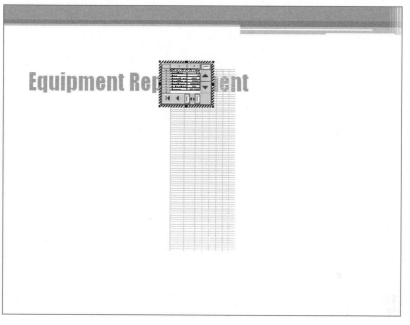

You have sized the frame so that it just fits the data.

7. Click outside the window to return to PowerPoint. Then point to the lower-right corner of the object, and drag down and to the right to enlarge it.

   Troubleshooting Be sure to point to the corner. Although you can't see it, you want to drag the sizing handle. If you drag the frame instead, you'll move the object instead of sizing it. If you drag down too much or to the right too much, you will expose empty cells. If that happens, click the Undo button, and try again.

8. Point to the frame (not to a handle), and drag the worksheet object to the center of the slide. Then double-click the worksheet object again.

   Once again, the object is displayed in an Excel window.

Now you can see that the columns are labeled with letters (A, B, C, and so on), and the rows are labeled with numbers (1, 2, 3, and so on).

You can reference each cell by its column letter followed by its row number (for example, A1). You can reference a block of cells by the cell in its upper-left corner and the cell in its lower-right corner, separated by a colon (for example, A1:C3).

9. Click cell **B2**, and notice in the **Number** group that the cell's contents are formatted as a percentage.

10. Click each of the other cells in column **B** in turn, and notice the contents of the formula bar (the box to the right of **fx** above the slide) and the format in the **Number** group.

11. Click cell **B2**, type **6**, and then press Enter.

    Excel uses formulas in cells B5, B6, and B8 to calculate the new cost of the equipment loan. The amount in cell B5 changed to $17,208, the amount in B6 changed to $619.494, and the amount in cell B8 changed to $1,180,506. These changes affect only the object on the slide; the data in the original Excel worksheet has not changed.

12. Select cell **A1**, which is merged with cell B1, and then on the Excel **Home** tab, in the **Font** group, click the **Fill Color** arrow. Under **Theme Colors** in the palette, click the second box in the green column (**Olive Green, Accent 3, Lighter 60%**).

13. Point to cell **A2**, and drag down to cell **A8**. Then click the **Fill Color** button to shade the selected cells with the default color.

14. Click a blank area of the slide.

    Excel closes, and the PowerPoint ribbon reappears.

15. Click the blank area again to deactivate the object.

    You can now see the results of your formatting.

You've successfully embedded and formatted a worksheet in a PowerPoint slide.

CLEAN UP Save the FinancialMeeting presentation, and then close it.

Key Points

- Use a table to organize information neatly in rows and columns.

- You can customize and format individual cells as well as the entire table.

- If the information you need already exists in an Excel worksheet, you can embed the worksheet in a slide. Double-clicking the worksheet object opens it in Excel so that you can edit it.

- If the information in the Excel worksheet is likely to change, you can link the slide to the source worksheet so that the slide is updated if the worksheet changes.

Chapter at a Glance

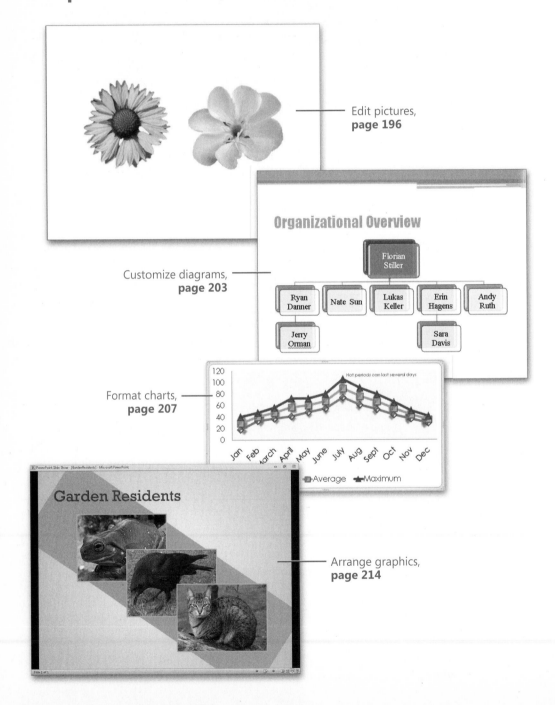

Edit pictures,
page 196

Organizational Overview

Customize diagrams,
page 203

Format charts,
page 207

Arrange graphics,
page 214

Garden Residents

8 Fine-Tune Visual Elements

In this chapter, you will learn how to

✔ Edit pictures.

✔ Customize diagrams.

✔ Format charts.

✔ Arrange graphics.

In Chapter 5, "Add Simple Visual Enhancements," you were introduced to the primary ways you can use graphic elements to convey information or dress up your slides. You inserted pictures and clip art images, created a diagram, plotted data in a chart, drew shapes, and eased the transition from one slide to another with a graphic effect. These simple techniques might be all you need to enhance your presentations. But if you need to manipulate graphic elements to produce more dramatic effects, you can push the Microsoft Office PowerPoint 2010 capabilities further to get just the result you are looking for.

In this chapter, you'll create a photo album and insert and manipulate photographs. Next, you'll manipulate shapes to customize an organization chart. Then you'll format a chart and save it as a template. Finally, you'll use various techniques to arrange graphics.

> **Practice Files** Before you can complete the exercises in this chapter, you need to copy the book's practice files to your computer. The practice files you'll use to complete the exercises in this chapter are in the Chapter08 practice file folder. A complete list of practice files is provided in "Using the Practice Files" at the beginning of this book.

Editing Pictures

From time to time in this book, we have alluded to the modern trend away from slides with bullet points and toward presentations that include more graphics. Successful presenters have learned that most people can't listen to a presentation while they are reading slides. So these presenters make sure most of their slides display graphics that represent the point they are making, giving the audience something to look at while they focus on what is being said.

PowerPoint 2010 gives you the tools you need to create graphic-intensive rather than text-intensive presentations. When you want to display a dynamic array of pictures in a presentation, you can use a photo album template to do the initial layout and then customize the album by adding frames of different shapes, as well as captions.

Tip To integrate the slide layouts from a photo album template into a more traditional presentation, create the photo album and then import its slides into the other presentation by clicking Reuse Slides at the bottom of the New Slide gallery. For information about reusing slides, see "Adding Slides with Ready-Made Content" in Chapter 2, "Work with Slides."

After you insert any picture into a presentation, you can modify it by using the buttons on the Format tab that is displayed on the ribbon only when the graphic is selected. For example, you can do the following:

- Remove the background by clicking the Remove Background button and then designating either the areas you want to keep or those you want to remove.

- Sharpen or soften the picture, or change its brightness or contrast, by choosing the effect you want from the Corrections gallery.

- Enhance the picture's color by making a selection from the Color gallery.

- Make one of the picture's colors transparent by clicking Set Transparent Color at the bottom of the gallery and then selecting the color.

- Choose an effect, such as Pencil Sketch or Paint Strokes, from the Artistic Effects gallery.

- Apply effects such as shadows, reflections, and borders, or apply combinations of these effects by choosing a predefined style from the Picture Styles gallery.

- Add a border consisting of one or more solid or dashed lines of whatever width and color you choose.

- Rotate the picture to any angle, either by dragging the green rotating handle or by clicking the Rotate button and then choosing a rotating or flipping option.

- Crop away the parts of the picture that you don't want to show on the slide. (The picture itself is not altered—parts of it are simply covered up.)

● Minimize the presentation's file size by clicking the Compress Pictures button and then choosing where or how the presentation will be viewed—for example, on the Web or printed—to determine the optimum resolution. You can also delete cropped areas of a picture to reduce file size.

In this exercise, you'll create a photo album displaying pictures of native plants. You'll crop, resize, remove the background, apply an artistic effect, and add captions. You'll also reuse a slide from another photo album, and apply a theme.

SET UP You need the NativePlant1 through NativePlant8 photographs and the PhotoAlbumTitleSlide presentation located in your Chapter08 practice file folder to complete this exercise. Open a blank presentation, and then follow the steps.

1. On the **Insert** tab, in the **Images** group, click the **Photo Album** button.

   The Photo Album dialog box opens.

2. Under **Insert picture from**, click **File/Disk**.

   The Insert New Pictures dialog box opens.

3. Navigate to your **Chapter08** practice file folder, click **NativePlant1**, hold down the Ctrl key, and click **NativePlant3** through **NativePlant5**. Then click **Insert**.

   The Photo Album dialog box now has four graphics files listed in the Pictures In Album list.

You can click each picture in turn to view it in the Preview box.

4. In the **Pictures in album** list, click **NativePlant4**, and then click the **Move Up** button to make it the second picture in the list.

5. Preview the pictures in turn, and then click the **Contrast** and **Brightness** buttons as necessary to give the four photographs a more even tone.

   You could also adjust the rotation of a picture, but in this case, that is not necessary.

6. In the **Album Layout** area, display the **Picture layout** list, and click **2 pictures**.

7. Display the **Frame shape** list, click **Rounded Rectangle**. Then click **Create**.

   PowerPoint creates a presentation called *Photo Album* that contains a title slide and two slides each containing two pictures.

On the title slide, PowerPoint inserts the user name stored in the PowerPoint Options dialog box.

Troubleshooting The appearance of buttons and groups on the ribbon changes depending on the width of the program window. For information about changing the appearance of the ribbon to match our screen images, see "Modifying the Display of the Ribbon" at the beginning of this book.

8. Save the presentation as **My Photo Album**.

9. Display **Slide 2**, and click the photo on the left. Then on the **Format** contextual tab, in the **Size** group, click the **Crop** arrow. In the list, point to **Aspect Ratio**, and then under **Portrait**, click **2:3**.

PowerPoint crops away parts of the picture, leaving a centered "window" over the photo, sized to the proportions you specified.

Cropping handles surround the active area so that if you want, you can adjust the cropped areas.

10. Click the photo on the right, and then repeat the cropping process in step 9.

11. In turn, select each photo, and drag the upper-left and bottom-right corner handles until the photos occupy the majority of the space on the slide.

    Tip When sizing the photo on the right, release the mouse button when the dotted guide appears, letting you know that the photo is aligned with the photo on the left.

12. Display slide **3**, and crop the photo on the left to **Square**, **1:1**. Then point inside the crop window, and drag to the left until the cropping window is centered on the flower.

    PowerPoint maintains the size of the crop window but moves the photo under the window to the left.

The image of the flower is centered in the crop window.

13. Click the photo on the right, and in the **Size** group, use the down arrow to reduce the height to **3"**. Then crop the photo to **Square**, **1:1**, adjusting the crop window so that all of the flower is showing.

14. Enlarge and align the photos so that they occupy the entire width of the slide.

15. Click the left photo, and in the **Adjust** group, click the **Remove Background** button.

The Background Removal contextual tab appears, and PowerPoint marks the areas of the photo that will be removed.

The thumbnail on the Slides tab shows what the flower will look like after its background is removed.

16. Drag the handles on the frame surrounding the flower until the entire flower is visible within the frame. Then in the **Close** group, click the **Keep Changes** button.

17. Repeat steps 15 and 16 to remove the background of the photo on the right. Then click a blank area of the slide.

The background is removed from both flower photos.

The flowers stand out vividly against the plain slide background.

18. Click the photo on the left, and then on the **Format** tab, in the **Adjust** group, click the **Artistic Effects** button.

Artistic Effects ▾

The Artistic Effects gallery appears.

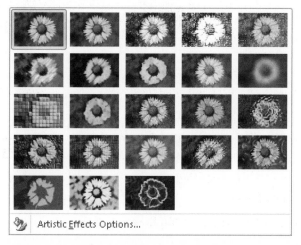

You can choose from a wide variety of effects in this gallery.

19. Point to each thumbnail in turn to see a live preview of the photo with the effect applied. Then click the third thumbnail in the second row (**Paint Brush**).

20. Repeat steps 18 and 19 for the photo on the right.

    The two photos now resemble paintings.

21. On the **Insert** tab, in the **Images** group, click the **Photo Album** arrow, and then click **Edit Photo Album**.

    The Edit Photo Album dialog box opens. This dialog box is the same as the Photo Album dialog box. With it, you can make changes to an existing photo album.

22. In the dialog box, under **Picture Options**, select the **Captions below ALL pictures** check box, and then click **Update**.

23. Replace the file names below each photograph with the following captions:

    NativePlant1 Achillea

    NativePlant4 Hedysarum

    NativePlant3 Gaillardia

    NativePlant5 Oenothera

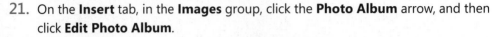

24. Click slide **1**, and on the **Home** tab, in the **Slides** group, click the **New Slide** arrow, and at the bottom of the gallery, click **Reuse Slides**.

    The Reuse Slides task pane opens.

25. In the **Reuse Slides** task pane, click **Browse**, and click **Browse File**. Then browse to your **Chapter08** practice file folder, and double-click the **PhotoAlbumTitleSlide** presentation.

    This presentation contains one slide that was based on a slide in the Contemporary Photo Album template available under the Sample Templates on the New page of the Backstage view.

26. In the **Reuse Slides** task pane, click **Slide 1** to insert it after the title slide of the My Photo Album presentation. Then close the task pane.

27. Delete the blank title slide. Then on the **Design** tab, in the **Themes** group, display the **Themes** gallery, and select a theme that showcases the photos.

    We chose the Trek theme.

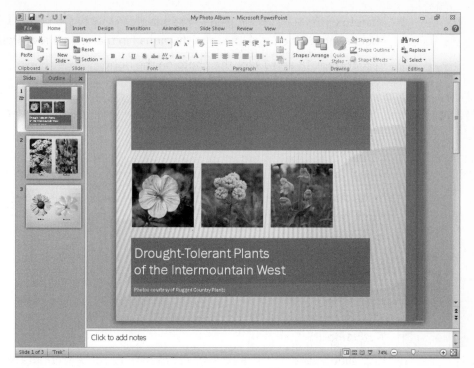

Careful theme selection can pull an entire presentation together.

✖ **CLEAN UP** Save the My Photo Album presentation, and then close it.

Customizing Diagrams

We've already told you how to use SmartArt to create a diagram, and we've shown you how to move and size it and apply simple formatting. But many diagrams involve different levels of information and benefit from more sophisticated formatting techniques. After you create a basic diagram, you can customize it at any time by clicking it and then using the commands on the Design and Format contextual tabs.

You can use the commands on the Design contextual tab to make changes such as the following:

● Add and change the hierarchy of shapes.

   Tip You can remove a shape by selecting it and then pressing the Delete key. You can also rearrange shapes by dragging them.

- Switch to a different layout of the same type or a different type.

  Tip If some of the text in the original diagram doesn't fit in the new layout, that text is not shown, but it is retained so that you don't have to retype it if you change the layout again.

You can use the buttons on the Format contextual tab to customize individual shapes in the following ways:

- Change an individual shape—for example, change a square to a star to make it stand out.
- Apply a built-in Shape Style.
- Change the color, outline, or effect of a selected shape.

Tip If you customize a diagram and then decide you preferred the original version, you can revert to the original by clicking the Reset Graphic button in the Reset group on the Design contextual tab.

In this exercise, you'll customize an organization chart by adding subordinate shapes. You'll change the layout of the chart as a whole and then change the color, size, and text of individual shapes.

SET UP You need the ReorganizationMeeting_start presentation located in your Chapter08 practice file folder to complete this exercise. Open the Reorganization-Meeting_start presentation, and save it as *ReorganizationMeeting*. Then follow the steps.

1. Display slide **5**, click the diagram to activate it, and then select the **Ryan Danner** shape for manipulation.

2. On the **Design** contextual tab, in the **Create Graphic** group, click the **Add Shape** arrow, and then click **Add Shape Below**.

   PowerPoint adds a shape to the organization chart.

3. Open the **Text** pane, click to the right of the bullet symbol, type **Jerry Orman**, and press Enter.

   PowerPoint adds a duplicate shape at the same level in the hierarchy.

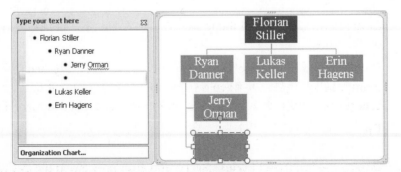

The colors of the shapes in the diagram reflect the theme color scheme

Troubleshooting Our instructions assume you are entering text in the Text pane. Typing and pressing Enter in a diagram shape enters a new paragraph in the same shape instead of creating a new shape.

4. Type **Nate Sun**.

5. In the **Text** pane, click to the right of **Erin Hagens**, press Enter, press Tab, and then type **Sarah Davis**.

   The new shape is a subordinate of Erin Hagens.

6. In the diagram, select the **Florian Stiller** shape for manipulation, click the **Add Shape** arrow in the **Create Graphic** group, and then click **Add Assistant**.

7. In the **Text** pane, click to the right of the arrow bullet symbol, and type **Andy Ruth**. Then close the **Text** pane.

8. In the diagram, select the **Nate Sun** shape for manipulation, and then in the **Create Graphic** group, click the **Promote** button.

   The selected shape moves up one level in the hierarchy.

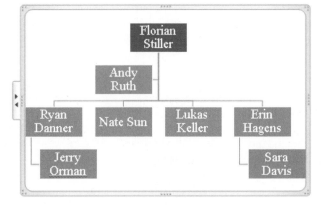

Nate Sun is now a peer of his former manager.

Troubleshooting Don't worry if your chart still shows the box and handles in the former location of the Nate Sun shape. It will disappear when you work on a different shape.

9. Drag the handles around the frame of the diagram until it fills the available space on the slide.

10. On the **Design** contextual tab, display the **Layouts** gallery, and point to each thumbnail in turn to see a live preview of the various layout options for an organization chart. Then click the second thumbnail in the second row (**Hierarchy**).

    Tip Some of the new PowerPoint 2010 layouts allow you to insert pictures of people as well as their names.

11. Display the **SmartArt Styles** gallery, and after previewing the available styles, under **3-D**, click the last thumbnail in the first row (**Cartoon**).

12. Andy Ruth is an assistant, not a manager, so select his background shape, and on the **Format** tab, in the **Shape Styles** group, click the **Shape Fill** arrow. Then under **Theme Colors** in the palette that appears, click the tan box (**Tan, Text 2**).

13. Click the **Florian Stiller** shape (not the text), and then in the **Shapes** group, click the **Larger** button three times.

    Troubleshooting Be sure to click the border of the shape. Otherwise, you will select the text for editing instead of the shape itself.

    The background shape grows with the selected shape.

14. In the **Shape Styles** group, click the **Shape Fill** arrow, and then in the palette, click the third box in the fifth column (**Gray-50%, Accent 1, Lighter 40%**)

15. Display the **WordArt Styles** gallery, explore the options, and then click the third thumbnail in the first row (**Fill – White, Drop Shadow**).

    The text in the shape is now a contrasting color.

16. Click outside the diagram frame.

    You can now see the final result.

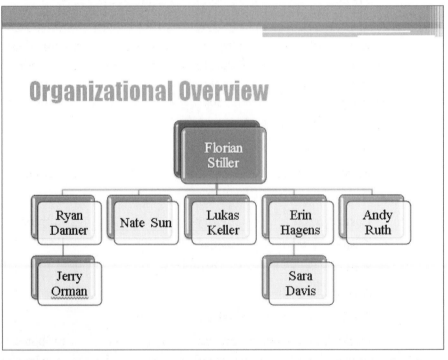

The number of employees that you want to include in an organization chart often determines which layout you choose.

CLEAN UP Save the ReorganizationMeeting presentation, and then close it.

Formatting Charts

You already know how to plot data in simple charts and how to edit that data in the associated Microsoft Excel worksheet. Often, you will need nothing more than these basic techniques to be able to convey your numeric data in a visual format. However, for those times when you need more than a basic chart, PowerPoint provides formatting capabilities that enable you to produce just the effect you want.

If you decide that the type of chart you selected doesn't adequately depict the most important characteristics of your data, you can change the type at any time. There are 11 chart types, each with two-dimensional and three-dimensional variations, and you can customize each aspect of each variation. Common chart types include the following:

- **Column charts** Used to show how values change over time.

- **Bar charts** Used to show the values of several items at one point in time.

- **Line graphs** Used to show erratic changes in values over time.

- **Pie charts** Used to show how parts relate to the whole.

If you don't want to spend a lot of time on a chart, you can apply the predefined combinations of formatting from the Chart Layouts and Chart Styles groups on the Design contextual tab to create sophisticated charts with a minimum of effort. However, if you want more control over the appearance of your chart, you can use the options on the Layout and Format contextual tabs. It is worth exploring these options so that you know how to do the following:

- Add shapes and pictures.

- Format individual elements such as titles, axes, data labels, and gridlines.

- Add trend lines, bars, and other lines.

- Customize the walls and floor or otherwise manipulate a three-dimensional chart.

- Customize the look of shapes.

- Add and format fancy text (WordArt).

- Arrange objects precisely.

- Precisely control the overall size of the chart.

You can double-click almost any chart object to change its attributes. For example, you can double-click an axis to display the Format Axis dialog box, where you can change the scale, tick marks, label position, line style, and other aspects of the axis. If you have trouble double-clicking some of the smaller chart elements, you can select the element you want to format from the Chart Elements list in the Current Selection group on the

Format tab, and then click the Format Selection button in the same group to display the Format dialog box for the selection.

If you make extensive modifications, you might want to save the customized chart as a template so that you can use it for plotting similar data in the future without having to repeat all the changes.

In this exercise, you'll modify the appearance of a chart by changing its chart type and style. You'll change the color of the plot area and the color of two data series. You'll then hide gridlines and change the layout to display titles and a datasheet. After adding an annotation in a text box, you'll save the chart as a template.

SET UP You need the LandscapingChart_start presentation located in your Chapter08 practice file folder to complete this exercise. Open the LandscapingChart_start presentation, and save it as *LandscapingChart*. Then follow the steps.

1. Display slide **14**, and click the blank area above the chart legend to activate the chart without selecting any of its elements.

   Troubleshooting Be sure to click a blank area inside the chart frame. Clicking any of its elements will activate that element, not the chart as a whole.

   PowerPoint displays the Design, Layout, and Format contextual tabs.

2. On the **Design** contextual tab, in the **Type** group, click the **Change Chart Type** button.

   The Change Chart Type dialog box opens.

Each chart category provides several different design options.

3. In the gallery on the right, under **Line**, double-click the fourth thumbnail (**Line with Markers**).

The column chart changes to a line chart, which depicts data by using colored lines instead of columns.

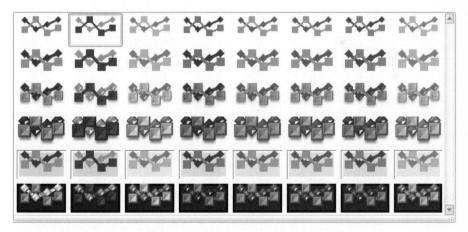

The temperature data plotted as a line chart.

4. In the **Chart Styles** group, click the **More** button.

The Chart Styles gallery appears.

You can quickly switch to a different color scheme or data marker style.

5. In the gallery, click the last thumbnail in the fourth row (**Style 32**).

The lines are now thicker, and the data markers are three-dimensional.

6. Move the pointer over the chart, and when a ScreenTip indicates you are pointing to the plot area, click to select it.

The plot area is the area between the axes that contains the data markers.

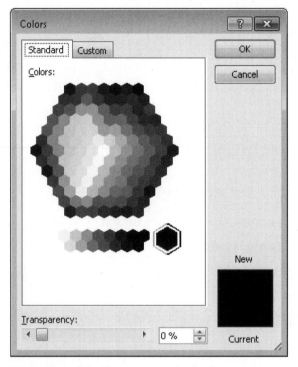

7. On the **Format** contextual tab, in the **Shape Styles** group, click the **Shape Fill** arrow, and then in the list, click **More Fill Colors**.

The Colors dialog box opens.

When none of the theme or standard colors meets your needs, you can pick a color in the Colors dialog box.

8. On the **Standard** page, click the pale yellow below and to the left of the center, and then click **OK**.

The plot area is now a pale yellow shade to distinguish it from the rest of the chart.

Tip To change several aspects of the plot area, right-click the area and then click Format Plot Area to open the Format Plot Area dialog box. You can then change the fill, border, shadow, and 3-D format in one location.

9. At the top of the **Current Selection** group, click the **Chart Elements** arrow, and then in the list, click **Series "Maximum"**.

   Tip If you have trouble selecting an element of the chart by clicking it, you can choose it from the Chart Elements list.

   An outline appears around the data points of the selected series.

10. In the **Current Selection** group, click the **Format Selection** button.

    The Format Data Series dialog box opens.

You can change several aspects of the selected data series in this dialog box.

11. In the left pane, click **Marker Fill**, and on the **Marker Fill** page, click **Solid Fill**. In the **Fill Color** area, click the **Color** button, and under **Standard Colors**, click the first box (**Dark Red**).

12. In the left pane, click **Line Color**. Then on the **Line Color** page, click **Solid line**, and change the color to the same dark red.

13. Repeat step 12 for the marker line color, and then click **Close**.

    The Maximum data series is now represented by the dark red color.

14. On the **Layout** tab, in the **Axes** group, click the **Gridlines** button, point to **Primary Horizontal Gridlines**, and then click **None** to remove the horizontal gridlines from the chart.

15. On the **Design** contextual tab, in the **Chart Layouts** group, click the **More** button.

    The Chart Layouts gallery appears.

You can quickly change the layout of the chart by selecting one of the predefined options.

16. In the gallery, click the first thumbnail in the second row (**Layout 4**).

    The legend now appears below the chart.

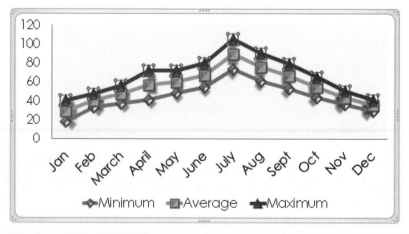

The plot area has expanded to occupy the area vacated by the legend.

Tip When you don't have a lot of data, choosing a layout that includes a datasheet—a table with all the values plotted in the chart—can clarify without adding clutter. In this case, we have too much data to add a datasheet.

17. On the **Layout** contextual tab, in the **Insert** group, click the **Text Box** button.

18. Point below the chart title and above the July maximum temperature, and then drag diagonally down and to the right until the text box stretches as far as the December data.

19. Type **Hot periods can last several days**. Then select the text, and on the **Home** tab, in the **Font** group, change the size to **10** points and the color to **Red**.

20. Click a blank area within the chart frame to release the text box selection.

    You can now see the results.

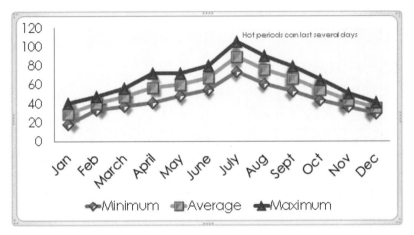

The annotated chart.

21. On the **Design** contextual tab, in the **Type** group, click the **Save As Template** button.

    The Save Chart Template dialog box opens and displays the contents of your Charts folder, which is a subfolder of your Templates folder.

    Troubleshooting If the *Charts* folder does not appear in the Address bar, navigate to the AppData\Roaming\Microsoft\Templates\Charts folder under your user profile.

22. With the **Charts** folder displayed in the **Address** bar, type **Temperature By Month** in the **File name** box, and then click **Save**.

23. In the **Type** group, click the **Change Chart Type** button, and then in the left pane of the **Change Chart Type** dialog box, click **Templates**. Then point to the icon under **My Templates** in the left pane.

A ScreenTip identifies this template as the one you just created.

In the future, you can click the custom template to create a chart with the same layout and formatting.

Tip To delete a custom chart template, click Manage Templates in the lower-left corner of the Change Chart Type dialog box, and then when Windows Explorer opens with your Charts folder displayed, right-click the template and click Delete. Confirm that you want to delete the template by clicking Yes, close Windows Explorer, and then close the Change Chart Type dialog box.

24. Click **Cancel** to close the dialog box.

✖ **CLEAN UP** If you don't want to keep the chart template, delete it by following the directions in the preceding tip. Then save and close the LandscapingChart presentation.

Arranging Graphics

After inserting pictures or drawing shapes in the approximate locations you want them on a slide, you can align them and change their stacking order by clicking the buttons in the Arrange group on the Format contextual tab.

Clicking the Align button gives you access to commands for aligning individual or multiple graphics in several ways. For example, you can:

- Align graphics vertically by the left or right edges or centerline, or horizontally by the top or bottom edges or centerline.

- Distribute graphics evenly within their current space, either horizontally or vertically.

- Align graphics relative to the slide that contains them or to other selected objects.

- Align graphics relative to a position on the slide.

- Align graphics against gridlines and adjustable horizontal and vertical guides.

Tip If you added pictures to a slide by clicking the Picture button in the Images group on the Insert tab, you can group them and then align and position them as a group the same way you would group shapes. However, if you have added them by clicking the Insert Picture From File button in a content placeholder, you cannot group them. For information about grouping shapes, see "Drawing Shapes" in Chapter 5, "Add Simple Visual Enhancements."

When graphics overlap each other, they are stacked. The stacking order is determined by the order in which you inserted the graphic. You can change the stacking order by selecting a graphic and then clicking the Bring Forward or Send Backward button to move the graphic to the top or bottom of the stack. To move the selected graphic forward in the stack one graphic at a time, click the Bring Forward arrow and then click Bring To Front in the list; to move it backward, click Send To Back in the Send Backward list.

Tip If you can't select a graphic because it is covered by others in the stack, click the Selection Pane button to display the Selection And Visibility task pane, and then select the graphic you want from the Shapes On This Slide list.

In this exercise, you'll align graphics in various ways, change their stacking order, and position them with the help of a grid and guidelines.

SET UP You need the GardenResidents_start presentation located in your Chapter08 practice file folder to complete this exercise. Open the GardenResidents_start presentation, and save it as *GardenResidents*. Then follow the steps.

1. On slide **1**, select the three pictures.

2. On the **Format** contextual tab, in the **Arrange** group, click the **Align** button, and then in the list, click **Distribute Vertically**.

   The middle picture moves down so that it is the same distance below the left picture as it is above the right picture.

3. In the **Arrange** group, click the **Align** button, and then click **Align Center**.

   The pictures are now stacked on top of each other.

Sometimes graphics are completely hidden when they are stacked.

4. Click away from the stack, and then click the top picture.

5. In the **Arrange** group, click the **Bring Forward** arrow, and then click **Bring to Front**.

   The top picture moves forward in the stack, obscuring the middle picture.

6. In the **Arrange** group, click the **Selection Pane** button.

   The Selection And Visibility task pane opens.

Selection and Visibility ▼ ✕

Shapes on this Slide:

Content Placeholder 11   👁

Content Placeholder 10   👁

Picture 12   👁

Rectangle 2   👁

Rectangle 2   👁

Show All   ▲ ▼

Hide All   Re-order

The top and middle pictures are designated as content placeholders because they were inserted into placeholders.

7. In the task pane, under **Shapes on this Slide**, click **Content Placeholder 10**.

   On the slide, the selection rectangle indicates that the middle picture is selected.

8. Close the **Selection and Visibility** task pane.

9. In the **Arrange** group, click the **Bring Forward** button.

   🔲 Bring Forward ▾

   The middle picture moves forward in the stacking order.

10. In the **Arrange** group, click the **Align** button, and then click **View Gridlines**.

    A faint dotted grid appears on the slide.

11. Drag the selected cat picture to the right and down, so that its right and bottom borders align with the first gridlines from the right and bottom edges of the slide.

12. Drag the crow picture so that its right and bottom borders align with the second gridlines from the right and bottom edges of the slide.

13. Drag the frog picture so that its right and bottom borders align with the third gridline from the right and bottom edges of the slide.

The pictures are now evenly stacked and spaced.

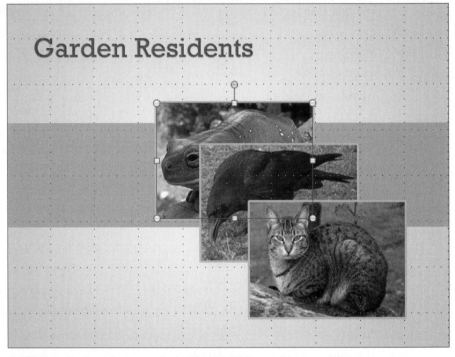

Gridlines make it easier to precisely align multiple graphics.

14. In the **Arrange** group, click the **Align** button, and then click **Grid Settings**.

The Grid And Guides dialog box opens.

In this dialog box, you specify the size of the grid and other options.

15. In the **Grid settings** area, clear the **Display grid on screen** check box.

16. In the **Guide settings** area, select the **Display drawing guides on screen** check box, and then click **OK**.

    The grid disappears, and vertical and horizontal guides span the slide.

17. Point to the vertical guide away from any text or objects, and drag it to the left, releasing it when the accompanying ScreenTip reads **3.50**. Then drag the horizontal guide down until its ScreenTip reads **0.50**.

    Troubleshooting If you move an object on the slide instead of a guide, click the Undo button, and then point outside the margins of the slide to drag the guide.

    The ScreenTips show in inches how far each guide is from the 0 mark in the center of the slide. As you drag, numbers are skipped because the Snap Objects To Grid check box is selected in the Grid And Guides dialog box.

    Tip The Snap Objects To Grid option snaps guides and graphics to an invisible grid. You can turn off this option, and you can set the spacing of the grid in the Grid And Guides dialog box.

18. Point to the selected frog picture, and drag it to the left until its left and bottom borders align with the guides.

19. Select all the pictures. Then on the **Format** tab, in the **Arrange** group, click the **Align** button, and in the list, click **Distribute Horizontally**.

20. Repeat step 19 to distribute the pictures vertically.

21. In the **Arrange** group, click the **Align** button, click **Grid Settings**, and in the **Grid and Guides** dialog box, clear the **Display drawing guides on screen** check box. Then click **OK**.

22. Click the shape behind the pictures, and drag the green rotating handle clockwise until the shape stretches diagonally across the slide. Then drag the shape's middle sizing handles until it is almost as wide as the pictures.

23. With the shape still selected, in the **Arrange** group, click the **Send Backward** arrow, and click **Send to Back**.

    The shape now sits behind the slide title as well as the pictures.

24. On the **View Shortcuts** toolbar in the lower-right corner of the program window, click the **Reading View** button.

    You can now see what the slide will look like during presentation delivery.

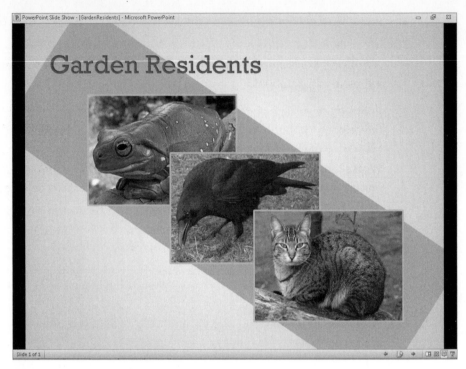

The finished slide in Reading view.

CLEAN UP Save the GardenResidents presentation, and then close it.

Alt Text

Alt (alternate) text is a title and description associated with a graphic object that enables people with vision or other impairments to determine what the object is. You can add alt text to your objects to improve the accessibility of presentations that will be viewed on the screen without a presenter.

To associate alt text with an object:

1. Right–click the object, and click the corresponding Format command.
2. In the left pane of the Format dialog box, click Alt Text.

   The Alt Text page is displayed.
3. Enter a title and a description for the graphic object, and then click Close.

Key Points

- A growing trend among presenters is to create graphic-intensive rather than text-intensive presentations.

- If you want to move beyond simple diagrams, you need to know how to manipulate levels of text in shapes and how to format individual shapes as well as the diagram as a whole.

- With all the sophisticated chart formatting tools PowerPoint provides, it is important to remember that to be effective, charts need to be simple enough for people to grasp key trends at a glance.

- Knowing how to manipulate graphics on a slide will help you position, align, and stack them to get the effect you want.

Chapter at a Glance

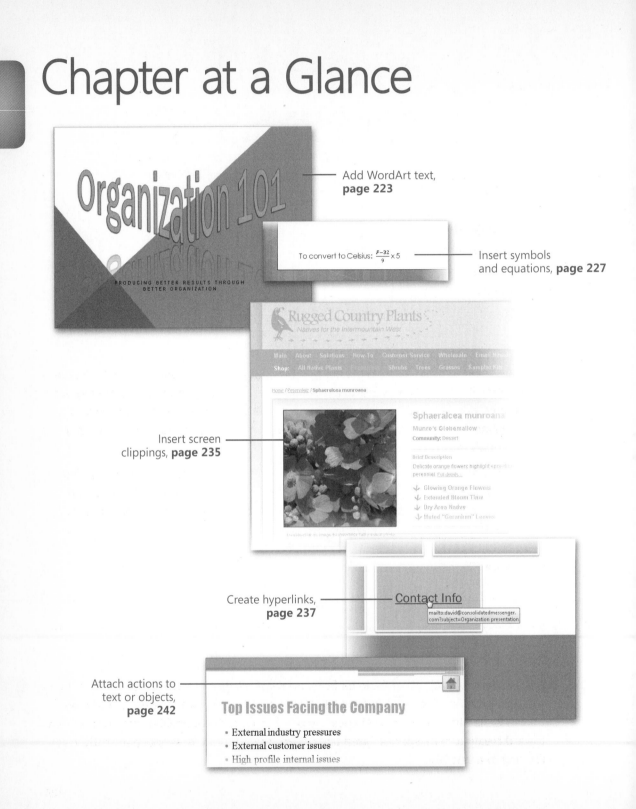

Add WordArt text, **page 223**

To convert to Celsius: $\frac{F-32}{9} \times 5$ — Insert symbols and equations, **page 227**

Insert screen clippings, **page 235**

Create hyperlinks, **page 237**

Attach actions to text or objects, **page 242**

9 Add Other Enhancements

In this chapter, you will learn how to

✔ Add WordArt text.

✔ Insert symbols and equations.

✔ Insert screen clippings.

✔ Create hyperlinks.

✔ Attach actions to text or objects.

We have looked at some of the more common graphic elements you can add to a slide to reinforce its concepts or to make it more attention grabbing or visually appealing, such as pictures, diagrams, and charts. But for some slides, you might need more specialized visual elements. You might also need to add navigation aids or ways to access supporting materials that are external to the presentation.

In this chapter, you'll use WordArt text to create a fancy title. You'll also insert a symbol, build a simple equation, and capture a screenshot from a Web page. Finally, you'll add hyperlinks and action buttons that jump to slides within a presentation, open files and message windows, and display Web pages.

> **Practice Files** Before you can complete the exercises in this chapter, you need to copy the book's practice files to your computer. The practice files you'll use to complete the exercises in this chapter are in the Chapter09 practice file folder. A complete list of practice files is provided in "Using the Practice Files" at the beginning of this book.

Adding WordArt Text

If you're familiar with WordArt in earlier versions of Microsoft PowerPoint, you're in for a surprise. WordArt has matured from the fun little tool you might have used in the past to create slide titles in molded shapes and gaudy colors. Its capabilities are now oriented toward creating more sophisticated text objects that you can move independently, just like text in a text box.

To insert WordArt text, you click the WordArt button in the Text group on the Insert tab and click a text style in the WordArt gallery. Then you enter the text in a text box that appears in the middle of the slide. You can edit the text, adjust the character formatting in the usual ways, and change the WordArt style at any time.

Tip You can also select existing text in a placeholder and then click a thumbnail in the WordArt Styles gallery to apply a fancy style to the text.

See Also For information about character formatting, see "Changing the Alignment, Spacing, Size, and Look of Text" in Chapter 4, "Format Slides."

When a WordArt text object is selected, you can use the commands on the Format contextual tab to format it to meet your needs. For example, from the Format tab, you can change the fill and outline colors, add effects such as shadows and beveled edges, and change the text direction and alignment.

In this exercise, you'll insert a new WordArt text object and then modify it.

 SET UP You need the Organization_start presentation located in your Chapter09 practice file folder to complete this exercise. Open the Organization_start presentation, and save it as *Organization*. Then follow the steps.

1. Display slide **1**. Then on the **Insert** tab, in the **Text** group, click the **WordArt** button.

   The WordArt gallery appears, displaying a list of styles.

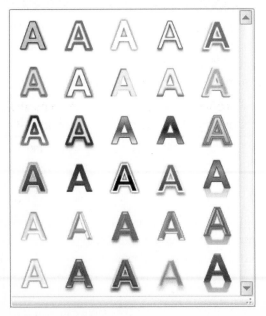

The WordArt gallery.

2. In the gallery, click the third thumbnail in the fifth row (**Fill – Orange, Accent 2, Warm Matte Bevel**).

   PowerPoint inserts a WordArt object in the slide.

The placeholder WordArt text is formatted according to the style you selected.

3. With the placeholder text selected, type **Organization 101**.

   The replacement text has the same style as the placeholder text.

4. Click the border of the WordArt object to select it for manipulation. Then move and resize the WordArt object so its frame spans the middle of the top half of the slide.

   Tip A WordArt object works just like any other text box. You click inside it to edit the text and you click its border to select the object as a whole. For information about text boxes, see "Adding Text Boxes" in Chapter 3, "Work with Slide Text."

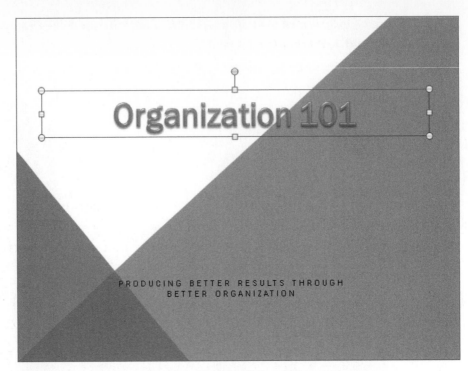

You can move and size a WordArt object just like any other text box.

5. Select the text, and on the **Format** contextual tab, in the **WordArt Styles** group, display the gallery, and try a few other styles. When you have finished exploring, click the second thumbnail in the first row (**Fill – None, Outline – Accent 2**).

6. With the text still selected, in the **WordArt Styles** group, click the **Text Fill** arrow. Then under **Theme Colors**, click the third box in the orange column (**Orange, Accent 2, Lighter 40%**).

7. In the **WordArt Styles** group, click the **Text Outline** arrow, and then under **Theme Colors**, click the third box in the third column (**Ice Blue, Background 2, Darker 50%**).

8. In the **WordArt Styles** group, click the **Text Effects** button, point to **Transform**, and then under **Warp**, click the last thumbnail in the first row (**Triangle Down**).

9. With the text still selected, click the **Text Effects** button again, point to **Reflection**, and then under **Reflection Variations**, click the second thumbnail in the second row (**Half Reflection, 4 pt offset**).

   The reflections vary by the amount of reflection shown and the starting point below the text.

10. Drag the pale blue handle in the middle of the bottom of the frame down until the reflection sits just above the subtitle.

   The letters in the middle of the WordArt object stretch so that the triangle effect is more exaggerated.

11. Click an edge of the slide to release the selection.

   You can now see the results.

You can use text effects to add drama to your presentation titles.

✖ **CLEAN UP** Save the Organization presentation, and then close it.

Inserting Symbols and Equations

Some slide text requires characters not found on a standard keyboard. These characters might include the copyright (©) or registered trademark (®) symbols, currency symbols (such as € or £), Greek letters, or letters with accent marks. Or you might want to add arrows (such as ↗ or ↖) or graphic icons (such as ☎ or ✈). PowerPoint gives you easy access to a huge array of symbols that you can easily insert into any slide. Like graphics, symbols can add visual information or eye-appeal to a slide. However, they are different from graphics in that they are characters associated with a particular font.

Keyboard Shortcut You can insert some common symbols by typing a keyboard combination. For example, if you type two consecutive dashes followed by a word and a space, PowerPoint changes the two dashes to a professional-looking em-dash—like this one. (This symbol gets its name from the fact that it was originally the width of the character m.) To use these keyboard shortcuts, display the Backstage view, click Options, and then, on the Proofing page of the PowerPoint Options dialog box, click AutoCorrect Options. On the AutoCorrect page of the AutoCorrect dialog box, ensure that the Replace Text As You Type check box is selected, and then select or clear check boxes in the Replace Text As You Type area of the AutoFormat As You Type page.

See Also For more information about keyboard shortcuts, see "Keyboard Shortcuts" at the end of this book.

You can insert mathematical symbols, such as π (pi) or $\sum$ (sigma, or summation), the same way you would insert any other symbol. But you can also create entire mathematical equations on a slide. You can insert some predefined equations, including the Quadratic Formula, the Binomial Theorem, and the Pythagorean Theorem, with a few clicks. If you need something other than these standard equations, you can build your own equations by using a library of mathematical symbols. Equations are accurately rendered mathematical formulas that appear in the slide as fields.

The buttons for inserting symbols and equations are in the Symbols group on the Insert tab.

● Clicking the Symbol button displays the Symbol dialog box, where you can select from hundreds of symbols and special characters in a variety of fonts.

The Symbol dialog box.

Tip The Recently Used Symbols area of the Symbol dialog box is dynamic. If you have already explored this dialog box, you will see the symbols you have added to your slides.

● Clicking the Equation arrow displays the Equation gallery of commonly used equations.

Area of Circle

$$A = \pi r^2$$

Binomial Theorem

$$(x + a)^n = \sum_{k=0}^{n} \binom{n}{k} x^k a^{n-k}$$

Expansion of a Sum

$$(1 + x)^n = 1 + \frac{nx}{1!} + \frac{n(n-1)x^2}{2!} + \cdots$$

Fourier Series

$$f(x) = a_0 + \sum_{n=1}^{\infty} \left(a_n \cos\frac{n\pi x}{L} + b_n \sin\frac{n\pi x}{L} \right)$$

Pythagorean Theorem

$$a^2 + b^2 = c^2$$

π Insert New Equation

Clicking a predefined equation adds it to the slide.

● Clicking the Equation button inserts a box where you can type an equation, and also adds the Design contextual tab to the ribbon. This tab provides access to mathematical symbols, structures such as fractions and radicals, and the Equation Options dialog box.

In this exercise, you'll add a symbol to a slide. Then you'll build a simple equation and display it in various ways.

SET UP You need the TemperatureCelsius_start presentation located in your Chapter09 practice file folder to complete this exercise. Open the TemperatureCelsius_start presentation, and save it as *TemperatureCelsius*. Then follow the steps.

1. Display slide **13**, and in the table, click to the right of **Winter**.

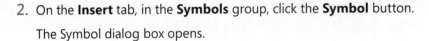

2. On the **Insert** tab, in the **Symbols** group, click the **Symbol** button.

   The Symbol dialog box opens.

3. In the dialog box, display the **Font** list, scroll to the bottom, and then click **Wingdings**.

   The Symbol dialog box now displays all the characters in the Wingdings font.

Wingdings is one of several symbol fonts available.

4. Click an icon that represents winter, such as the snowflake in the fourth row. Then click **Insert**, and click **Close**.

   PowerPoint inserts the selected symbol at the cursor.

5. Repeat step 4 to insert symbols for **Spring**, **Summer**, and **Fall**, switching to different fonts if necessary to find the symbols you want.

   Each season now has a symbol.

Seasonal Temperatures			
	Winter❄	Spring✿	Summer☀	Fall✖
Minimum	18	41	73	43
Average	29	57	89	54
Maximum	40	72	105	65

You can select a symbol and format it by clicking buttons in the Font group of the Home tab.

6. Click a blank area of the slide to deselect the table. Then on the **Insert** tab, in the **Symbols** group, click the **Equation** button.

A text box containing an equation field appears near the middle of the slide, and the Design contextual tab appears on the ribbon.

7. Click the border of the text box to select it for manipulation, and drag it to the lower-left corner of the slide.

In the text box, the equation field appears as a placeholder that you can replace with your equation.

The Design contextual tab includes symbols and structures for building an equation.

Troubleshooting The appearance of buttons and groups on the ribbon changes depending on the width of the program window. For information about changing the appearance of the ribbon to match our screen images, see "Modifying the Display of the Ribbon" at the beginning of this book.

8. Click anywhere in the equation placeholder, and press the Home key to position the cursor at the left end of the placeholder, before the equation field. Then type **To convert to Celsius:** (including the colon and a space).

9. Click the equation placeholder, and on the **Design** contextual tab, in the **Structures** group, click the **Fraction** button.

   The Fraction gallery appears.

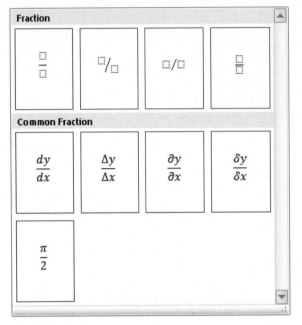

This gallery provides ready-made common fractions as well as the structures for creating your own fractions.

10. In the gallery, click the first thumbnail in the first row (**Stacked Fraction**).

    The structure for a simple fraction is inserted in the field at the cursor.

11. Click the top box in the fraction structure, and type **F-32**. Then click the bottom box, and type **9**.

12. Click the blank area to the right of the equation field. Then press the Spacebar, type **x**, press the Spacebar, and type **5**. Then click a blank area of the slide.

This equation subtracts 32 from the Fahrenheit temperature and divides the result by 9, and then multiplies that result by 5 to yield the Celsius temperature. PowerPoint has taken care of formatting the fraction so that it looks professional.

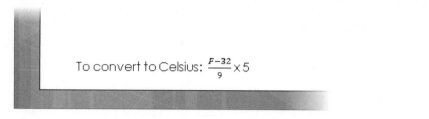

To convert to Celsius: $\frac{F-32}{9} \times 5$

The F variable in the equation is automatically formatted as italic.

13. Click the fraction, and then on the **Design** contextual tab, in the **Tools** group, click the **Linear** button.

The format of the fraction changes.

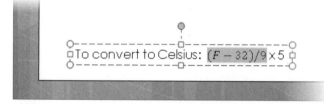

To convert to Celsius: $(F-32)/9 \times 5$

The fraction is easier to edit in Linear format.

14. Right-click the fraction, point to **Math Options**, and then click **Professional**.

15. Right-click the fraction again, point to **Math Options**, and then click **Change to Skewed Fraction**.

16. Right-click again, point to **Math Options**, and then click **Change to Stacked Fraction**.

✖ **CLEAN UP** Save the TemperatureCelsius presentation, and then close it.

Setting Math AutoCorrect Options

If you frequently create slides that contain mathematical formulas, you don't have to rely on the Design contextual tab to insert mathematical symbols. Instead, you can type a predefined combination of characters and have PowerPoint automatically replace it with a corresponding math symbol. For example, if you type \infty, PowerPoint replaces the characters with the infinity symbol.

This replacement is made possible by the Math AutoCorrect feature. You can view all the predefined combinations by displaying the Backstage view, clicking Proofing, and then clicking AutoCorrect Options. Then in the AutoCorrect dialog box, click the Math AutoCorrect tab.

The Math AutoCorrect page of the AutoCorrect dialog box.

Tip You can create custom Math AutoCorrect entries in the same way you create text AutoCorrect entries. For information, see "Correcting and Sizing Text While Typing" in Chapter 3, "Work with Slide Text."

Inserting Screen Clippings

These days, many people rely on the Web as a source of the information they use in their daily life. Sometimes that information is presented in a graphic that would be useful in a PowerPoint presentation. Included in PowerPoint 2010 is a screen clipping tool that you can use to capture an image of anything that is visible on your computer screen.

After you display the content you want to include in a slide, you switch to PowerPoint and click the Screenshot button in the Images group on the Insert tab. You can then insert a screen clipping in one of two ways:

● Clicking a window thumbnail in the Screenshot gallery inserts a picture of that window into the slide at the cursor.

● Clicking Screen Clipping at the bottom of the gallery enables you to drag across the part of the screen you want to capture, so that only that part is inserted as a picture into the slide.

In this exercise, you'll capture a screen clipping from a Web site and then insert it into a slide.

SET UP You need the DesertPlants_start presentation located in your Chapter09 practice file folder to complete this exercise. Open the DesertPlants_start presentation, and save it as *DesertPlants*. Then follow the steps.

1. Display slide **2**, and then at the right end of the program window title bar, click the **Minimize** button.

2. Start your Web browser, and display a Web site from which you want to capture a screen clipping.

   For example, we searched for pictures of desert plants.

3. On the Windows Taskbar, click the button for the **DesertPlants** presentation. Then on the **Insert** tab, in the **Images** group, click the **Screenshot** button.

   A gallery displays the open windows from which you can capture a screen clipping.

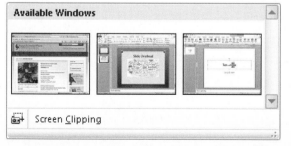

Clicking the thumbnail of a window inserts an image of the window in the slide.

4. At the bottom of the gallery, click **Screen Clipping**.

The PowerPoint program window is minimized on the Windows Taskbar, and a translucent white layer covers the entire screen.

Tip If you change your mind about capturing the screen clipping, press the Esc key to remove the white layer.

5. On the Web page, point to the upper-left corner of the image you want, and drag down and to the right to select it.

For example, we dragged across a picture of a desert flower.

As you drag, the white layer is removed from the selected area so that you can see what you are selecting.

When you release the mouse button, PowerPoint inserts the screen clipping into the center of the slide.

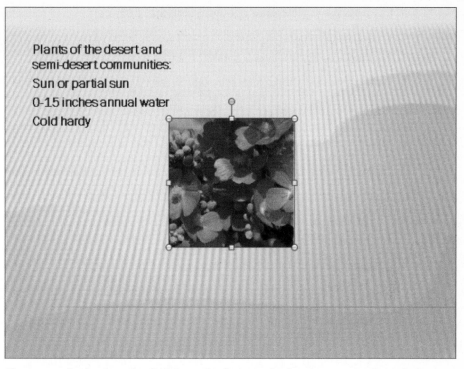

The screen clipping is a picture that can be formatted using the commands on the Format contextual tab, just like any other picture.

See Also For information about formatting pictures, see "Inserting Pictures and Clip Art Images" in Chapter 5, "Add Simple Visual Enhancements" and "Editing Pictures" in Chapter 8, "Fine-Tune Visual Elements."

CLEAN UP Save the DesertPlants presentation, and then close it.

Creating Hyperlinks

Presentations that are intended to be viewed electronically often include hyperlinks to provide access to supporting information. That information might be on a hidden slide, in another presentation, in a file on your computer or your organization's network, or on a Web site. You can also use a hyperlink to open an e-mail message window so that people viewing the presentation can easily contact you.

You can attach a hyperlink to any selected object, such as text, a graphic, a shape, or a table. Clicking the hyperlinked object then takes you directly to the linked location. Editing the object does not disrupt the hyperlink; however, deleting the object also deletes the hyperlink.

In this exercise, you'll create one hyperlink that opens an e-mail message window and another that opens a document. You'll also create a hyperlink with an informative ScreenTip that starts the default Web browser and jumps to a specific Web page.

SET UP You need the OrganizationLinks_start presentation and the Procedures document located in your Chapter09 practice file folder to complete this exercise. Be sure an e-mail program is configured on your computer and connect to the Internet before beginning this exercise. Open the OrganizationLinks_start presentation, and save it as *OrganizationLinks*. Then follow the steps.

1. Display slide **8**, and in the lower-right shape, select the words **Contact Info**.

2. On the **Insert** tab, in the **Links** group, click the **Hyperlink** button.

   Keyboard Shortcut Press Ctrl+K to open the Insert Hyperlink dialog box.

   The Insert Hyperlink dialog box opens.

3. Under **Link to**, click **E-mail Address**.

   The dialog box options change to those needed for an e-mail hyperlink.

Insert Hyperlink		? ✕
Link to:	**Text to display:** Contact Info	ScreenTip...
Existing File or Web Page	**E-mail address:**	
	Subject:	
Place in This Document	**Recently used e-mail addresses:**	
	mailto:margie@margiestravel.com?subject=Flora%20Fauna%20inquiry mailto:andrew@consolidatedmessenger.com	
Create New Document		
E-mail Address		OK Cancel

If you have already created links to e-mail addresses, they appear in the Recently Used E-Mail Addresses box.

4. In the **E-mail address** box, type **david@consolidatedmessenger.com**, and then in the **Subject** box, type **Organization presentation**.

   Notice that PowerPoint changes the entry in the E-mail Address box to *mailto:david@consolidatedmessenger.com*.

5. Click **OK**, and then click away from the diagram.

The text is now underlined and gray, the color designated by the presentation's theme for hyperlinks.

You can attach hyperlinks to the shapes in a diagram as easily as you can to text or a graphic.

6. On the **View Shortcuts** toolbar, click the **Reading View** button.

7. Click **Contact Info**.

   Your default e-mail program displays a message window with the specified e-mail address entered in the To box and the specified subject entered in the Subject box.

8. Close the message window without sending the message, and then press Esc to return to Normal view.

9. Display slide **4**, and then click the graphic.

10. On the **Insert** tab, in the **Links** group, click the **Hyperlink** button, and then in the **Insert Hyperlink** dialog box, under **Link to**, click **Existing File or Web Page**.

    The list box in the center changes to show the contents of the last folder you accessed.

You can use the Look In box to find a file on your computer, or you can click the Browse The Web button to locate a Web site.

11. With the contents of the **Chapter09** folder displayed, double-click the **Procedures** document.

12. Switch to Reading view, point to the graphic to see the path of the hyperlinked file displayed as a ScreenTip, and then click the graphic.

    Tip The pointer changes to a pointing hand when you move it over a hyperlinked object. Any time the pointer has this shape, you can click to follow a hyperlink.

    Microsoft Word 2010 opens and displays a document about office procedures.

13. Close Word, and then press Esc to return to Normal view.

14. Display slide **5**, and then click the clock to the left of the table.

15. In the **Links** group, click the **Hyperlink** button, and then in the upper-right corner of the **Insert Hyperlink** dialog box, click **ScreenTip**.

    The Set Hyperlink ScreenTip dialog box opens.

You can specify the text that will appear when someone points to the clock graphic.

16. In the **ScreenTip text** box, type **Check out this book**, and then click **OK**.

17. Back in the **Insert Hyperlink** dialog box, in the **Address** box, type **http://go.microsoft.com/fwlink/?LinkId=192151**, and then click **OK**.

18. Display the slide in Reading view, and point to the clock graphic.

    PowerPoint displays the ScreenTip you entered.

19. Click the graphic.

    Your Web browser starts, and if you are connected to the Internet, you are taken to the Web page for our book *Microsoft Outlook 2010 Step by Step*.

20. Close the browser window, and then press Esc to return to Normal view.

 CLEAN UP Save the OrganizationLinks presentation, and then close it.

Attaching the Same Hyperlink to Every Slide

If you want the same hyperlink to appear on every slide in a presentation, you need to attach the hyperlink to text or an object on the presentation's slide master.

To attach hyperlinks to slide master objects:

1. On the View tab, in the Master Views group, click the Slide Master button.

2. In Slide Master view, click the primary master (the top thumbnail). Then create a text box and enter text or insert an object to which you can apply the link.

   Tip You cannot attach a hyperlink to the default placeholders.

3. Select the text or object.

4. On the Insert tab, in the Links group, click the Hyperlink button.

5. In the Insert Hyperlink dialog box, set up the hyperlink as usual, and then click OK.

6. Switch to Reading view, and move through the presentation's slides, checking for the presence of the hyperlink.

   Because you inserted the hyperlink on the primary master, the link appears on all the slides in the presentation.

Attaching Actions to Text or Objects

In addition to attaching hyperlinks to text or objects by clicking the Hyperlink button, you can attach them by clicking the Action button, which is also in the Links group on the Insert tab. In the dialog box that opens, you can specify whether the action should take place when you point to the linked text or object or when you click it. You can designate a target to which PowerPoint should jump if the link is pointed to or clicked, or designate an action to perform such as starting a program or playing a sound.

If attaching an action to existing text or an object on a slide doesn't suit your needs, you can insert an action button. PowerPoint provides navigation action buttons (Back, Forward, Beginning, End, Home, and Return) and display action buttons (Document, Help, Information, Movie, and Sound) as well as a generic action button that you can customize.

In this exercise, you'll select a word in a bulleted list and attach an action that displays a hidden slide when the word is clicked. You'll also attach a sound that plays when you point to a slide title. Finally, you'll create action buttons that you can click to move between presentation slides and an overview slide.

SET UP You need the MeetingAction_start presentation located in your Chapter09 practice file folder to complete this exercise. Open the MeetingAction_start presentation, and save it as *MeetingAction*. Then follow the steps.

1. Display slide **8**, switch to Reading view, and then click the **Next** button to move to the next slide. Press Esc to return to Normal view.

   On the Slides tab of the Overview pane, notice that PowerPoint skipped from slide 8 to slide 10 because slide 9 is hidden. Let's create an action to display this slide when appropriate.

   See Also For information about hiding slides, see "Adapting Presentations for Different Audiences" in Chapter 14, "Prepare for Delivery."

2. On slide **8**, select the words **Equipment replacement**.

Action

3. On the **Insert** tab, in the **Links** group, click the **Action** button.

   The Action Settings dialog box opens.

The Mouse Click page of the Action Settings dialog box.

4. On the **Mouse Click** page, in the **Action on click** area, click **Hyperlink to**, display the list, and then click **Slide**.

   The Hyperlink To Slide dialog box opens.

The slide number of the hidden slide is enclosed in parentheses.

5. In the **Slide title** list, click **(9) Equipment Replacement**.

   You want to be able to click the words *Equipment replacement* to go to the slide containing the replacement costs, when appropriate.

6. Click **OK** to close the **Hyperlink to Slide** dialog box, and then click **OK** again to close the **Action Settings** dialog box.

   The words *Equipment replacement* are now underlined and displayed in the color assigned by the theme to hyperlinks.

7. Display slide **4**, and select **How Did We Do?**

8. In the **Links** group, click the **Action** button, and then in the **Action Settings** dialog box, click the **Mouse Over** tab.

   This page of the dialog box is almost identical to the Mouse Click page.

9. Below the **Action on mouse over** area, click **Play sound**, display the list of built-in sounds, click **Applause**, and then click **OK**.

   The title is now underlined and displayed in the hyperlink color.

10. Switch to Reading view, and then point to **How Did We Do?**.

    The Applause sound plays.

11. Right-click the screen, point to **Go to Slide**, and then click **8 Key Spending Areas**.

12. In the bulleted list, click **Equipment replacement**.

    PowerPoint displays the hidden slide.

13. Press Esc to return to Normal view, and then display slide **6**.

14. On the **Insert** tab, in the **Illustrations** group, click the **Shapes** button.

    The Shapes gallery appears.

15. Under **Action Buttons** at the bottom of the gallery, click the **Action Button: Home** icon.

    The pointer changes to a cross.

16. In the upper-right corner of the slide, drag the cross pointer to create a **Home** action button about half an inch square.

     When you release the mouse button, the Action Settings dialog box opens with the Hyperlink To option selected and First Slide in the box below. At the bottom of the dialog box, the Highlight Click check box is selected, but dimmed to indicate that you cannot change this setting.

17. Display the **Hyperlink to** list, and click **Slide**.

     The Hyperlink To Slide dialog box opens.

18. In the **Slide title** list, click **2. Agenda**, and then click **OK** twice.

19. With the action button still selected on the slide, on the **Format** contextual tab, in the **Shape Styles** group, click the **More** button, and then in the gallery, click the pale green thumbnail in the fourth row (**Subtle Effect – Olive Green, Accent 2**). Then click away from the button.

     The color of the Home action button is now compatible with the background.

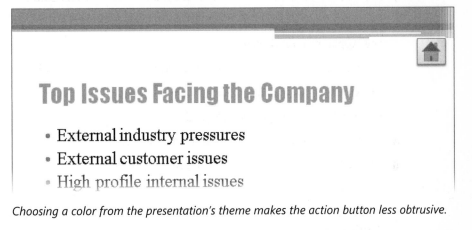

Choosing a color from the presentation's theme makes the action button less obtrusive.

When you click the action button in Reading view or Slide Show view, you'll jump to slide 2, which is an overview of slides 3 through 11. Referring back to this slide after showing half of the listed topics is a good idea, but suppose you need a quick way of jumping back to slide 6 so that you can resume the discussion.

20. Display slide **2**, and then on the **Insert** tab, in the **Illustrations** group, click the **Shapes** button.

    The Shapes gallery appears.

21. Under **Action Buttons** at the bottom of the gallery, click the **Action Button: Return** icon. Then in the upper-right corner of the slide, drag the cross pointer to create a **Return** action button about half an inch square.

    When you release the mouse button, the Action Settings dialog box opens with the Hyperlink To option set to Last Slide Viewed.

22. Click **OK** to close the **Action Settings** dialog box.

23. Change the color of the action button to one that is compatible with the background.

    The button is all ready for action.

The unobtrusive Return button.

24. Display slide **6**, switch to Reading view, and then click the **Home** action button to jump to slide **2**.

25. On slide **2**, click the **Return** action button to jump back to slide **6**, and then click the mouse button to display slide **7**.

26. Press Esc to return to Normal view.

❌ **CLEAN UP** Save the MeetingAction presentation, and then close it.

Key Points

- Fancy titles created with WordArt can have much more impact than regular text.

- The Symbols dialog box provides access not only to the symbols you might need for a slide but also to little icons that can add pizzazz.

- You can construct complex math equations on your slides and have PowerPoint display them in traditional math formats.

- You can capture graphical information from Web sites or other programs for use on your slides.

- In electronic presentations, you can add hyperlinks to text or objects to directly link to another slide or to a presentation, file, or Web address.

- Action buttons also provide convenient ways to jump to other locations, play sounds, or run programs when you click or point to them.

Chapter at a Glance

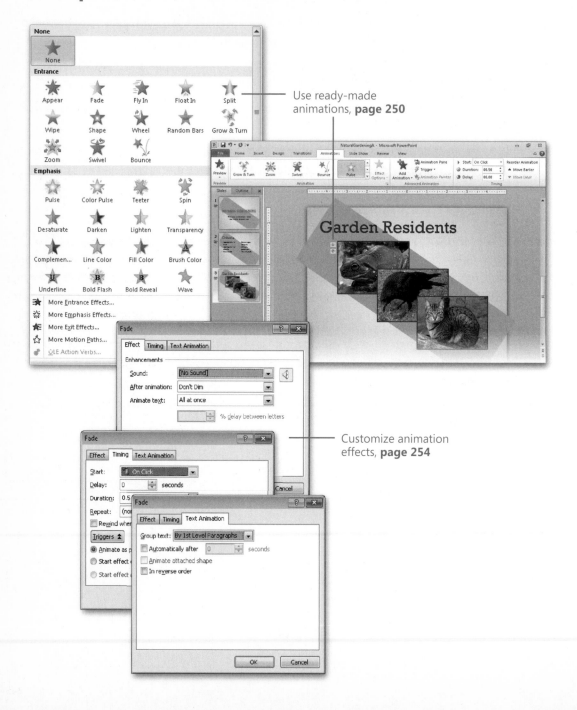

Use ready-made animations, **page 250**

Customize animation effects, **page 254**

10 Add Animation

In this chapter, you will learn how to

✔ Use ready-made animations.

✔ Customize animation effects.

The difference between an adequate presentation and a great presentation often lies in the judicious use of dynamic effects. By incorporating animation, you can grab and keep the attention of your audience. You can emphasize key points, control the focus of the discussion, and entertain in ways that will make your message memorable.

With Microsoft PowerPoint 2010, you have so many opportunities to add pizzazz to your slides that it is easy to end up with a presentation that looks more like an amateur experiment than a professional slide show. When you first start adding animation to your slides, it is best to err on the conservative side. As you gain more experience, you'll learn how to mix and match effects to get the results you want for a particular audience.

In this chapter, you'll apply predefined animations to titles, bullet points, and pictures on slides. Then you'll see how to change some of the animation settings to create custom animation schemes.

Practice Files Before you can complete the exercises in this chapter, you need to copy the book's practice files to your computer. The practice files you'll use to complete the exercises in this chapter are in the Chapter10 practice file folder. A complete list of practice files is provided in "Using the Practice Files" at the beginning of this book.

Using Ready-Made Animations

With all the options available for creating engaging and lively presentations in PowerPoint 2010, you no longer have to settle for static presentations, especially if you are delivering the presentation from a computer. By applying various types of animations to the text and graphics on your slides, you can keep your audience focused and reinforce the message of your presentation. For example, you can animate text so that it appears on the screen only when you want to discuss it, or you can animate objects such as shapes or pictures.

You can animate text or an object to make it enter or leave a slide with a particular effect, to emphasize it in a certain way, or to move it across the slide along a particular path. Entrance effects are the most common. To apply one of the 13 ready-made entrance effects, you click the element you want to animate and then select the effect from the Animation gallery. To help you decide which effect to use, you can point to each in turn to see a live preview.

To really emphasize an element, you can animate it with more than one effect. And if you combine animation effects and want to apply the same combination to another object, you can simply copy the set with the Animation Painter, which functions the same way as the Format Painter.

Tip Animations can become tiresome, so it's best to choose one entrance effect for all the objects on your slides, varying only those objects you particularly want to emphasize.

In this exercise, you'll apply predefined animations to a title and subtitle on one slide, bullet points on another slide, and pictures on another.

SET UP You need the NaturalGardeningA_start presentation located in your Chapter10 practice file folder to complete this exercise. Open the NaturalGardeningA_start presentation, and save it as *NaturalGardeningA*. Then follow the steps.

1. With slide **1** displayed in Normal view, click the slide title.

2. On the **Animations** tab, in the **Animation** group, click the **More** button.

   The Animation gallery appears.

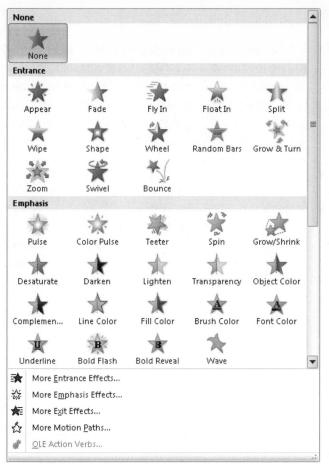

There are many built-in animation effects to choose from.

3. Point to the handle in the lower-right corner of the gallery, and drag upward until you can see a couple of rows of animation thumbnails and the title of the slide.

4. Preview all of the **Entrance** animations, and then click the **Shape** thumbnail.

   PowerPoint displays a live preview of the animation effect. A box containing the number 1 appears to the left of the title, indicating that this element will be the first one animated on this slide.

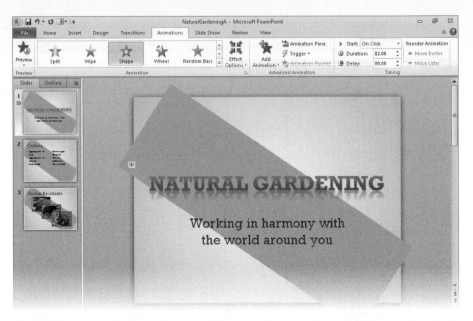

On the Slides tab in the Overview pane, the animation icon below the slide number indicates the presence of some form of animation on the slide.

Troubleshooting The appearance of buttons and groups on the ribbon changes depending on the width of the program window. For information about changing the appearance of the ribbon to match our screen images, see "Modifying the Display of the Ribbon" at the beginning of this book.

5. Apply the **Shape** animation to the slide's subtitle.

   A box containing the number 2 appears to the left of the subtitle.

6. Display slide **2**, click anywhere in the left content placeholder, and apply the **Shape** animation.

   PowerPoint displays each bullet point in turn with the selected animation effect. Boxes containing the numbers 1 through 3 appear to the left of the bullet points to indicate the order of their animations on the slide.

7. Repeat step 6 for the right placeholder.

8. In the **Preview** group, click the **Preview** button.

   PowerPoint displays all the animations on slide 2 in the order specified by their animation boxes.

9. Display slide **3**, click the frog picture, and apply the **Shape** animation.

10. In the **Advanced Animation** group, click the **Add Animation** button, and then in the **Animation** gallery, under **Emphasis**, click **Pulse**.

11. Click the **Preview** button to see both the **Shape** and **Pulse** animations in action.

   PowerPoint first makes the frog picture appear with the Shape animation and then quickly expands and shrinks the picture, positioning it on the slide at its normal size. Boxes containing the numbers 1 and 2 appear to the left of the picture.

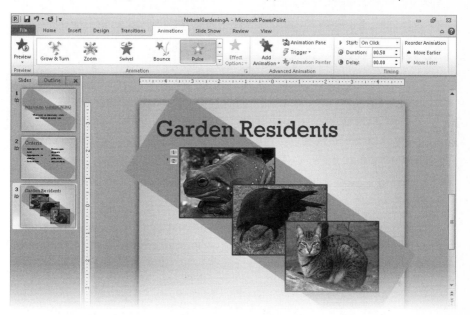

Two animation effects are applied to the frog picture.

12. Click the frog picture. Then in the **Advanced Animations** group, click the **Animation Painter** button, and click the crow picture.

   The animations you applied to the frog picture are copied to the crow picture. Boxes containing the numbers 3 and 4 appear adjacent to the crow picture.

13. Repeat step 12 to copy the two animations to the cat picture.

14. Preview the animations on this slide.

15. Click slide **1**, and then on the **View Shortcuts** toolbar, click the **Reading View** button.

    The title slide is displayed without the title or the subtitle.

16. In the lower-right corner of the program window, click the **Next** button repeatedly to display the animation effects on all three slides, and then click again to return to Normal view.

✖ CLEAN UP Save the NaturalGardeningA presentation, and then close it.

Customizing Animation Effects

The majority of professional presenter-led slide shows don't require much in the way of animation, and you might find that transitions and ready-made animation effects will meet all your animation needs. However, for those occasions when you want a presentation to have a little more pizzazz, PowerPoint provides a variety of options for creating your own animation schemes.

Tip Animation is often useful for self-running presentations, where there is no presenter to lead the audience from one concept to another.

If you would rather create your own animation scheme, you can select the text or object you want to animate, apply an entrance effect, and then add the following types of ready-made effects:

- **Emphasis** You can increase or decrease the importance of the element by changing its font, size, or style; by making it grow or shrink; or by making it spin.

- **Exit** You can animate the way that the element leaves the slide.

- **Motion Path** You can move the element around on the slide in various ways, such as diagonally to the upper-right corner or in a circular motion.

If none of the predefined effects in the Add Animation gallery meets your needs, you can display more effects by clicking an option at the bottom of the gallery. These options display dialog boxes with professionally designed animations in four categories: Basic, Subtle, Moderate, and Exciting.

Clicking an animation in a dialog box displays a live preview of its action when applied to the selected object on the slide.

After you apply an animation effect, you can fine-tune its action by using the commands on the Animations tab in the following ways:

- Click the Effect Options button to specify the direction, shape, or sequence of the animation. (The options vary depending on the type of animation you apply.)

- Click the Trigger button to specify what action will trigger the animation. For example, you can specify that clicking a different object on the slide will animate the selected object.

- As an alternative to clicking the mouse button to build animated slides, you can have PowerPoint build the slide for you by changing the Start setting from On Click to With Previous or After Previous.

- To control the implementation speed of each animation, you can change the Duration setting. You can also delay an animation effect by changing the Delay setting.

- You can change the order of an animation effect by clicking its box on the slide and then clicking the Move Earlier or Move Later buttons.

You can make additional animation adjustments by displaying the Animation pane. This pane shows all the animations applied to the active slide.

The Animation pane.

Clicking the arrow that appears when you click an animation in the Animation pane displays a menu of actions. Clicking Effect Options on that menu provides access to an effect-specific dialog box where you can refine that type of animation in the following ways:

- You can specify whether the animation should be accompanied by a sound.
- You can dim or hide the element after the animation, or you can have it change to a specific color.
- If the animation is applied to text, you can animate all the text at once or animate it word by word or letter by letter.
- In addition to the Start, Delay, and Duration settings that you can specify from the Timing group on the Animations tab, you can repeat an animation and specify what will trigger its action.
- If a slide has more than one level of bullet points, you can animate different levels separately.

● If an object has text, you can animate the object and the text together (the default) or separately, or you can animate one but not the other.

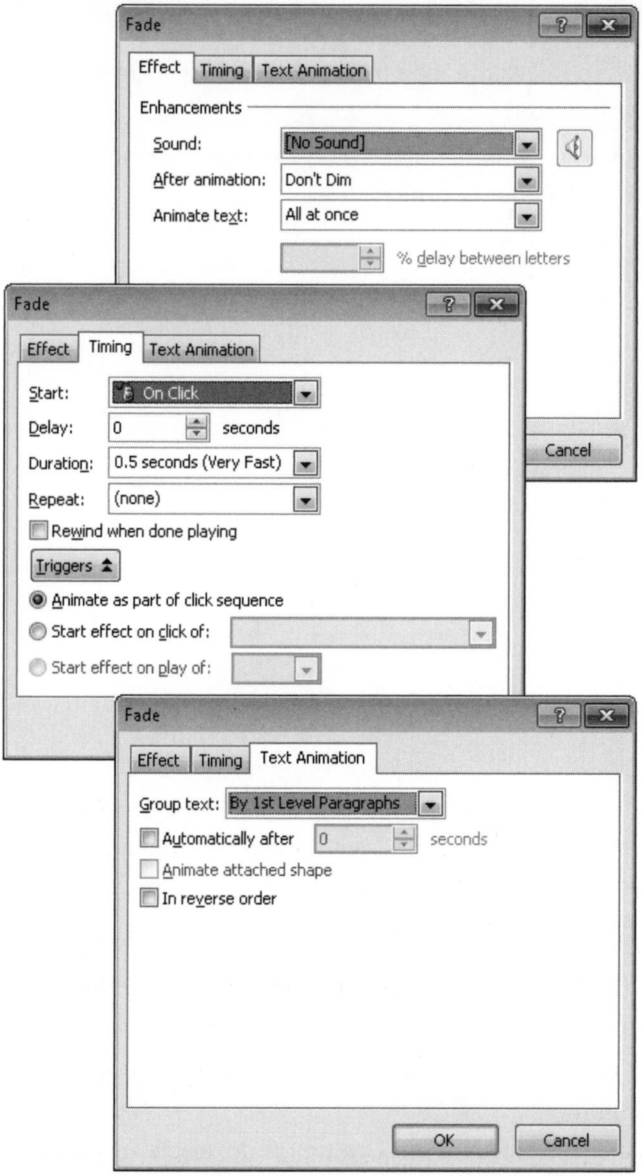

Fade

Effect | Timing | Text Animation

Enhancements

Sound: [No Sound]

After animation: Don't Dim

Animate text: All at once

□ % delay between letters

Cancel

Fade

Effect | Timing | Text Animation

Start: On Click

Delay: 0 seconds

Duration: 0.5 seconds (Very Fast)

Repeat: (none)

☐ Rewind when done playing

Triggers ⬍

◉ Animate as part of click sequence

○ Start effect on click of:

○ Start effect on play of:

Fade

Effect | Timing | Text Animation

Group text: By 1st Level Paragraphs

☐ Automatically after 0 seconds

☐ Animate attached shape

☐ In reverse order

OK | Cancel

The pages of the Fade dialog box (one of the effect-specific dialog boxes).

In this exercise, you'll apply effects to an existing animation and change when it starts. Then you'll add sound to a bulleted list, make words appear letter-by-letter, and make them dim to a different color when they have been discussed.

Effect
Options ▾

➡ **SET UP** You need the NaturalGardeningB_start presentation located in your Chapter10 practice file folder to complete this exercise. Open the NaturalGardeningB_start presentation, and save it as *NaturalGardeningB*. Then follow the steps.

1. With slide **1** displayed, click the slide title, and then in the **Animation** group, click the **Effect Options** button.

    The Shape entrance animation applied to this title has several Direction and Shapes options but only one Sequence option.

Direction
🞧 In
🞥 Out
Shapes
⬤ Circle
◼ Box
◆ Diamond
✚ Plus
Sequence
☰ As One Object

    The Effect Options gallery for the Shape animation.

2. Preview all the options, and then set **Shape** to **Diamond** and **Direction** to **Out**.

    Troubleshooting Always select the shape first. By default, the In direction is applied to each shape.

3. Change the effect options of the subtitle to match those of the title.

4. With the subtitle still selected, in the **Timing** group, display the **Start** list, and click **After Previous**.

5. Switch to Reading view, and preview the animation effects on slide **1**.

    You no longer have to click to make the subtitle appear.

6. Switch back to Normal view, display slide **2**, and then click anywhere in the bulleted list on the left.

7. In the **Advanced Animation** group, click the **Animation Pane** button.

The Animation pane opens.

8. If the **Animation** pane shows only the first animation in each content placeholder, click the chevrons for each placeholder to expand their contents.

   Tip If you have several animations on a slide, being able to expand and hide sets of animations can help you focus on the ones you want to work with.

9. In the **Animation** pane, click animation **1**. Then click the arrow that appears, and in the menu, click **Effect Options**.

   The Circle dialog box opens.

The Effect page of the Circle dialog box.

10. In the **Enhancements** area, display the **Sound** list, and click **Chime**.

11. Display the **After animation** list, and in the palette, click the rightmost red box.

12. Display the **Animate text** list, and click **By letter**.

13. Click the **Timing** tab, display the **Duration** list, and click **3 seconds (Slow)**. Then click **OK**.

    PowerPoint demonstrates the effects of your changes on the slide. The Shape animation doesn't work very well with the selected effect options.

14. On the slide, click the left placeholder.

    In the Animation pane, all the animations for the left content placeholder are selected.

    You can now apply animation effects to all the bullet points at once.

15. Apply the **Float In** entrance animation to the entire placeholder, and then in the **Animation** pane, click the arrow to the right of the selected animations, and click **Effect Options**.

    The Float Up dialog box opens. (By default, the direction of the Float In animation is Up.)

16. On the **Effect** page, set **Sound** to **Chime**, **After animation** to the red box on the right side of the palette, and **Animate text** to **By letter**.

17. On the **Timing** page, set **Duration** to **3 seconds (Slow)**. Then click **OK**.

    PowerPoint demonstrates the effects of your changes on the slide.

18. Make any additional adjustments you want to your custom animation scheme. When you are satisfied, use the **Animation Painter** to copy the animation effects of the bulleted list on the left to the one on the right.

   PowerPoint demonstrates the effects of the bulleted list on the right.

 19. Switch to Reading view, and click the **Next** button repeatedly to display the animated bullet points on slide **3**.

20. When all the bullet points are visible and dimmed to red, click the **Next** button again to return to Normal view.

✖ CLEAN UP Close the Animation pane. Then save and close the NaturalGardeningB presentation.

Key Points

- Used judiciously, animated text and graphics add interest to your slides.
- Combinations of the ready-made animations will probably meet almost all of your animation needs.
- You decide how and when the animation occurs, and you can even customize an effect with a sound.

Chapter at a Glance

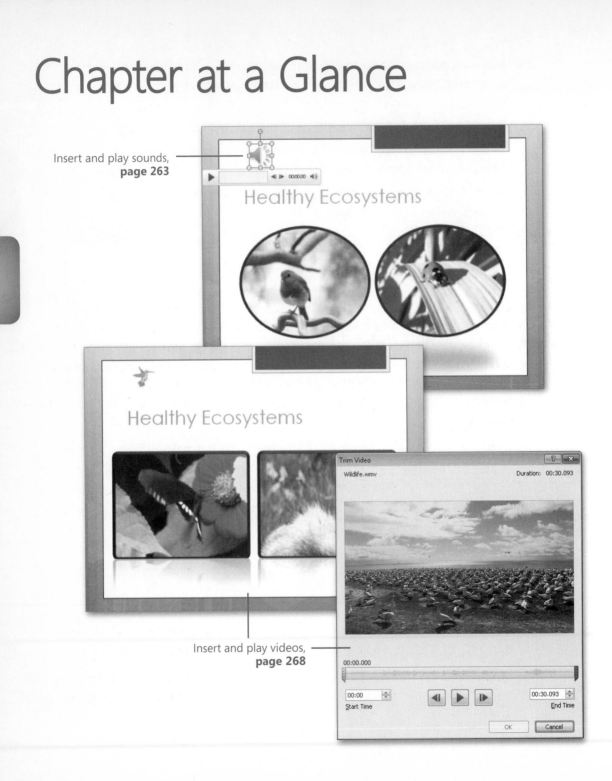

Insert and play sounds,
page 263

Insert and play videos,
page 268

11 Add Sound and Movies

In this chapter, you will learn how to

✔ Insert and play sounds.

✔ Insert and play videos.

A Microsoft PowerPoint presentation is usually created to convey a lot of information in a short time. That information can be in the form of text, graphics, charts, and tables, but it might also consist of audio content. And sometimes the best way to ensure that your audience understands your message is to show a video. For example, if your company has developed a short advertising video, it makes more sense to include the video in a presentation about marketing plans than to try and describe it with bullet points or even pictures.

In this chapter, you'll insert a sound clip and a sound file and make various adjustments to their settings. You'll also insert two video files, edit one of them, and format them both.

> **Practice Files** Before you can complete the exercises in this chapter, you need to copy the book's practice files to your computer. The practice files you'll use to complete the exercises in this chapter are in the Chapter11 practice file folder. A complete list of practice files is provided in "Using the Practice Files" at the beginning of this book.

Inserting and Playing Sounds

In "Adding Transitions" in Chapter 5, "Add Simple Visual Enhancements," you added sound to a slide transition. You can also insert the following types of sounds:

● **Audio files** You can insert an audio file—for example, a speech or interview—by clicking the Audio button in the Media group on the Insert tab, and then selecting the file.

- **Sound clips** You can insert a sound clip by clicking the Audio arrow in the Media group on the Insert tab, and then clicking Clip Art Audio to display the Clip Art task pane, where you can search for and select the sound you want. Clicking Find More At Office.com at the bottom of the task pane takes you to the Office.com Web site, where you can search for additional sounds.

  See Also For information about using the Clip Art task pane, see "Inserting Pictures and Clip Art Images" in Chapter 5, "Add Simple Visual Enhancements."

- **Recorded sounds** You can record a sound or narration and attach it to a slide, all from within PowerPoint.

  See Also For information about recording sounds, see the sidebar "Recording Presentations" in Chapter 14, "Prepare for Delivery."

After you add a sound object, it appears on the slide represented by an icon. When the sound object is selected, a play bar appears below its icon with controls for playing the sound, and PowerPoint adds Format and Playback contextual tabs to the ribbon. You can change the icon as follows:

- Drag the object to locate it anywhere on the slide.
- Drag its sizing handles to make it larger or smaller.
- Use commands on the Format tab to change its appearance, in much the same way that you would format a picture.
- Click the Change Picture button to replace the default icon with a picture.

You can modify the sound itself on the Playback tab, as follows:

- Click the Trim Audio button in the Editing group to edit the sound so that only part of it plays.
- Specify Fade In and Fade Out settings to have the sound gradually increase and decrease in volume.
- Click the Volume button to adjust the volume to Low, Medium, or High, or to mute the sound.
- Specify whether the sound plays:
  - ○ Automatically when the slide appears.
  - ○ Only if you click its icon.
  - ○ Throughout the presentation.

- Select the Hide During Show check box to make the sound object invisible while the presentation is displayed in Reading view or Slide Show view.

- Select the Loop Until Stopped check box to have the sound play continuously until you stop it.

- Select the Rewind After Playing check box to ensure that the sound starts from the beginning each time it is played.

To play a sound, you must have a sound card and speakers installed. In Normal view, you can test the sound associated with a slide by clicking its icon and then either clicking the Play/Pause button on its play bar or clicking the Play button in the Preview group on the Playback contextual tab.

In this exercise, you'll insert a sound clip into a slide, adjust the position of the sound object, change its picture, and make various other adjustments to its settings. Then you'll insert an audio file into another slide and make the file play continuously throughout a presentation.

SET UP You need the HealthyEcosystemsA_start and AGKCottage_start presentations, the Bird picture, and the Amanda audio file located in your Chapter11 practice file folder. Open the AGKCottage_start presentation, and save it as *AGKCottage*. Then open the HealthyEcosystemsA_start presentation, and save it as *HealthyEcosystemsA*. Be sure to turn on your computer's speakers for this exercise. (If you do not have a sound card and speakers, you can still follow the steps, but you won't be able to hear the sound.) With HealthyEcosystemsA displayed on your screen, follow the steps.

1. On the **Insert** tab, in the **Media** group, click the **Audio** arrow, and then click **Clip Art Audio**.

   The Clip Art task pane opens, displaying thumbnails of common sound clips.

2. In the **Search for** box, type **birds**, and then click **Go**.

   The task pane now displays thumbnails of bird calls.

3. Click any thumbnail, click the arrow that appears, and then click **Preview/ Properties**.

The Preview/Properties dialog box for the sound clip you selected opens.

Preview/Properties

Name:	00441655.wav
Type:	Wave Sound
Resolution:	
Size:	2409 KB
Created:	
Orientation:	Landscape
Open with:	Windows Media Player

Keywords:

ambient
audio
birds
birdsongs
crows
environments
iStockphoto
music styles
nature
sounds
soundscapes
sparrows
summers

Caption: Birds at dawn
Provided by: iStockphoto

< Previous Refresh Next > Edit Keywords...

Paths
File: C:\Users\Sidney Higa\AppData\Local\Microsoft\Windows\Temporary Internet Files\Content.IE5\UFY5RW
Catalog: http://office2010.microsoft.com

Close

When you display this dialog box, PowerPoint downloads and plays the sound clip.

Troubleshooting The sound clips available from Office.com change frequently, so don't worry if you don't see the Birds At Dawn clip in your Clip Art task pane. Just use a different clip.

4. Click **Close** to close the dialog box, and continue previewing sound clips.

5. When you are ready, double-click a sound clip that you think is appropriate for the slide, and then close the **Clip Art** task pane.

   We chose Birds Singing. A small speaker icon representing the sound object appears in the middle of the slide, along with a play bar. It is hard to see the icon because it is on top of the picture.

6. Drag the sound object to the upper-left corner of the slide.

   The play bar moves with the sound object.

The handles around the sound object indicate that you can resize it, just like any other object.

7. On the play bar, click the **Play/Pause** button to hear the sound.

   The sound plays. Now let's change the picture associated with the object.

8. With the sound object selected, on the **Format** contextual tab, in the **Adjust** group, click the **Change Picture** button. Then in the **Insert Picture** dialog box, double-click the **Bird** picture in your **Chapter11** practice file folder.

9. On the **Playback** contextual tab, in the **Audio Options** group, display the **Start** list, and click **Automatically**. Then select the **Loop until Stopped** check box.

10. On the **View Shortcuts** toolbar, click the **Reading View** button.

    PowerPoint plays the sound clip.

11. Move the pointer over the bird representing the sound object, and when the play bar appears, click the **Play/Pause** button. Then press the Esc key to return to Normal view.

12. Display the **AGKCottage** presentation, and view it in Reading view, pressing Esc after a few slides.

    This presentation would benefit from a "sound track."

13. With slide **1** displayed, on the **Insert** tab, in the **Media** group, click the **Audio** button. Then in the **Insert Audio** dialog box, double-click the **Amanda** file in your **Chapter11** practice file folder.

14. On the **Playback** tab, In the **Audio Options** group, display the **Start** list, and then click **Play across slides**. Then select the **Hide During Show** and **Loop until Stopped** check boxes.

15. Switch to Reading view.

    The audio file plays while PowerPoint moves from slide to slide.

16. Press Esc to stop the presentation and return to Normal view.

✖ **CLEAN UP** Save and close the HealthyEcosystemsA and AGKCottage presentations.

Inserting and Playing Videos

In keeping with the trend toward more visual presentations, PowerPoint 2010 has new video capabilities that broaden the range of videos you can use and what you can do with them. You can insert the following types of movies in slides:

- **Video files** You can insert a digital video that has been saved as a file in one of two ways: If a slide's layout includes a content placeholder, you can click the Insert Movie Clip button in the placeholder. You can also click the Video button in the Media group on the Insert tab. Either way, the Insert Video dialog box opens so that you can select the file.

- **Videos from Web sites** For information, see the sidebar "Inserting Videos from Web Sites" later in this chapter.

- **Clip art videos** Clip art videos are animated graphics, rather than real videos. Clicking the Video arrow in the Media group on the Insert tab and then clicking Clip Art Video displays the Clip Art task pane, where you can search for and select the clip you want. Clicking Find More At Office.com at the bottom of the task pane takes you to the Microsoft Office Online Web site, where you can search for additional clips. When you insert a clip art video, it appears as a picture on the slide, and PowerPoint adds a Format contextual tab to the ribbon so that you can adjust the way the picture looks. The clip moves only when you display the slide in Reading view or Slide Show view, and you cannot adjust its action.

    See Also For information about using the Clip Art task pane, see "Inserting Pictures and Clip Art Images" in Chapter 5, "Add Simple Visual Enhancements."

Both video files and videos from Web sites appear on the slide as video objects that you can size and move to meet your needs. When you select a video object, PowerPoint adds Format and Playback contextual tabs to the ribbon. You can change the way the object appears on the slide as follows:

● Drag the object to locate it anywhere on the slide.

● Drag its sizing handles to make it larger or smaller.

● Use commands on the Format tab to change its appearance, in much the same way that you would format a picture.

You can modify the video itself on the Playback tab, as follows:

● Click the Trim Video button in the Editing group to edit the video so that only part of it plays.

  Tip You can find out the total playing time of a video by displaying the Trim Video dialog box.

● Specify Fade In and Fade Out settings to have the video gradually appear and disappear.

● Click the Volume button to adjust the volume to Low, Medium, or High, or to mute the sound.

● Specify whether the video plays:

  ○ Automatically when the slide appears.

  ○ Only if you click the object.

● Select the Play Full Screen check box to have the video occupy the entire slide space while playing.

● Select the Hide While Not Playing check box to make the video object invisible while the presentation is displayed in Reading view or Slide Show view.

● Select the Loop Until Stopped check box to have the video play continuously until you stop it.

● Select the Rewind After Playing check box to ensure that the video starts from the beginning each time it is played.

In Normal view, you can test the video associated with a slide by clicking the video object and then either clicking the Play/Pause button on its play bar or clicking the Play button in the Preview group on the Playback contextual tab.

In this exercise, you'll insert two videos into a slide, adjust the size of their objects, format the objects, and make various other adjustments to their settings.

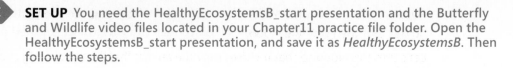

SET UP You need the HealthyEcosystemsB_start presentation and the Butterfly and Wildlife video files located in your Chapter11 practice file folder. Open the HealthyEcosystemsB_start presentation, and save it as *HealthyEcosystemsB*. Then follow the steps.

1. In the **Slide** pane, in the left content placeholder, click the **Insert Media Clip** button.

2. In the **Insert Video** dialog box, double-click the **Butterfly** file in your **Chapter11** practice file folder.

   The video is inserted as an object in the content placeholder with a play bar below it.

The play bar is similar to the one for a sound object.

3. On the play bar, click the **Play/Pause** button to watch the video.

4. Repeat steps 1 through 3 to insert the **Wildlife** video in the right content placeholder, and then play the video.

Let's trim this video so that it shows only the animal that looks like a big ground squirrel.

5. With the **Wildlife** video selected, on the **Playback** contextual tab, in the **Editing** group, click the **Trim Video** button.

The Trim Video dialog box opens.

You can advance through the video frame by frame to identify the start and end times.

6. Drag the green start marker to the right until it sits at about the **00:17.020** mark. Then click the **Next Frame** button, pausing after each click, until the first ground squirrel frame comes into view at the **00:17.288** mark.

7. Drag the red stop marker to the left until it sits at about the **00:20.900** mark. Then click the **Next Frame** button, pausing after each click, until the last ground squirrel frame comes into view at the **00:20.799** mark.

8. Click **OK**. Then play the trimmed video.

9. Click the **Butterfly** video object, and on the **Format** tab, in the **Size** group, click the **Height** arrow until the object is **3** inches tall.

   The width of the object increases proportionally. Let's make the Wildlife object the same size.

10. Click the **Wildlife** object, and in the **Size** group, change its **Height** to **3**.

    Because this video object is now too wide, we need to crop it from the left.

11. Right-click the object, and click **Format Video**. Then in the **Format Video** dialog box, click the **Crop** tab.

    The settings on this page take the trial-and-error out of any cropping task.

The Crop page of the Format Video dialog box.

12. In the **Crop position** area, change the **Width** setting to **4"**. Then click **Close**.

13. Drag the objects until they are evenly spaced on the slide, using the **Align** com-
    mands in the **Arrange** group as necessary to line them up.

14. With both objects selected, click the **More** button in the **Video Styles** group.
    The Video Styles gallery appears.

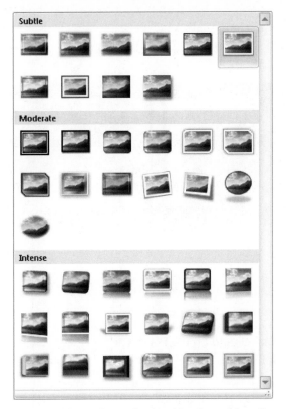

You can select a frame for the video from this gallery.

Tip In addition to formatting a video with a ready-made video style, you can choose
from the Video Shape, Video Border, and Video Effects galleries to create your own
combinations. Just be careful not to overdo it.

15. Under **Intense**, click the fifth thumbnail in the first row (**Reflected Bevel, Black**).
    Then click away from the objects.

You can now see the results.

The two video objects have rounded frames and reflections.

16. Click the **Butterfly** object, and on the **Playback** contextual tab, in the **Video Options** group, click the **Volume** button, and then click **Mute**.

17. In the **Video Options** group, display the **Start** list, and click **Automatically**. Then select the **Loop until Stopped** check box.

18. Click the **Wildlife** object, set **Volume** to **Mute**, leave **Start** set to **On Click**, and select the **Loop until Stopped** check box.

19. Switch to Reading view, and preview and pause the **Butterfly** video. Then preview and pause the **Wildlife** video.

20. Press Esc twice to return to Normal view.

✖ **CLEAN UP** Close the HealthyEcosystemsB presentation without saving your changes.

Inserting Videos from Web Sites

If you find a video on a public Web site that you want to use to illustrate a point in a presentation, you might be able to insert a link to the video into a slide. The format of the video must be supported by Windows Media Player, and the owner of the video must have made it available to the public. You can tell which videos are publicly available by right-clicking the video and looking for a Copy Embed HTML command. If you do not see this command, the owner has secured the video, and you cannot play it from anywhere but the site on which it is published.

To insert a link to a video on a Web site:

1. Display the video, right-click it, and then click Copy Embed HTML.

2. Display the slide into which you want to insert the video.

3. On the Insert tab, in the Media group, click the Video arrow, and then click Video From Web Site.

   The Insert Video From Web Site dialog box opens.

4. In the dialog box, click in the text box, and then press Ctrl+V (the keyboard shortcut for the Paste command).

   The copied embed code is inserted at the cursor.

A link to a video available from YouTube.

5. Click OK.

To view the video, switch to Reading view or Slide Show view, and then click the Play/Pause button. PowerPoint then uses the embed code to locate and play the video. Provided the video remains available in its original location, and provided you have an active Internet connection, you will be able to access and play the video from the slide at any time.

Key Points

- Audio and video clips can convey information or simply add interest.
- Use the sounds that come with PowerPoint, or supply your own audio files.
- After you insert an audio or video object, you can change the way it looks and the way it plays to suit your needs.

Additional Techniques

Chapter at a Glance

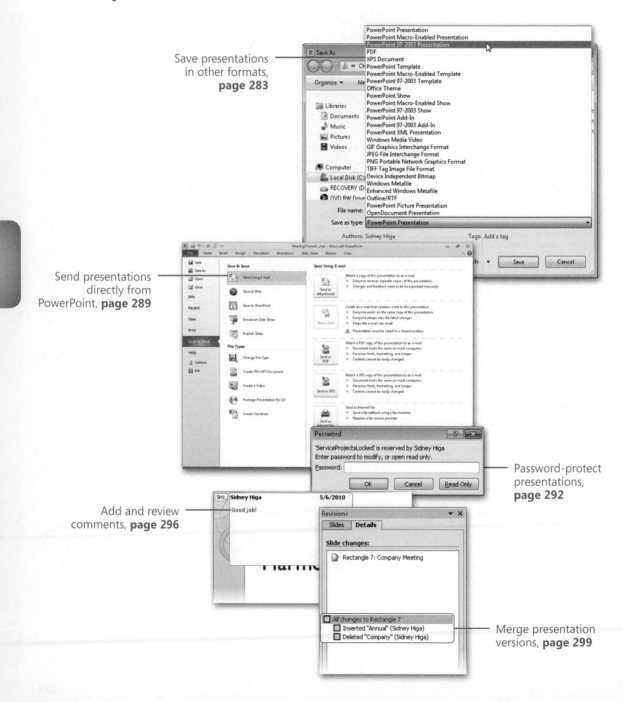

Save presentations in other formats, **page 283**

Send presentations directly from PowerPoint, **page 289**

Password-protect presentations, **page 292**

Add and review comments, **page 296**

Merge presentation versions, **page 299**

12 Share and Review Presentations

In this chapter, you will learn how to

✔ Collaborate with other people.

✔ Save presentations in other formats.

✔ Send presentations directly from PowerPoint.

✔ Password-protect presentations.

✔ Add and review comments.

✔ Merge presentation versions.

In today's workplace, many presentations are developed collaboratively by a team of people. You might be the lead developer of some presentations that are reviewed by your colleagues and managers, and you might be a reviewer of other presentations. With Microsoft PowerPoint 2010, you can collaborate on the development of presentations in new and exciting ways.

Even if you are not collaborating on a presentation with a team, you can easily attach a presentation to an e-mail message and send it to someone for review. If you want to send it to someone who doesn't have PowerPoint 2010 installed on his or her computer, you can save the presentation in a different file format so that your colleague can read it. If you want to be sure that only authorized people can review a presentation, you can assign a password.

These days, most presentations are reviewed on the screen. With PowerPoint, it's easy to insert comments, ask questions, and respond to comments made by others. If you send a presentation out for review and then receive back a copy with changes, you can merge the reviewed version with your version to simplify the process of reviewing and accepting or rejecting changes.

In this chapter, we'll first discuss the new PowerPoint coauthoring capabilities., and then you'll save presentations in a couple of different formats. You'll send a presentation via e-mail directly from PowerPoint and then password-protect another presentation. You'll review, add, delete, and hide comments, and finally, you'll merge two versions of the same presentation.

> **Practice Files** Before you can complete the exercises in this chapter, you need to copy the book's practice files to your computer. The practice files you'll use to complete the exercises in this chapter are in the Chapter12 practice file folder. A complete list of practice files is provided in "Using the Practice Files" at the beginning of this book.

Collaborating with Other People

You might need to collaborate with other people on the development of a presentation for your company or organization. Or perhaps you are serving on a committee or working with a team of students or volunteers on a presentation that requires input from everyone. No matter what the circumstances, it can be difficult to keep track of different versions of a presentation produced by different people. With PowerPoint 2010, however, it is now possible to store one version of the presentation that can be worked on by multiple people simultaneously.

To develop a presentation with other users, you need to save it to a Microsoft SharePoint 2010 site. Display the Save & Send page of the Backstage view, click Save To SharePoint, and then use the settings in the Save As dialog box to save the presentation to the site. You then continue to work on it from the site. When another contributor begins making changes to the file stored on the site, PowerPoint alerts you to that person's presence. You can display a list of the other people who are actively working on the presentation and their availability.

As the people working on the presentation make changes, PowerPoint keeps track of them. At any point, you can display the Info page of the Backstage view to see the status of the presentation. When you finish working with the presentation, you save and close it as usual. The next time you open it, you'll see the changes made by anyone who has worked on the presentation in the meantime. In this way, several people can work effi-ciently on a presentation, whether they are in the same office building, on the other side of town, or in a different time zone, without fear that their changes will not make it into the final version or that their changes will overwrite someone else's.

If your organization has implemented the PowerPoint 2010 Web App on a server, team members who travel frequently can review presentations while on the road. With the Web App, you can review a presentation stored on your organization's server on any computer running Windows Internet Explorer 7, Internet Explorer 8, FireFox 3.5, or Safari 4 on the Mac. The presentation looks very similar to the way it does in PowerPoint on a desktop computer or portable computer, and you can make changes just as you would in PowerPoint.

You can also save a presentation to a Windows Live SkyDrive location and share it with other people from there. SkyDrive is part of Windows Live Online Services, a suite of useful programs that is available over the Internet from your computer or from mobile devices, such as portable computers or smart phones. You can visit www.windowslive.com/Online/ to learn about these services. All you need to start using them is a Windows Live ID.

You save a presentation to SkyDrive by displaying the Save & Send page of the Backstage view, clicking Save To Web, and then specifying the location where you want to save the file. You can make the presentation publicly available by saving it in the Public folder, or you can save it in your My Documents folder and then assign access permissions to specific people. You and colleagues who can access the file can then work on it by using the PowerPoint Web App from the site.

If you have a Windows smartphone, you can also use the PowerPoint 2010 Mobile App to view and edit presentations.

The Web App and the Mobile App allow you to continue collaborating with your team no matter where you are. Although a more in-depth discussion of these programs is beyond the scope of this book, if you are a "road warrior," you will certainly want to research them further.

Broadcasting Presentations

Suppose you work with a team whose members are located in various cities in the United States, as well as Denmark and New Zealand. You have developed a presentation to explain the results of your team's work to your managers, and you want to review the presentation with the team. You don't have much time for this review, and you don't want anyone to be able to change the content of the slides.

PowerPoint has the ideal solution for this situation: You can use a broadcast service to make the presentation available over the Internet, so that team members can see the presentation in their Web browsers and give feedback via a conference call.

To broadcast a presentation:

1. Display the Save & Send page of the Backstage view, click Broadcast Slide Show in the center pane, and then click Broadcast Slide Show in the right pane.

   Tip You can also click the Broadcast Slide Show button in the Start Slide Show group on the Slide Show tab.

   The Broadcast Slide Show dialog box opens.

2. Click Start Broadcast to connect to the service.

   The service displays a link to the Web site from which the presentation will be broadcast.

3. Click Send In Email, and when your e-mail program displays a message containing the link, enter the e-mail addresses of the reviewers, and click Send.

4. In the Broadcast Slide Show dialog box, click Start Slide Show.

   The first slide is displayed in Slide Show view.

5. Click through the slides.

   Everyone watching the presentation in their Web browser can see all transitions and animations, just as if they were watching the show in the room where you are presenting it.

6. When you reach the last slide, click again to return to Normal view. Then click End Broadcast in the Broadcast View banner at the top of the workspace, and confirm that you want to end the broadcast in the message box.

Saving Presentations in Other Formats

When you save a PowerPoint presentation, the default file format is the PowerPoint 2010 .pptx format. To save a presentation in a different file format, you display the Backstage view, click Save As to open the Save As dialog box, and then change the Save As Type setting to the format you want to use.

If you want to save the file so that it can be used with an earlier version of PowerPoint, you need to save it in the .ppt format. You do this by changing the Save As Type setting to PowerPoint 97-2003 Presentation.

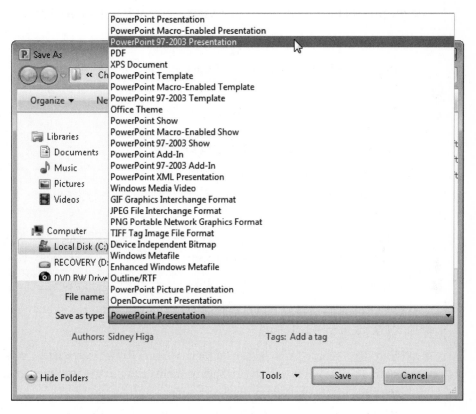

You can save presentations in many different formats.

If you are confused by the wide variety of formats, you might want to display the Save & Send page of the Backstage view and click Change File Type to display descriptions of some of the common formats.

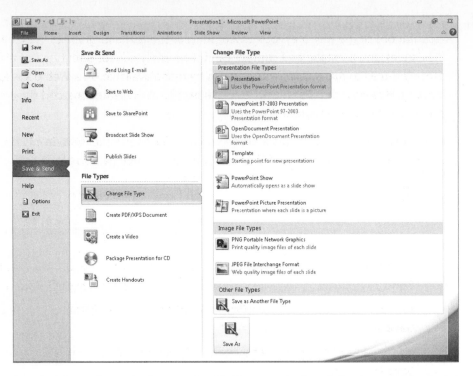

Use the information under Presentation File Types on the Save & Send page of the Backstage view to help you decide what format to save in.

The format you choose will depend on what you want other people to be able to do with the presentation. If you want people to be able to view the presentation with a minimum of fuss, you might want to save it in PowerPoint Show (.ppsx) format. These files open automatically in Slide Show view. If you want people to be able to see the content of a presentation but not change it, you can save the presentation in one of two formats:

- **PDF (.pdf)** This format is preferred by commercial printing facilities. You should also use this format if you know that recipients have a PDF reader, such as Adobe Acrobat Reader, installed on their computer.

- **XPS (.xps)** This format precisely renders all fonts, images, and colors on recipients' computers.

Both the PDF and XPS formats are designed to deliver presentations as electronic representations of the way they look when printed. The text and graphics in .pdf and .xps files are essentially static and content cannot be easily edited. Both types of files can be sent by e-mail to many recipients and can be made available on a Web page for downloading. However, the files are no longer PowerPoint presentations, and they cannot be opened, viewed, or edited in PowerPoint.

In this exercise, you'll first save a presentation as a PowerPoint Show. Then you'll save one slide of a presentation in XPS format, and you'll view the .xps file.

SET UP You need the CottageShow_start and WaterUse_start presentations located in your Chapter12 practice file folder to complete this exercise. Open first the WaterUse_start presentation and then the CottageShow_start presentation. Then follow the steps.

1. With slide **1** of the **CottageShow_start** presentation active, display the **Save & Send** page of the Backstage view, and in the center pane, click **Change File Type**.

2. In the right pane, click **PowerPoint Show**. Then at the bottom of the pane, click **Save As**.

   The Save As dialog box opens with the PowerPoint Show format selected in the Save As Type box.

3. Change the file name to **CottageShow**, and then click **Save**.

4. Display Windows Explorer, navigate to your **Chapter12** practice file folder, and double-click **CottageShow**.

   The presentation opens in Slide Show view and advances automatically from slide to slide while playing the embedded music.

5. Press Esc to end the presentation.

   PowerPoint stops the show and returns to Normal view.

6. Switch to the **WaterUse_start** presentation, and display slide **7**.

   Let's save only this slide in XPS format.

7. Display the **Save & Send** page of the Backstage view. In the center pane, click **Create PDF/XPS Document**, and then in the right pane, click **Create PDF/XPS**.

   The Publish As PDF Or XPS dialog box opens.

8. Display the **Save as type** list, and click **XPS Document**.

The dialog box is designed only for the PDF and XPS formats.

This dialog box looks like an expanded Save As dialog box.

9. In the **File name** box, change the name to **WaterUse**.

10. In the **Optimize for** area, click **Minimum size (publishing online)**.
    Then click **Options**.

    The Options dialog box opens.

You can choose from these options to tailor the .xps file to your needs.

11. In the **Range** area, click **Current slide**.

    Tip If you are saving this presentation in a different format to send it for review, you might want to select the Include Hidden Slides check box in the Publish Options area to ensure that the reviewer sees all the slides. Similarly, you might want to select the Include Comments And In Markup check box to ensure that he or she can evaluate all the available information in the presentation.

12. In the **Include non-printing information** area, clear the **Document properties** check box, and then click **OK**.

13. Back in the **Publish as PDF or XPS** dialog box, select the **Open file after publishing** check box, and then click **Publish**.

The slide is saved in XPS format. Because you indicated that you wanted to open the file after saving it, the XPS Viewer starts and displays the file.

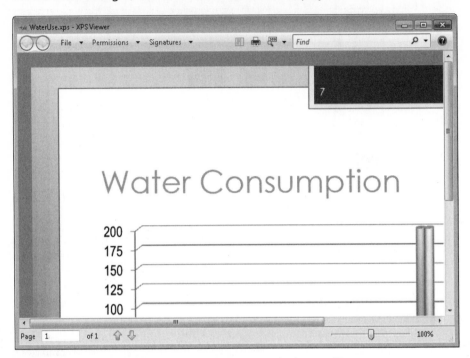

Only slide 7 of the PowerPoint presentation appears in the .xps file.

Tip The XPS Viewer window includes two toolbars, one below the title bar and one at the bottom of the window. You can use the commands on the top toolbar to save a copy of the file, specify who can access the file, attach a digital signature, print the file, and search for particular words or phrases. You can use the tools on the bottom toolbar to move back and forth among pages, and zoom in or out.

✖ CLEAN UP Close the XPS Viewer, and then close the WaterUse_start presentation.

Sending Presentations Directly from PowerPoint

After you create a presentation, you can quickly send it via e-mail from the Save & Send page of the Backstage view, without starting your e-mail program.

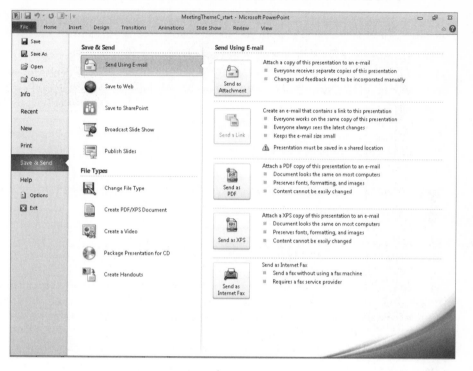

You can send a file in PPTX, PDF, or XPS format.

Clicking Send As Attachment opens a message window with the current presentation already attached as a PPTX file. All you have to do is enter the e-mail addresses of anyone you want to receive the message and its attachment. If you want, you can modify the subject line, which contains the name of the presentation you're sending.

Tip If you are working on a presentation that is stored on a server and you want other people who have access to the server to review that particular file, you can send an e-mail message with a link to the file by clicking Send A Link on the Save & Send page of the Backstage view.

Similarly, you can click Send As PDF or Send As XPS to have PowerPoint save and attach a version of the presentation in the corresponding file format.

In addition to sending a presentation as an e-mail attachment from within PowerPoint, if you have signed up with an Internet fax service provider, you can send the presentation as a fax. Although the exact terms vary from one Internet fax service provider to another, these services all enable you to send and receive faxes from your computer without needing a fax machine or dedicated fax line. After establishing an Internet fax service account, you can send the current presentation as a fax by clicking Send As Internet Fax on the Save & Send page. Then all you have to do is follow the procedure specified by your fax service provider.

Tip If you do not sign up with an Internet fax service provider before clicking Send As Internet Fax, a message box appears. Clicking OK opens a Web page where you can choose a fax service provider.

In this exercise, you'll attach three presentations to an e-mail message so that you can simulate sending them for review.

SET UP You need the MeetingThemeA_start, MeetingThemeB, and MeetingThemeC presentations located in your Chapter12 practice file folder to complete this exercise. Open the MeetingThemeA_start presentation and save it as *MeetingThemeA*. Be sure to have an e-mail program installed on your computer and an e-mail account set up before beginning this exercise. Microsoft Outlook 2010 is recommended. You can use another e-mail program, but the steps for attaching and sending a message might vary from those given in this exercise. Then with the MeetingThemeA presentation open, follow the steps.

1. Display the **Save & Send** page of the Backstage view.

2. With **Send Using E-mail** selected in the center pane, click **Send as Attachment** in the right pane.

   PowerPoint starts your default e-mail program, and a message window opens.

   Troubleshooting You might be prompted to supply your user name and password to access your e-mail account.

PowerPoint enters the name of the presentation in the Subject line and attaches the presentation to the message.

3. In the **To** box, type your own e-mail address.

4. In the message content pane, type **Please review the attached presentations, and let me know which theme you prefer.**

   You can format the text of the message in the same way you would the text on a slide.

5. On the **Message** tab, in the **Include** group, click the **Attach File** button.

   The Insert File dialog box opens.

6. Navigate to your **Chapter12** practice file folder.

7. Click **MeetingThemeB**, hold down the Ctrl key, click **MeetingThemeC**, and then click **Insert**.

   In the message window, the Attached box shows that three files are attached to the message.

8. On the **Message** tab, in the **Tags** group, click the **High Importance** button.

   If the message recipient is using Outlook, the message header will display a red exclamation mark to indicate that it is important.

9. In the message header, click the **Send** button.

   Outlook sends the e-mail message with the attached presentations. You'll receive the message the next time Outlook connects to your mail server.

   ✖ **CLEAN UP** Close the MeetingThemeA presentation.

Adding Digital Signatures

When you create a presentation that will be circulated to other people via e-mail or the Web, you might want to attach a digital signature, which is an electronic stamp of authentication. The digital signature confirms the origin of the presentation and indicates that no one has tampered with the presentation since it was signed.

To add a digital signature to a PowerPoint presentation:

1. Display the Info page of the Backstage view.

2. In the center pane, click the Protect Presentation button, and then click Add A Digital Signature.

    If a digital signature is not already stored on this computer, a dialog box opens.

3. If you want to obtain a signature from a third-party company such as ARX CoSign or IntelliSafe, click Signature Services From The Office Marketplace to display a Web site with instructions.

4. If you want to create your own signature, click OK. Then in the Get A Digital ID dialog box, click Create Your Own Digital ID, and click OK. When PowerPoint displays the Signature Setup dialog box, specify your name, title, organization, and e-mail address, and click OK.

5. In the Sign dialog box, enter the purpose for signing the presentation, if you want, and click Sign. Then when a message tells you that the signature has been saved with the presentation, click OK.

    The Info page now indicates that the presentation is signed and final. When you click any of the other ribbon tabs, an info bar at the top of the presentation discourages editing by announcing that the presentation is final, and the ribbon commands are hidden.

Password-Protecting Presentations

Sometimes you might want only specified people to be able to view a presentation. Or you might want some people to only be able to view it and others to be able to change it. In both cases, you can control who has access to the presentation and what they can do by assigning one or more passwords to the presentation.

You can assign two types of passwords to a presentation:

- **Password to open** When you assign a password that must be entered to open the presentation, the presentation is encrypted so that only people with the password can view the presentation.

- **Password to modify** When you assign a password that must be entered to modify the presentation, people who don't have the password can open a read-only version but they cannot make changes or save a copy with a different name.

When you try to open a presentation to which a password has been assigned, the Password dialog box opens. If the password must be entered to open the presentation, you must enter the exact password—including capitalization, numbers, spaces, and symbols. If the password must be entered to modify the presentation, you can either enter the exact password to open it or click Read-Only to open a version that you can view but not modify.

In this exercise, you'll assign a password that people must type in order to modify a presentation. You'll open a read-only version of the password-protected presentation and then enter the password to open a version that you can edit.

SET UP You need the ServiceProjects_start presentation located in your Chapter12 practice file folder. Open the ServiceProjects_start presentation, and save it as *ServiceProjects*. Then follow the steps.

1. Display the Backstage view, and then click **Save As**.

   The Save As dialog box opens.

2. At the bottom of the dialog box, click **Tools**, and then in the list, click **General Options**.

   The General Options dialog box opens.

You can set encrypted (Password To Open) or unencrypted (Password To Modify) passwords in this dialog box.

> **Tip** You can set an encrypted password by displaying the Info page of the Backstage view, clicking Protect Presentation, and then clicking Encrypt With Password.

3. In the **Password to modify** box, type **P@ssword**.

   To keep your password confidential, black dots appear in place of the characters you type.

   > **Important** In this exercise, we use a common password that is easy to type. For maximum protection, use a password of at least eight characters that includes a combination of uppercase and lowercase letters, digits, and punctuation symbols. Write it down and keep it in a safe place. Otherwise, if you forget the password, you will not be able to open the presentation.

4. Click **OK**.

   The Confirm Password dialog box opens.

5. In the **Reenter password to modify** box, type **P@ssword**, and then click **OK**.

   > **Troubleshooting** If the two passwords you enter do not match exactly, PowerPoint displays a message. Click OK in the message box, click Cancel in the Confirm Password dialog box, and then repeat steps 3 through 5.

6. With the contents of your **Chapter12** practice file folder displayed in the **Save As** dialog box, replace the name in the **File name** box with **ServiceProjectsLocked**, and then click **Save**.

   PowerPoint saves a new version of the presentation with the password in place. To test the password protection, you need to close the presentation and open it again.

7. Display the Backstage view, and then click **Close**.

8. Display the Backstage view, and then in the **Recent Presentations** list, click **ServiceProjectsLocked**.

   The Password dialog box opens.

Passwords are case sensitive, so be sure to type the exact combination of uppercase and lowercase letters.

9. In the **Password** box, type **password**, and then click **OK**.

   A message box tells you that the password you have typed is incorrect.

10. Click **OK** in the message box, and then in the **Password** dialog box, click **Read Only**.

    A read-only version of the ServiceProjectsLocked presentation opens, displaying slide 1 in Normal view. In the title bar at the top of the screen, the presentation is designated as *(Read-Only)*.

11. On the slide, double-click **and** in the presentation title, and then press Delete.

    Pressing the Delete key has no effect, because you cannot modify the presentation.

12. Close the presentation, and then reopen it.

13. In the **Password** dialog box, type **P@ssword** in the **Password** box, and then click **OK**.

    The presentation opens, displaying slide 1 in Normal view. There is no Read-Only designation in the title bar, indicating that you can modify and save changes to the presentation.

    Tip To remove the password from a password-protected presentation, open it using the password, display the Save As dialog box, click Tools, and then click General Options. In the General Options dialog box, remove the password from the password box(es), and click OK. Then click Save to overwrite the password-protected version.

CLEAN UP Close the ServiceProjectsLocked presentation.

Information Rights Management

If your organization has implemented Information Rights Management (IRM) or if you sign up for the free IRM trial service from Microsoft, you can restrict who can change, print, or copy a presentation, and you can limit these permissions for a specified period of time. Your system administrator might also establish policies to further restrict how presentations can be manipulated and circulated, and he or she might provide templates for confidential or otherwise sensitive presentations.

For more information about IRM, display the Info tab of the Backstage view, click Protect Presentation, and then click Restrict Permission By People. In the list, click Restricted Access. If the Windows Rights Management client is not installed on your computer, the Service Sign-Up wizard starts. Click the Learn More About This Free Service From Microsoft link to open a Web site with information about the free trial service.

Adding and Reviewing Comments

The development of a presentation, especially one that will be delivered to clients, shareholders, or other important people, is often a collaborative effort, with several people contributing ideas and feedback. Even if you are developing a presentation for your own purposes, you might want to ask other people to review and comment on it before declaring a presentation final.

If you are asked to review a presentation, you can give feedback about a slide without disrupting its text and layout by clicking the New Comment button in the Comments group on the Review tab, and then typing in a comment box. Clicking away from the comment box hides the comment but leaves a small comment icon with your initials and a number. If you add a comment without first selecting an object on the slide, the comment icon appears in the upper-left corner of the slide. If you select an object such as the title or a graphic before adding the comment, the comment icon appears in the upper-right corner of the object. In either case, pointing to the icon displays the comment temporarily and clicking the icon displays the comment until you click somewhere else.

You can manage and review comments by clicking these buttons in the Comments group:

- **Show Markup** Clicking this button hides all the comment icons so that you can view the slides without extraneous clutter.

- **Edit Comment** Clicking this button displays the comment box associated with the active comment icon and places a cursor at the end of the comment text so that you can make additions or changes.

   Tip You can quickly activate a comment for editing by double-clicking it.

- **Delete** Clicking this button deletes the active comment icon and its comment box. To delete all the comments on the current slide or all the comments in the entire presentation, select that option in the Delete list.

- **Previous and Next** Clicking these buttons moves backward or forward through the comments, displaying the comment box of each one in turn.

See Also For information about marking up slides with an electronic pen while reviewing a presentation, see "Delivering Presentations" in Chapter 6, "Review and Deliver Presentations."

In this exercise, you'll add and edit comments in a presentation, move among the comments, delete a comment, and hide and display comments. Then you'll remove all comments from the presentation.

SET UP You need the HarmonyReview_start presentation located in your Chapter12 practice file folder to complete this exercise. Open the HarmonyReview_start presentation, and save it as *HarmonyReview*. Then follow the steps.

1. With nothing selected on slide **1**, on the **Review** tab, in the **Comments** group, click the **New Comment** button.

   PowerPoint adds a comment icon containing your initials and the number 1 to the upper-left corner of the slide, and opens a comment box.

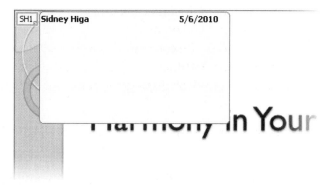

The comment box contains your user name and today's date.

Tip Comment boxes include the user name and initials you specified the first time you started any program in the Microsoft Office 2010 system. To change this information, display the PowerPoint Options dialog box, and on the General page, under Personalize Your Copy Of Microsoft Office, change the entries in the User Name and Initials boxes, and click OK.

2. In the comment box, type **Feng shui not mentioned. Good or bad?**

3. Click away from the comment box to close it.

4. Point to the comment icon to display the comment, and then move the pointer away from the icon to close the box again.

5. Move to slide **2**, click anywhere in the bulleted list, and in the **Comments** group, click the **New Comment** button.

6. In the comment box, type **A graphic would add interest here**, and then click away from the comment box.

Because this comment is attached to the bulleted list, its icon appears in that placeholder.

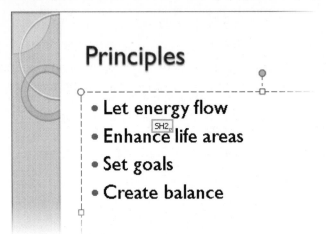

This is the second comment in the presentation, so the comment icon shows your initials and the number 2.

7. With the comment icon on slide **2** selected, in the **Comments** group, click the **Edit Comment** button.

The comment box opens so that you can edit the comment.

8. Click to the left of the word **graphic**, type **tasteful**, press the Spacebar, and then click away from the comment box to close it.

9. Move back to slide **1**, double-click the word **Your** in the title, and add a comment that says **Should this be "the"?**

10. At the top of the slide, click comment icon **1** to open its comment box, and then in the **Comments** group, click the **Next** button.

PowerPoint closes the first comment box and displays the next comment.

11. In the **Comments** group, click the **Previous** button to move back to the first comment.

12. With the first comment displayed, in the **Comments** group, click the **Delete** button.

    The comment is deleted from the slide.

13. In the **Comments** group, click the **Show Markup** button to turn it off.

    The comment icon attached to the title on slide 1 disappears.

14. Move to slide **2** to verify that the comment icon is hidden there also.

15. In the **Comments** group, click the **Show Markup** button to redisplay the comment icons, and then click the comment icon on the active slide.

16. In the **Comments** group, click the **Delete** arrow, and then in the list, click **Delete All Markup in this Presentation**.

17. When asked to confirm that you want to delete all the comments, click **Yes**.

    Both the remaining comments are removed.

 CLEAN UP Save the HarmonyReview presentation, and then close it.

Merging Presentation Versions

Sometimes you might want to compare two versions of the same presentation. For example, if you have sent a presentation out for review by a colleague, you might want to compare his or her edited version with the original presentation so that you can incorporate the changes you like and reject those you don't.

Instead of comparing two open presentations visually, you can tell PowerPoint to compare the presentations and merge the differences into one presentation. The differences are recorded in the merged presentation as revisions. From within that one presentation, you can view the suggested changes and accept or reject them.

In this exercise, you'll merge two versions of the same presentation. You'll then review the changes and accept those you like.

SET UP You need the MeetingCompareA_start and MeetingCompareB_start presentations located in your Chapter12 practice file folder to complete this exercise. Open the MeetingCompareA_start presentation, save it as *MeetingCompareA*, and then close it. Then open the MeetingCompareB_start presentation, and save it as *MeetingCompareB*. With that presentation open, follow the steps.

Compare

1. On the **Review** tab, in the **Compare** group, click the **Compare** button.

   The Choose File To Merge With Current Presentation dialog box opens.

2. With the contents of your **Chapter12** practice file folder displayed, double-click **MeetingCompareA**.

   PowerPoint compares the two presentations and incorporates the differences into MeetingCompareB. To the right, it displays the Revisions task pane, with the Details tab active.

The orange revision box at the bottom of the screen tells you that the displayed slide has been deleted from MeetingCompareA.

Troubleshooting The appearance of buttons and groups on the ribbon changes depending on the width of the program window. For information about changing the appearance of the ribbon to match our screen images, see "Modifying the Display of the Ribbon" at the beginning of this book.

3. In the orange revision box at the bottom of the screen, select the check box to accept the slide deletion.

The slide disappears, and an icon between slide 8 and slide 9 on the Slides tab of the Overview pane indicates that you have accepted the change.

4. Point to the icon on the **Slides** tab.

A ScreenTip tells you that you can click the icon to see which slide has been deleted.

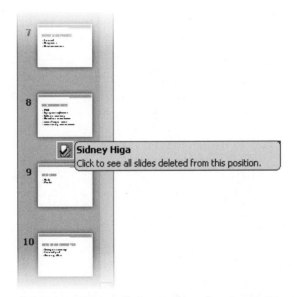

If you change your mind, you can easily reinsert slides
that you've deleted by clicking the icon.

5. Click the icon.

PowerPoint displays the revision box. If you want to reinstate the deleted slide, you can clear the check box.

6. Scroll to the top of the **Slides** pane, and click slide **1**.

   The Slide Changes area of the Revisions task pane tells you that there is a change on this slide.

7. Click **Rectangle 7: Company meeting**.

   The revision box tells you that Sidney Higa deleted the word *Company* and inserted the word *Annual*.

You can choose individual changes or accept or reject all of them.

8. In the revision box, select the **All changes to Rectangle 7** check box.

9. On the **Review** tab, in the **Compare** group, click the **Next** button.

   PowerPoint displays slide 2, and the Revisions task pane indicates that Sidney Higa made changes to the bulleted list.

10. In the revision box, select the **Deleted "our"** check box. Then reverse this step and clear the check box again.

    You can flip back and forth to determine whether or not you like each change.

11. Accept all the changes, and then click the **Next** button.

12. Review and accept the remaining changes. When PowerPoint displays a message that it has reached the end of all changes, click **Continue** to return to the first change.

    PowerPoint displays the revision box for the deleted slide. Let's keep this change.

13. Click the **Next** button.

14. With slide **1** displayed, on the **Review** tab, in the **Compare** group, click the **Reject** button to restore the original slide title.

15. To apply all the decisions you have made, in the **Compare** group, click the **End Review** button. Then confirm that you want to end the review by clicking **Yes** in the message box.

    PowerPoint accepts all the changes and closes the Revisions task pane.

 **CLEAN UP** Save the MeetingCompareB presentation, and then close it.

Key Points

- If your organization has a SharePoint site, you and your colleagues can collaborate on a presentation. Or you can collaborate on a presentation stored in a Windows Live SkyDrive space.

- You can save a presentation in several different file formats, including PowerPoint Show, PDF, and XPS.

- You can send a presentation for review via e-mail. When you receive the reviewed versions, you can merge them so that all the changes are recorded in one presentation.

- Assigning a password ensures that only people who know the password can review and work on the presentation.

- When you review a presentation created by someone else, you can add comments to give feedback. You can also use comments in your own presentations to remind yourself of outstanding issues and tasks.

Chapter at a Glance

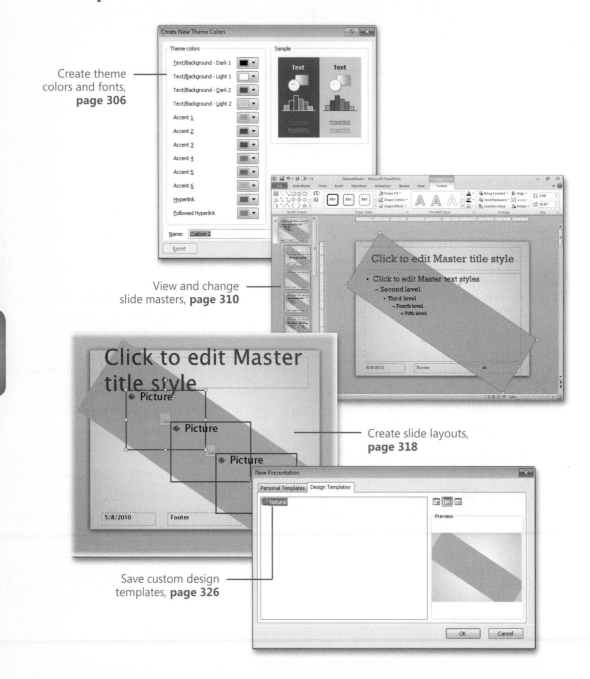

Create theme colors and fonts, **page 306**

View and change slide masters, **page 310**

Create slide layouts, **page 318**

Save custom design templates, **page 326**

13 Create Custom Presentation Elements

In this chapter, you will learn how to

✔ Create theme colors and fonts.

✔ View and change slide masters.

✔ Create slide layouts.

✔ Save custom design templates.

In addition to using the built-in design elements of Microsoft PowerPoint 2010, you can create your own color schemes, font sets, layouts, and templates. Why would you want to create your own elements rather than using those that come with PowerPoint? If your organization has established a corporate or brand image through the use of a logo, a color scheme, or other visual cues, you might be required to incorporate that branding into presentations that will be seen outside the organization. Even if branding is not an issue, you might want to establish a unique look for all your presentations to identify your work.

In this chapter, you'll create a color scheme and font set and then save the color/font combination as a new theme. You'll view and edit the slide masters for a presentation, changing the layout, text formatting, and bullet formatting, and adding a picture to the background. You'll then create a master layout, save a presentation as a design template, and create a presentation based on the template.

> **Practice Files** Before you can complete the exercises in this chapter, you need to copy the book's practice files to your computer. The practice files you'll use to complete the exercises in this chapter are in the Chapter13 practice file folder. A complete list of practice files is provided in "Using the Practice Files" at the beginning of this book.

Creating Theme Colors and Fonts

One simple way to dress up a presentation is to apply a theme to make its colors, fonts, formatting, graphics, and other elements consistent from slide to slide. You can then switch to a different predefined color scheme and font set without otherwise affecting the overall look of the theme.

If none of the ready-made color schemes or font sets meets your needs, you can create your own and use it with any theme. If you want to be able to use your custom color scheme/font set combination with other presentations, you can save the combination as a new theme that you can then apply to another presentation with a few clicks of the mouse button.

Tip You can set a custom theme, or any theme, as the default for all new presentations by right-clicking the theme's thumbnail in the Themes gallery and then clicking Set As Default Theme.

The simplest way to create a color scheme or font set is by altering an existing one. After you add the new scheme to the Colors gallery or font set to the Fonts gallery, you can apply it to an entire presentation by clicking the scheme in the Custom section of the gallery. You can apply it to the current slide only by right-clicking it and then clicking Apply To Selected Slides.

Tip You don't have to create a custom color scheme or font set to be able to apply the particular combination of colors or fonts used on one slide to another slide. You can display the slide with the formatting you want to reuse, click the Format Painter button in the Clipboard group on the Home tab, and then click the slide to which you want to copy the formatting.

In this exercise, you'll create a color scheme and font set for a photo album and make them available for reuse. Then you'll save the color/font combination as a new theme that you can apply to any presentation.

SET UP You don't need any practice files to complete this exercise; just follow the steps.

1. Display the **New** page of the Backstage view, click **Sample Templates**, and double-click **Classic Photo Album**. Then save the presentation with the name **My Photo Album**.

   This presentation is very somber. Let's keep the classic look but make it more lively.

2. On the **Design** tab, in the **Themes** group, click the **Colors** button.

   The Colors gallery appears. The Technic color scheme is currently applied to the presentation.

3. In the gallery, click the **Pushpin** color scheme.

   This scheme has some interesting colors, but the presentation title is too sedate.

4. In the **Themes** group, click the **Colors** button, and then at the bottom of the gallery, click **Create New Theme Colors**.

The Create New Theme Colors dialog box opens.

Each color scheme consists of 12 colors assigned to the 12 possible design elements of a presentation.

5. Click the **Text/Background - Light 2** box to display a color palette.

6. Under **Theme Colors**, click the fifth box in the top row (**Orange, Accent 1**).

The Sample pane changes to show the new color combination.

7. Click the **Accent 1** box, and under **Theme Colors** in the palette, click the fourth box in the top row (**Ice Blue, Text 2**).

You have switched the two colors.

8. Click the **Text/Background - Light 1** box, and at the bottom of the palette, click **More Colors**.

The Colors dialog box opens.

9. If the **Standard** tab is not displayed, click it.

This tab displays a color wheel.

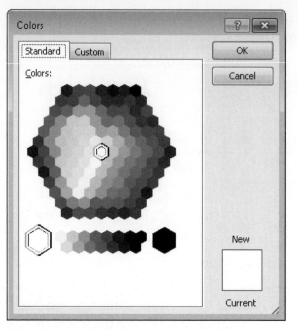

The Standard page of the Colors dialog box.

10. In the color wheel, click a lime green color, and then click **OK**.

11. In the **Name** box at the bottom of the **Create New Theme Colors** dialog box, change the name of the new theme to **My Custom Colors**, and then click **Save**.

    PowerPoint applies the change to the slides and adds a theme with the new color scheme to the left end of the Themes gallery.

    Troubleshooting Sometimes PowerPoint doesn't update the text of the slides with the new color scheme. If that happens, click the text placeholder, press Ctrl+A to select all its text, and then press Ctrl+Spacebar. This removes any local formatting and reapplies the formatting defined in the attached theme.

12. In the **Themes** group, click the **Fonts** button, and then in the **Fonts** gallery, click **Aspect** as a starting point for a new font set.

13. Click the **Fonts** button again, and then at the bottom of the gallery, click **Create New Theme Fonts**.

    The Create New Theme Fonts dialog box opens.

When choosing fonts, try to find a combination that reflects the tone of your presentation.

14. Click the **Heading font** arrow, and then in the list, click **Arial Rounded MT Bold**.

    The Sample pane shows the new font combination.

15. In the **Name** box at the bottom of the dialog box, change the name of the new font set to **My Custom Fonts**, and then click **Save**.

16. In the **Themes** group, click first the **Colors** button and then the **Fonts** button, and notice that your combinations are listed under **Custom** in the respective galleries.

17. In the **Themes** group, click the **More** button, and then at the bottom of the gallery, click **Save Current Theme**.

    The Save Current Theme dialog box opens, displaying the contents of your Document Themes folder. Saving custom themes in this folder ensures that they are available in the gallery for use in other presentations.

18. In the **File name** box at the bottom of the dialog box, change the name of the new theme to **My Theme**, and then click **Save**.

19. Save the **My Photo Album** presentation, and then close it.

20. Open a new, blank presentation. Then on the **Design** tab, in the **Themes** group, point to the second thumbnail in the gallery.

    PowerPoint displays the ScreenTip *My Theme* below the thumbnail.

21. Click the **My Theme** thumbnail to apply the custom theme to the new presentation.

    Tip Custom themes, color schemes, and font sets are saved in the C:\Users\<*username*>\ AppData\Roaming\Microsoft\Templates\Document Themes folder. To delete a custom theme, color scheme, or font set, navigate to the folder, right-click the item, and then click Delete.

✖ **CLEAN UP** Close the blank presentation without saving your changes.

Viewing and Changing Slide Masters

When you create a presentation, the slides take on the characteristics of the template on which it is based. PowerPoint templates use masters to determine their basic design. By default, PowerPoint presentations have three masters:

- **Slide master** This set of masters controls the look of all the slides in a presentation, including the theme, text placement, background graphics, and other slide elements. The set contains a master design for most of the layouts you are likely to use.

- **Handout master** This master controls the look of any handouts you prepare for distribution to your audience.

- **Notes master** This master controls the look of speaker notes (if you choose to print them).

    See Also For information about handouts and speaker notes, see "Preparing Speaker Notes and Handouts" in Chapter 6, "Review and Deliver Presentations."

When you create a presentation, its slides assume the design of its corresponding set of slide masters. The slide masters contain placeholders for a title, bullet points, or other content, depending on the particular layout. Most slide masters also contain placeholders for the date and time, footer information, and slide number. The placeholders control the position of the elements on the slide. Text placeholders also control the formatting of their text.

On an individual slide, you can make changes to the design elements provided by the master, but you can change the basic design only on the master. When you change a design element on the master, all the slides reflect the change.

Tip To override the master design for a particular slide, you use commands on the Home and Design tabs. For example, you can remove a background graphic from a slide by clicking the Hide Background Graphics button in the Background group on the Design tab.

To make changes to a presentation's masters, you need to switch to Slide Master view by clicking the Slide Master button in the Master Views group on the View tab. In this view, the Overview pane on the left displays the primary master, which controls the base layout, followed by all the available layout variations. The layout selected in the Overview pane is displayed in the Slide pane on the right. PowerPoint adds a Slide Master tab to the ribbon and hides the tabs that aren't needed in this view.

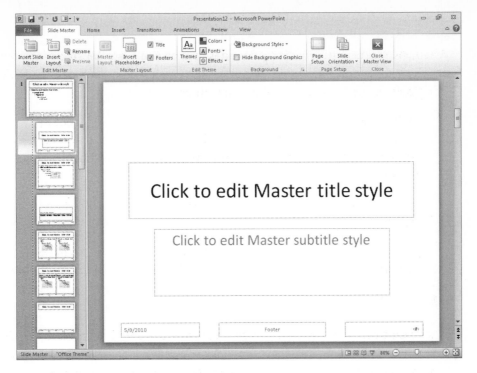

The slide masters for a new blank presentation.

Troubleshooting The appearance of buttons and groups on the ribbon changes depending on the width of the program window. For information about changing the appearance of the ribbon to match our screen images, see "Modifying the Display of the Ribbon" at the beginning of this book.

By clicking buttons on the Slide Master tab, you can make the following adjustments:

- Make another set of masters available to the presentation and preserve that set so that it remains available even if it is not currently used in the presentation.

- Add a new layout with the same background, title, and footer style to which you can add your own placeholders.

- Delete or rename a selected layout.

- Specify which placeholders will be included on the selected layout.

- Select and fine-tune the theme applied to the master set.

- Control the background color, texture, and graphics.

- Set the default page setup for the presentation.

Clicking the Close Master View button in the Close group on the Slide Master tab returns you to the view from which you switched to Slide Master view. You can also click any view button on the View Shortcuts toolbar at the right end of the status bar to close Slide Master view.

While you are working in Slide Master view, you can use the buttons on the other tabs in the following ways:

- Format a text placeholder on a master by selecting it and then clicking buttons in the Font and Paragraph groups on the Home tab.
- Add objects such as graphics and WordArt text to a master by clicking buttons on the Insert tab.
- Apply transitions by clicking buttons on the Transitions tab.
- Animate parts of a slide by clicking buttons on the Animations tab.
- Use the proofing and language tools on the Review tab.

For slides designed to contain text, you can format bulleted lists by specifying the bullet's size, shape, and color. You can also control the indenting of various bullet levels and the distance between the bullet and its text by displaying the rulers and moving markers, as follows:

- **First Line Indent** The upper triangle controls the first line of the paragraph.
- **Hanging Indent** The lower triangle controls the left edge of the remaining lines of the paragraph.
- **Left Indent** The small square controls how far the entire paragraph sits from the edge of the text object.

These indent markers...

...control this bullet point.

You can click any bullet point to see its indent markers on the horizontal ruler.

To adjust the relationship between the first and remaining lines of a bullet point, you drag the First Line Indent and Hanging Indent markers to the left or right on the ruler. To adjust the distance of the bullet point from the edge of the text object, you drag the Left Indent marker.

In this exercise, you'll view a presentation's masters in Slide Master view. Then you'll add a graphic to the background, change character formatting, and change the font scheme. Then you'll change bullet characters and adjust bullet spacing. Finally, you'll remove the footer placeholders from the title slide layout.

SET UP You need the NaturalMaster_start presentation located in your Chapter13 practice file folder to complete this exercise. Open the NaturalMaster_start presentation, and save it as *NaturalMaster*. Display the rulers, and then follow the steps.

1. With slide **1** displayed in Normal view, on the **View** tab, in the **Master Views** group, click the **Slide Master** button.

   You are now in Slide Master view. The Overview pane on the left shows thumbnails of the primary master and the layouts in this set. The first layout—the Title Slide layout, which controls the presentation's title slide—is selected and appears in the Slide pane to the right. Notice that, other than the gradient background, the masters don't reflect the formatting of the slides, which has been applied manually on a slide-by-slide basis. Let's implement the formatting in the masters so that we don't have to do it manually on each slide.

2. On the **View Shortcuts** toolbar, click the **Normal** button. Then on slide **1**, click the diagonal shape to select it, and copy it.

   Keyboard Shortcut Press Ctrl+C to copy a selected item.

   See Also For more information about keyboard shortcuts, see "Keyboard Shortcuts" at the end of this book.

3. Switch back to Slide Master view. Then in the **Overview** pane, click the primary master (the top thumbnail), and paste the diagonal shape into that master.

   Keyboard Shortcut Press Ctrl+V to paste a cut or copied item.

   Because the primary master controls the basic characteristics of all the layouts, the graphic fills their backgrounds as well. The shape is selected, so PowerPoint adds the Format contextual tab to the ribbon.

4. On the **Format** tab, in the **Arrange** group, click the **Send Backward** arrow, and then click **Send to Back**.

   PowerPoint moves the shape behind the other elements on the primary master.

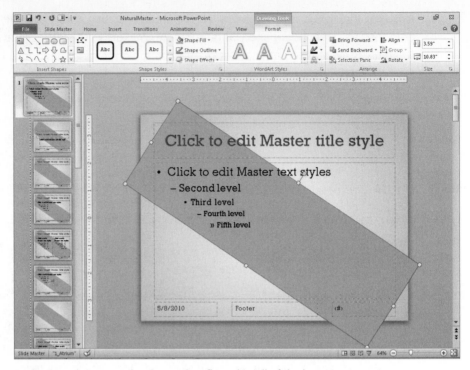

In the Overview pane, the change is reflected in all of the layouts.

5. Switch to Normal view, and on slide **1**, select and delete the shape that was drawn manually on the slide.

   The appearance of the slide remains the same, because the shape is now supplied by the slide master.

6. Click anywhere in the title placeholder, select all the text, and then on the **Home** tab, in the **Clipboard** group, click the **Format Painter** button.

   Keyboard Shortcut Press Ctrl+A to select all the text in a placeholder.

7. Switch back to Slide Master view, where the Title Slide layout is selected by default, and drag the **Format Painter** pointer across the text in the placeholder for the presentation's title.

   PowerPoint copies the local character formatting of the title on slide 1 to the master Title Slide layout.

8. Enlarge the title placeholder by dragging its handles upward and toward the edges of the slide. Then click away from the placeholder to see the result.

   The newly formatted title fits on two lines.

On any slide you create with the Title Slide layout, the title will now be formatted as shown on this master.

9. Repeat steps 6 and 7 to copy the formatting of the subtitle on the presentation's title slide to the master Title Slide layout.

10. Repeat steps 6 and 7 again to copy the formatting of the title of slide **2** in the presentation to the title of the primary master.

    PowerPoint copies the character formatting of slide 2's title to the primary master's title, and in the Overview pane, all the layouts with slide titles now reflect this change.

    Tip At its bigger size, the title placeholder text breaks to two lines and overflows its placeholder. However, if you want slide titles in the presentation to be only one line long, you shouldn't adjust the size of the placeholder.

11. With the primary master still selected, on the **Slide Master** tab, in the **Edit Theme** group, click the **Fonts** button, and then in the **Fonts** gallery, click **Concourse**.

    The primary master and all the layouts change to reflect the new font scheme.

12. In the bulleted list placeholder, click anywhere in the phrase **Click to edit Master text styles**. Then on the **Home** tab, in the **Paragraph** group, click the **Bullets** arrow, and at the bottom of the gallery, click **Bullets and Numbering**.

    The Bullets And Numbering dialog box opens.

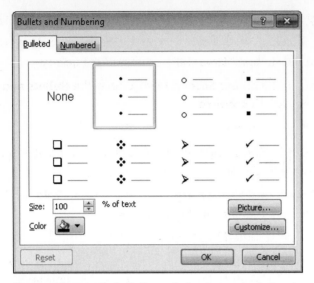

You can change the bullet's symbol, color, and relative size.

13. Click **Picture**.

The Picture Bullet dialog box opens.

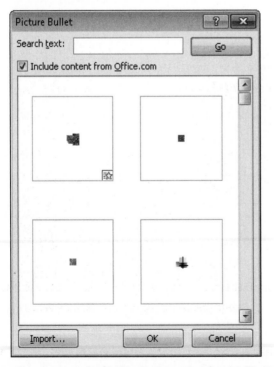

Choosing a picture bullet in place of a standard bullet can add character to your presentation.

14. Scroll through the gallery of images, click any dark red image you like, and then click **OK**.

    We chose the red sunburst toward the bottom of the gallery.

15. Click anywhere in the phrase **Second level**, display the **Bullets and Numbering** dialog box, and click **Customize**.

    The Symbol dialog box opens.

16. Change the **Font** to **Wingdings**, and double-click a symbol that is compatible with the picture you selected for the first-level bullet.

17. Back in the **Bullets and Numbering** dialog box, set the **Color** of the new bullet to **Dark Red** and its **Size** to **90**, and then click **OK**.

    All the layouts with bulleted lists reflect your changes.

18. Click the first-level bullet point, and on the horizontal ruler, drag the **Hanging Indent** marker to the right to the **0.5** inch mark. Then click the second-level bullet point, and drag its Hanging Indent marker to the **1** inch mark.

    The First Line Indent marker remains where it is, but the Left Indent marker moves with the Hanging Indent marker.

In both the first-level and second-level bullet points, the distance between the bullet and the text has increased.

19. Display the **Title Slide** layout, and on the **Slide Master** tab, in the **Master Layout** group, clear the **Footers** check box.

The date, footer information, and slide number placeholders are removed from the Title Slide layout.

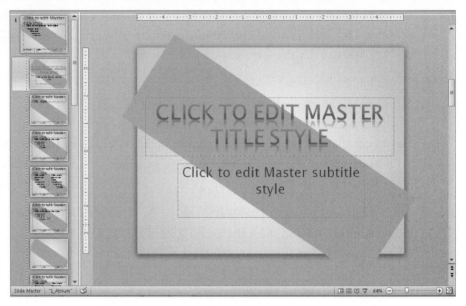

The footers are still in place on all the other master layouts.

Tip You cannot remove the footer placeholders from the primary master. You must remove them from the individual layouts.

20. Switch to Normal view, and display each slide in turn, noticing the effects of your changes to the slide masters.

 CLEAN UP Save the NaturalMaster presentation, and then close it.

Creating Slide Layouts

PowerPoint 2010 comes with many standard layouts—enough to suit most presentations. However, one of the slides in a presentation might require a completely different layout. If the same custom layout is likely to be used more than once in a presentation, you can save time by adding the layout to the slide master set so that you can use it anytime you need it. Clicking the Insert Layout button in the Edit Master group on the Slide

Master tab adds a new layout to the master set, with a title but no other content. You can then insert placeholders and arrange and format them the way you want them.

In this exercise, you'll create a master layout with placeholders for a title and a paragraph of text. Then you'll create another master layout with placeholders for a title and pictures.

 SET UP You need the NaturalLayout_start presentation located in your Chapter13 practice file folder to complete this exercise. Open the NaturalLayout_start presentation, and save it as *NaturalLayout*. Then follow the steps.

1. Switch to Slide Master view. Then with the **Title Slide** layout displayed, on the **Slide Master** tab, in the **Edit Master** group, click the **Insert Layout** button.

   PowerPoint adds a new layout after the Title Slide layout.

2. In the **Master Layout** group, click the **Insert Placeholder** arrow.

   The Placeholder gallery appears.

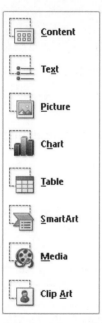

You can draw placeholders for any of these types of content.

3. In the **Placeholder** gallery, click **Text**. Then move the cross pointer over the slide, and drag to create a text placeholder the width of the title placeholder and about **3** inches high.

Use the vertical ruler to judge the placeholder's size, and drag from about the upper 1.5 inch mark to the lower 1.5 inch mark.

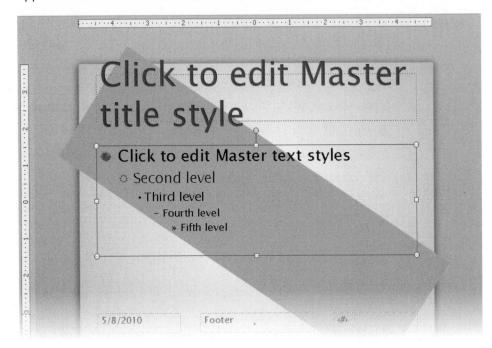

When you finish dragging, PowerPoint adds the five default bullet levels defined in the primary master to the text placeholder.

4. In the text placeholder, point to the bullet to the left of **Fifth level**, and when the cursor changes to a four-headed arrow, click to select the bullet point. Then press Delete.

5. Repeat step 4 for **Fourth level**, **Third level**, and **Second level**.

6. With the cursor at the end of the first-level bullet point, on the **Home** tab, in the **Paragraph** group, click the **Bullets** arrow. Then when the **Bullets** gallery appears, click **None**.

7. With the placeholder still selected, select all the text, and then in the **Font** group, click the **Italic** button.

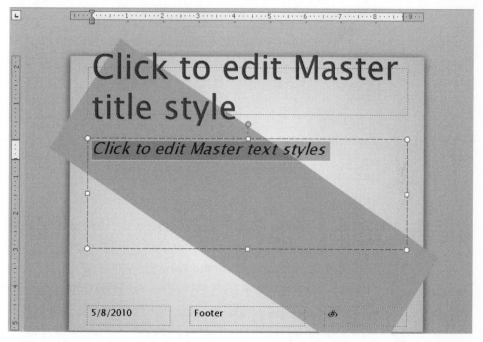

Keyboard Shortcut Press Ctrl+I to italicize the selected text.

The text placeholder is now formatted to display an italic paragraph, instead of a bulleted list.

On the horizontal ruler, the indent markers show that the paragraph is no longer formatted with a hanging indent.

8. On the **Slide Master** tab, in the **Master Layout** group, click the **Insert Layout** button to add another layout to the master set.

9. Switch to Normal view, and display slide **3**. Then select the cat, crow, and frog pictures, and copy them.

10. Switch to Slide Master view, display the new master layout (the third one), and paste in the pictures.

The pictures now appear on the layout master.

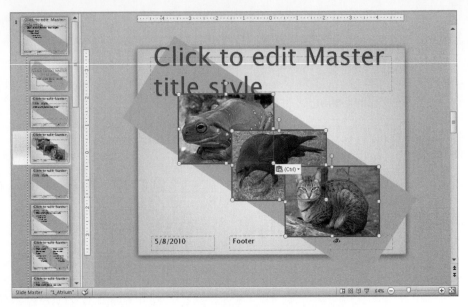

If you want the pictures to show up on all slides, paste them into the primary master instead.

To make it easier to add pictures to slides with this layout, let's replace the pictures with placeholders.

11. Click the frog picture, and on the **Format** contextual tab, in the **Arrange** group, click the **Selection Pane** button to open the **Selection and Visibility** task pane.

    Notice that the frog picture is designated as Picture 5.

12. On the **Slide Master** tab, in the **Master Layout** group, click the **Insert Placeholder** arrow, click **Picture** in the gallery, and then drag a picture placeholder directly on top of the frog picture.

    PowerPoint adds a Picture Placeholder to the Shapes On This Slide list in the Selection And Visibility task pane.

13. In the task pane, click **Picture 5**, and then press Delete.

    The frog picture is deleted, leaving the picture placeholder occupying its spot in the slide.

14. Repeat steps 11 through 13 to replace the crow and cat pictures with picture placeholders. Then close the **Selection and Visibility** task pane.

15. Select the bottom picture placeholder, and on the **Format** tab, in the **Shape Styles** group, use the **Shape Outline** command to give the placeholder a **Dark Red** frame that is **3 pt** wide.

16. Use the **Format Painter** command to copy the frame of the bottom picture placeholder to the other two picture placeholders.

This layout now accommodates any three pictures arranged diagonally on the slide.

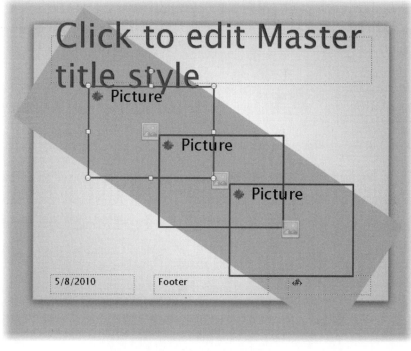

Each picture placeholder contains an Insert Picture From File button.

17. With the picture layout still selected, on the **Slide Master** tab, in the **Edit Master**
group, click the **Rename** button.

The Rename Layout dialog box opens.

The name will identify the layout in the New Slide gallery.

18. In the **Layout name** box, type **My 3-Picture**, and then click **Rename**.

19. On the **Overview** tab, point to the layout.

PowerPoint displays a ScreenTip with the name of the layout.

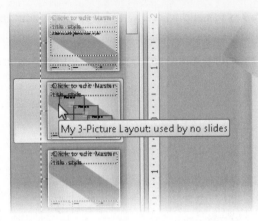

The ScreenTip also tells you how many slides are using this layout.

20. Repeat steps 17 and 18 to rename the first layout master you created as **My Text Paragraph**.

21. Switch to Normal view. Then with slide **3** selected, click the **New Slide** arrow.

The New Slide gallery appears.

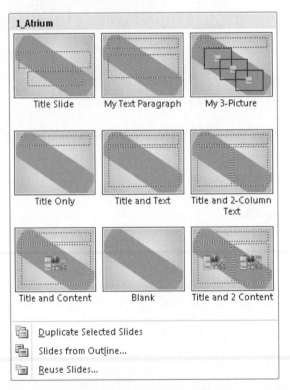

The gallery now includes your custom layouts.

22. In the gallery, click **My Text Paragraph**. Then add another slide, clicking **My 3-Picture** in the gallery.

23. Test the new layouts by adding a title and a paragraph to slide **4** and a title and pictures to slide **5**.

    We added the photographs from Rugged Country Plants that you will find in your Chapter13 practice file folder to slide 5.

This slide is based on the custom My 3-Picture layout.

CLEAN UP Save the NaturalLayout presentation, and then close it.

Saving Custom Design Templates

Suppose you have spent a lot of time customizing the masters of a particular presentation and you think you might want to use the new design for future presentations. Or suppose your company requires that all official presentations use a customized set of masters that include a logo, contact information, a specific background, and bullets and text in colors that reflect the company's branding. In cases like these, you can save a customized presentation as a design template. You can then use it as the basis for new presentations by clicking My Templates on the New page of the Backstage view and then double-clicking the custom template in the New Presentation dialog box.

Tip For a template to be available in the New Presentation dialog box, it must be stored in the default Templates folder. If you store a template in a different folder, you can browse to that folder and double-click the template file to start PowerPoint and open a new presentation based on the template.

In this exercise, you'll save a presentation as a template and then create a presentation based on the template.

SET UP You need the NaturalTemplate_start presentation located in your Chapter13 practice file folder to complete this exercise. Open the NaturalTemplate_start presentation, and save it as *NaturalTemplate*. Then follow the steps.

1. Display the **Save & Send** page of the Backstage view, and in the center pane, click **Change File Type**.

2. In the right pane, click **Template**, and then at the bottom of the pane, click **Save As**.

   The Save As dialog box opens with the Save As Type option already set to PowerPoint Template.

3. In the **File name** box, type **Natural**.

4. Navigate to your **C:\Users\<*username*>\AppData\Roaming\Microsoft\ Templates** folder, and then on the toolbar, click **New folder**.

5. With the name **New folder** selected, type **Design Templates**, and press Enter.

6. Double-click the **Design Templates** folder, and click **Save**.

   PowerPoint saves the template in the specified folder. You can now edit the template and save it as you would any other presentation.

7. With the title slide displayed, select all the text in the title placeholder, and press the Delete key. Then click away from the placeholder.

   In place of the title, you now see the instruction to click to add the presentation's title.

8. Repeat step 7 for the subtitle.

9. On the **Slides** tab in the **Overview** pane, click slide **2**. Then hold down the Shift key, and click slide **5**.

10. With slides **2** through **5** selected, press Delete.

    The template now contains only the title slide.

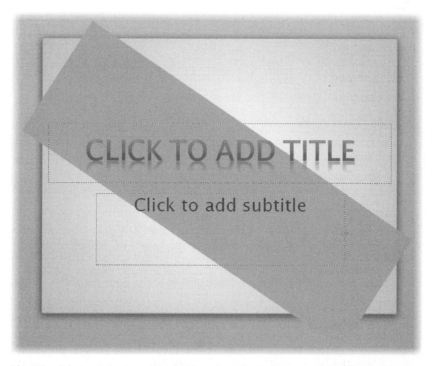

The title slide contains two placeholders that are empty except for placeholder instructions.

11. On the Quick Access Toolbar, click the **Save** button, and then close the template.

    Keyboard Shortcut Press Ctrl+S to save the presentation.

12. Display the **New** page of the Backstage view, and in the top row of the center pane, click **My templates**.

13. When the **New Presentation** dialog box opens, click the **Design Templates** tab, and then click (don't double-click) the **Natural** template.

PowerPoint displays a thumbnail of the template in the Preview pane.

The three buttons above the Preview pane control the view of the template files listed in the left pane. You can display the files in Large Icons, List, or Details view.

14. Click **OK**.

PowerPoint opens a new presentation based on your custom template.

Tip If the Document Information Panel opens so that you can enter properties for this new presentation, click the Close button at the right end of the title bar to close it.

15. On the **Home** tab, in the **Slides** group, click the **New Slide** arrow, and then in the **New Slide** gallery, click the **My Text Paragraph** layout.

16. Add one slide of each layout to the presentation, and then display each in turn to see what it looks like.

✖ CLEAN UP Close the presentation without saving your changes.

Key Points

- If the themes, color schemes, and font sets that come with PowerPoint 2010 don't meet your needs, you can create your own and then make any combination available to all your presentations as a custom theme.

- The slide master set controls the basic design of all slides in a presentation. You can make global changes by editing text and objects on the primary master and on the layout variations in the set.

- To create your own layouts, you can manipulate existing objects on the masters. Or you can add an entirely new layout and build it from scratch.

- After setting up a presentation to look the way you want, you can save it as a design template for use as the basis for other presentations.

Chapter at a Glance

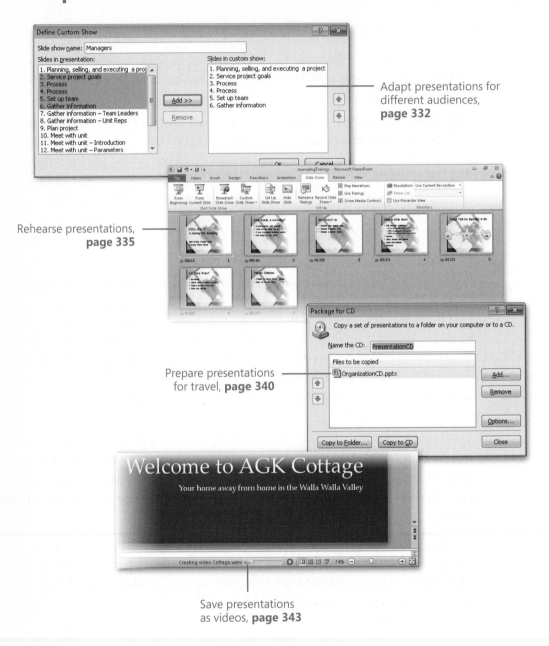

Adapt presentations for different audiences, **page 332**

Rehearse presentations, **page 335**

Prepare presentations for travel, **page 340**

Save presentations as videos, **page 343**

14 Prepare for Delivery

In this chapter, you will learn how to

✔ Adapt presentations for different audiences.

✔ Rehearse presentations.

✔ Prepare presentations for travel.

✔ Save presentations as videos.

The goal of all the effort involved in creating a presentation is to be able to effectively deliver it to a specific audience. With Microsoft PowerPoint 2010, you can deliver presentations in several different ways, and you need to prepare the presentation accordingly to ensure its success.

If your presentation will be delivered in person, you might want to hide individual slides that are not appropriate to show to all audiences. If you know that you'll be giving variations of the same presentation to different audiences, you can prepare a master set of slides and then save subsets as separate presentations that you'll show to each type of audience. You can tailor the speed at which slides appear, to appropriately fit your presentation to the allotted time. Finally, if you are delivering the presentation at a remote location, you'll want to use the Package For CD feature to ensure that you take all the necessary files with you.

If you cannot travel to deliver your presentation in person to an audience in a remote location or if your audience is in scattered locations, you might want to save your presentation as a video so that you can distribute it over your network or via the Web. This new PowerPoint 2010 capability makes it easy to reach a wide audience with little extra effort.

In this chapter, you'll adapt a presentation for two audiences, first by creating a custom slide show, and then by hiding a slide. You'll rehearse a presentation so that you can have PowerPoint set slide timings. You'll also save a presentation package on a CD. Finally, you'll save a presentation as a video.

> **Practice Files** Before you can complete the exercises in this chapter, you need to copy the book's practice files to your computer. The practice files you'll use to complete the exercises in this chapter are in the Chapter14 practice file folder. A complete list of practice files is provided in "Using the Practice Files" at the beginning of this book.

Adapting Presentations for Different Audiences

If you plan to deliver variations of the same presentation to different audiences, you should prepare one presentation containing all the slides you are likely to need for all the audiences. Then you can select slides from the presentation that are appropriate for a particular audience and group them as a custom slide show. When you need to deliver the presentation for that audience, you open the main presentation and show the subset of slides by choosing the custom slide show from a list.

For example, suppose you need to pitch an idea for a new product or service to both a team of project managers and a company's executive team. Many of the slides would be the same for both groups, but the presentation to the executive team would include more in-depth competitive and financial analysis. You would develop the executive team's presentation first and then create a custom slide show for the project managers by using a subset of the slides in the executive presentation.

During a presentation, you might sometimes want to be able to make an on-the-spot decision about whether to display a particular slide. You can give yourself this flexibility by hiding the slide so that you can skip over it if its information doesn't seem useful to a particular audience. If you decide to include the slide's information in the presentation, you can display it by pressing the letter H or by using the Go To Slide command.

In this exercise, you'll select slides from an existing presentation to create a custom slide show for a different audience. You'll also hide a slide and then see how to display it when necessary.

SET UP You need the SeviceShows_start presentation located in your Chapter14 practice file folder to complete this exercise. Open the ServiceShows_start presentation, and save it as *ServiceShows*. Then follow the steps.

Custom
Slide Show ▾

1. On the **Slide Show** tab, in the **Start Slide Show** group, click the **Custom Slide Show** button, and then click **Custom Shows**.

    The Custom Shows dialog box opens.

2. Click **New**.

    The Define Custom Show dialog box opens.

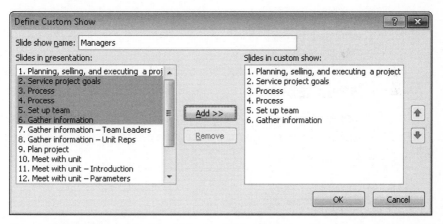

The default custom show name is selected in the Slide Show Name box.

3. In the **Slide show name** box, type **Managers**.

4. In the **Slides in presentation** list, click slide **1**, and then click **Add**.

    Slide 1 appears as Slide 1 in the Slides In Custom Show box on the right.

5. In the **Slides in presentation** list, click slide **2**, hold down the Shift key, and click slide **6**. Then click **Add**.

    The slides appear in sequential order in the Slides In Custom Show box on the right.

You can change the order of the slides by clicking the Up or Down arrow to the right of the Slides In Custom Show box.

6. Add slides **9**, **10**, and **14** through **16**, and then click **OK**.

    Of the 16 slides in the presentation, you have chosen 11 to show to managers.

7. In the **Custom Shows** dialog box, click **Show** to start the custom slide show.

8. Click the mouse button to advance through all the slides, including the blank one at the end of the show.

9. In Normal view, on the **Slide Show** tab, in the **Start Slide Show** group, click the **Custom Slide Show** button.

   The Managers custom show has been added to the list. Clicking this option will run the custom slide show.

10. In the list, click **Custom Shows**.

11. In the **Custom Shows** dialog box, verify that **Managers** is selected, and then click **Edit**.

   The Define Custom Show dialog box opens.

12. In the **Slides in custom show** list, click slide **3**, and then click **Remove**.

   PowerPoint removes the slide from the custom slide show, but not from the main presentation.

13. Click **OK** to close the **Define Custom Show** dialog box, and then click **Close** to close the **Custom Shows** dialog box.

14. On the **Slides** tab of the **Overview** pane, click slide **3**, and then in the **Set Up** group, click the **Hide Slide** button.

   On the Slides tab, PowerPoint puts a box with a diagonal line around the number 3, and dims the slide contents to indicate that it is hidden.

Slide 3 is hidden.

Tip You can also right-click the slide thumbnail and then click Hide Slide.

15. Display slide **2**, and switch to Reading view. Then click the **Next** button.

    Because slide 3 is hidden, PowerPoint skips from slide 2 to slide 4.

16. Click the **Previous** button to move back to slide **2**.

17. Right-click anywhere on the screen, point to **Go to Slide**, and then click **(3) Process**.

    The number is in parentheses because the slide is hidden. When you click it, the hidden slide appears in Reading view.

18. Press Esc to return to Normal view.

✖ **CLEAN UP** Save the ServiceShows presentation, and then close it.

Rehearsing Presentations

As you already know, when delivering a presentation, you can move from slide to slide manually by clicking the mouse button, pressing keys, or clicking commands, or you can have PowerPoint display each slide for a predefined length of time and then display the next slide. In automatically advancing presentations, the length of time a slide appears on the screen is controlled by its slide timing.

To apply a timing to one slide, to a group of slides, or to an entire presentation, you first select the slides, and then under Advance Slide in the Timing group on the Transitions tab, you select the After check box and enter the number of minutes and/or seconds you want each slide to remain on the screen. By default, each slide timing is divided equally among the animated items on that particular slide. So if a slide has a title and four bullet points that are all animated and you assign a timing of 1 minute to the slide, the five elements will appear at 12-second intervals.

Tip If you are delivering the presentation in Slide Show view and want to prevent PowerPoint from advancing to the next slide according to a slide timing, press the letter S on your keyboard, or right-click the current slide and click Pause. To continue the presentation, press the letter S again, or right-click the slide and click Resume.

If you don't know how much time to allocate for the slide timings of a presentation, you can rehearse the presentation while PowerPoint automatically tracks and sets the timings for you, reflecting the amount of time you spend on each slide during the rehearsal. During the presentation, PowerPoint displays each slide for the length of time you indicated during the rehearsal. In this way, you can synchronize an automatic slide show with a live narration or demonstration.

In this exercise, you'll set the timing for one slide and then apply it to an entire presentation. Then you'll rehearse the presentation and have PowerPoint set slide timings according to the amount of time you display each slide during the rehearsal.

SET UP You need the JournalingTimings_start presentation located in your Chapter14 practice file folder to complete this exercise. Open the JournalingTimings_start presentation, and save it as *JournalingTimings*. Then follow the steps.

1. On the **Transitions** tab, in the **Timing** group, in the **Advance Slide** area, select the **After** check box, and then at the right end of the adjacent box, click the up arrow three times to change the setting to **00:03.00**.

   Because both check boxes in the Advance Slide area are selected, the slide will advance either after 3 seconds or when you click the mouse button.

   Tip The ability to click the mouse in addition to setting slide timings is useful when you're running short on time during a presentation and need to speed things up.

2. On the **View Shortcuts** toolbar, click the **Reading View** button.

   Slide 1 is displayed for 3 seconds, and then PowerPoint moves to slide 2.

3. Press Esc to return to Normal view, and then on the **View Shortcuts** toolbar, click the **Slide Sorter** button.

   Below the lower-left corner of slide 1 is the slide timing you just applied.

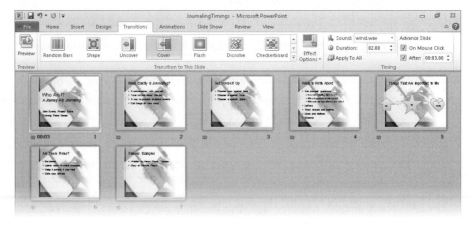

Slide 1 is the only slide with a slide timing.

Troubleshooting The appearance of buttons and groups on the ribbon changes depending on the width of the program window. For information about changing the appearance of the ribbon to match our screen images, see "Modifying the Display of the Ribbon" at the beginning of this book.

Apply To All **4.** With slide **1** selected, in the **Timing** group, click the **Apply To All** button.

The slide timing you applied to slide 1 is now applied to all the slides.

Tip When you click Apply To All, all the transition effects of the current slide are copied to the other slides. If you have applied different transitions to different slides, those individually specified transitions are overwritten. So it's a good idea to apply all the effects that you want the slides to have in common first. Then you can select individual slides and customize their effects. For information about transitions, see "Adding Transitions" in Chapter 5, "Add Simple Visual Enhancements."

5. Switch to Reading view, watch as the slides advance, and then when the black screen is displayed, click the mouse button to return to Slide Sorter view.

6. Select slide **1**. In the **Advance Slide** area of the **Timing** group, clear the **After** check box, and then click **Apply To All**.

The slide timings disappear from below the slides.

7. With slide **1** selected, on the **Slide Show** tab, in the **Set Up** group, click the **Rehearse Timings** button.

PowerPoint switches to Slide Show view, starts the presentation, and displays the Rehearsal toolbar in the upper-left corner of the screen.

Recording
0:00:01   0:00:01

A Slide Time counter is timing the length of time slide 1 remains on the screen.

8. Wait several seconds, and then on the **Rehearsal** toolbar, click the **Next** button.

The counter starts over at 0:00:00.

9. Work your way slowly through the presentation, clicking **Next** to move to the next slide.

Let's repeat the rehearsal for the current slide.

10. On the **Rehearsal** toolbar, click the **Repeat** button to reset the slide time for that slide to 0:00:00.

A message appears, advising that the recording has been paused.

11. In the message box, click **Resume Recording**.

Tip If you want to start the entire rehearsal over again, click the Close button on the Rehearsal toolbar, and when a message asks whether you want to keep the existing timings, click No.

When you reach the end of the presentation, a message box displays the elapsed time for the presentation and asks whether you want to apply the recorded slide timings.

12. Click **Yes**.

    The screen switches back to Slide Sorter view.

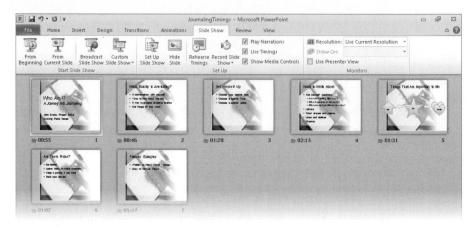

The recorded timings have been added below each slide.

13. Click the **Transitions** tab.

    The timing for the active slide, slide 1, appears in the After box in the Advance Slide area of the Timing group.

14. If the **After** setting for slide **1** is not a whole second, click the **Up** button to the right of the box to adjust the time up to the next whole second.

    You can manually adjust the timing of any slide by selecting it and changing the setting in this box.

15. Switch to Reading view.

    The slides advance according to the recorded timings.

16. Press Esc at any time to stop the presentation.

✖ CLEAN UP Save the JournalingTimings presentation, and then close it.

Recording Presentations

For a really smooth delivery, you might want to record your presentation so that you can hear yourself in action and correct any flaws before you have to perform before a live audience. You might also want to record a presentation that people will view on their own computers rather than at a speaker-led meeting. When you record a presentation, you can specify whether you want to record only slide and animation timings or only narrations and laser pointer movements, and you can record an entire presentation or only a specific slide.

To record a presentation:

1. Ensure that your computer has a sound card, microphone, and speakers. Test the microphone before beginning the recording.

2. Open the presentation you want to record.

3. With slide 1 displayed, on the Slide Show tab, in the Set Up group, click the Record Slide Show button.

   Tip If you don't want to record the entire presentation, click the Record Slide Show arrow, and then click Start Recording From Current Slide.

   The Record Slide Show dialog box opens.

4. If you don't want to record timings or narrations and laser pointer movements, clear the corresponding check box. Then click Start Recording.

   PowerPoint switches to Slide Show view, starts the presentation, and displays the Recording toolbar in the upper-left corner of the screen. A Slide Time counter tracks the length of time the slide remains on the screen.

5. Discuss the points associated with the current slide, just as if you were delivering the presentation to a live audience, and then on the shadow navigation toolbar in the lower-left corner of the screen, click the Next button to move to the next slide.

   Tip You can pause the recording by clicking the Pause button on the Recording toolbar, and you can repeat the recording for the current slide by clicking the Repeat button. You can stop recording by pressing the Esc key.

6. When you have finished delivering the presentation, press the Esc key to stop recording.

   The presentation is displayed in Slide Sorter view. The narration appears on each slide as a sound object and the slide timings appear below the lower-left corner of each slide.

7. Test the recording by running the presentation in Reading view.

   Each slide is accompanied by its recorded narration.

If you are not satisfied with the narration for a particular slide, you can delete its sound icon just like any other object, and then record that slide again.

If you are archiving a presentation and want to add comments to a specific slide, you don't have to record the entire presentation. Click the slide in Normal view, and on the Insert tab, in the Media group, click the Audio arrow, and then click Record Audio. After recording your comments, name the sound file for that slide, and click OK. The narration is then attached to a sound icon on the slide.

Preparing Presentations for Travel

When you develop a presentation on the computer from which you'll be delivering it, you'll have all the fonts, linked objects, and other components of the presentation available when the lights go down and you launch your first slide. However, if you'll deliver your presentation from a different computer, you need to ensure that the fonts, linked objects, and any other necessary items will all be available when you need them.

With PowerPoint 2010, you can use the updated Package For CD feature to help you gather all the presentation components and save them to a CD or other type of removable media so that they can be transported to a different computer. Linked and embedded items, such as fonts, sounds, videos, and any other files used by the presentation are included in the presentation package by default. You also have the option of assigning a password to open or modify the presentation, and of using the Document Inspector to remove any personal or confidential information from the packaged file.

Tip PowerPoint 2010 does not support the direct burning of content to a DVD. If you prefer to burn to a DVD rather than a CD, first use the Package For CD feature to create a presentation package in a folder on your computer, and then use DVD-burning software to copy the package to the DVD.

You can add more than one presentation to the same presentation package, and you can include files not specifically related to the presentation. If you add more than one presentation, you can specify the order in which the presentations should run. PowerPoint assembles all the files, adds an autorun file, and creates a folder of supporting files.

To run a packaged presentation from CD on a computer that does not have PowerPoint 2010 installed, you need the Microsoft PowerPoint Viewer. With previous versions of PowerPoint, the PowerPoint Viewer was automatically included with the packaged presentation. However, the Viewer cannot run presentations saved in the new PowerPoint 2010 format from a CD; it must be installed on the computer. So before you can use PowerPoint Viewer, you need to download and install it from the Microsoft Download Center Web site.

Tip When you insert the presentation CD into your CD/DVD drive, the AutoPlay dialog box opens so that you can indicate whether you want to display an HTML introductory screen (called a *splash screen*) for the presentation. This screen provides a link for downloading the Viewer. After the Viewer is installed, clicking the name of the presentation on the HTML splash screen theoretically runs the presentation. However, at the time of writing, the Viewer downloaded by following this process does not work with presentations in PowerPoint 2010 format. This issue might have been resolved by the time you read this book.

In this exercise, you'll use Package For CD to create a presentation package on a CD.

→ **SET UP** You need the OrganizationCD_start presentation and the Procedures document located in your Chapter14 practice file folder to complete this exercise. Be sure to have a blank CD available. If your computer does not have a CD/DVD burner, you can follow along with the exercise by creating a presentation package in a folder. Open the OrganizationCD_start presentation, and save it as *OrganizationCD*. Then follow the steps.

1. Display the **Save & Send** page of the Backstage view, click **Package Presentation for CD**, and then click **Package for CD**.

   The Package For CD dialog box opens.

   You can add files or remove files from the Files To Be Copied list.

2. In the **Name the CD** box, type **Organization**.

3. Click **Options**.

   The Options dialog box opens.

   By default, the presentation's linked files, and embedded TrueType fonts will be included in the presentation package.

Tip Be sure to leave the Embedded TrueType Fonts check box selected if the presentation includes fonts that don't come with the version of Windows running on the presentation computer or with the Microsoft Office 2010 programs. Then the presentation will look the same on a computer on which the fonts aren't installed as it does on your computer. You can embed fonts when you package a presentation, or you can do it when you first save the presentation. (Only TrueType and OpenType fonts can be embedded.) In the Save As dialog box, click Tools, click Save Options, and on the Save page, select the Embed Fonts In The File check box. Then click Embed Only The Characters Used In The Presentation to embed only the characters in the font set that are actually used, or click Embed All Characters to embed the entire font set.

4. Select the **Inspect presentations for inappropriate or private information** check box, and then click **OK**.

5. Insert a blank CD in your CD/DVD burner, and if the **AutoPlay** dialog box opens, close it.

6. In the **Package for CD** dialog box, click **Copy to CD**.

   Troubleshooting If your computer does not have a CD/DVD burner, click Copy To Folder instead. Then in the Copy To Folder dialog box, specify the folder in which you want to store the package, clear the Open Folder When Complete check box, and click OK.

7. When PowerPoint asks you to verify that you want to include linked content, click **Yes**.

   The Document Inspector opens so that you can inspect the presentation file for personal or confidential information.

   See Also For information about the Document Inspector, see "Finalizing Presentations" in Chapter 6, "Review and Deliver Presentations."

8. Click **Inspect**. When the inspection results are displayed, click **Remove All** to the right of **Document Properties and Personal information**. Then click **Close**.

   PowerPoint copies the files required for the OrganizationCD presentation to CD and then ejects the disk.

This message tells you that the packaging operation was successful.

9. Click **No** to indicate that you don't want to copy the same package to another CD.

10. Click **Close** to close the **Package for CD** dialog box.

   If you have access to a different computer, you should now test whether you can run the presentation from the CD. If the other computer does not have PowerPoint 2010 installed on it, you might want to download and install the 2010 version of the PowerPoint Viewer, which is not available at the time of writing this book.

✖ **CLEAN UP** Close the OrganizationCD presentation.

Saving Presentations as Videos

In Chapter 12, "Share and Review Presentations," you saved a presentation as a PowerPoint show so that viewers with PowerPoint 2010 installed on their computers could click the file name and automatically open and run the presentation based on its slide timings. If you want to share a presentation with viewers who might not have PowerPoint 2010 installed on their computers, the simplest way to ensure that everyone can view the presentation is to turn it into a video.

In PowerPoint 2010, creating presentation videos couldn't be easier. However, video files can be quite large, so before you create your video, you might want to ensure that your presentation is as compact as possible by compressing pictures and media to the smallest size that is suitable for the intended use.

When you are ready to turn the presentation into a video, you simply click Create A Video on the Save & Send page of the Backstage view, and specify the following:

● The size that is most suitable for your intended output. You can choose Large or Small depending on the size of the device on which the presentation will be viewed, or Medium for presentations that will be viewed from the Internet or DVD.

● Whether to use recorded timings and narrations. If the presentation has no slide timings or narration, you are given the opportunity to create them before saving the video.

After specifying these options, you click Create Video. The Save As dialog box opens with the Save As Type option already set to Windows Media Video. Then all you have to do is name the file and specify a location. Depending on the size of the presentation and the amount of media and linked files it contains, the creation process can take quite a while, so be patient!

In this exercise, you'll save a presentation with slide timings as a video optimized for distribution via the Internet.

 SET UP You need the CottageVideo_start presentation located in your Chapter14 practice file folder to complete this exercise. Open the CottageVideo_start presentation, and save it as *CottageVideo*. Then follow the steps.

1. On slide **1**, click the photo. Then on the **Format** contextual tab, in the **Adjust** group, click the **Compress Pictures** button.

   The Compress Pictures dialog box opens.

   Compress Pictures

   Compression options:

   ☑ Apply only to this picture
   ☑ Delete cropped areas of pictures

   Target output:

   ○ Print (220 ppi): excellent quality on most printers and screens
   ○ Screen (150 ppi): good for Web pages and projectors
   ○ E-mail (96 ppi): minimize document size for sharing
   ◉ Use document resolution

   [OK]   [Cancel]

   The descriptions after each output type help you select the appropriate setting.

2. Clear the **Apply only to this picture** check box to compress all the pictures in the presentation. Then with **Use document resolution** selected, click **OK**.

   Tip For any presentation, you can compact the size of its media files by clicking Compress Media on the Info page of the Backstage view, and then choosing the intended output category.

3. Display the Backstage view, click **Save & Send**, and then in the center pane, click **Create a Video**.

   The right pane changes to display the options related to videos.

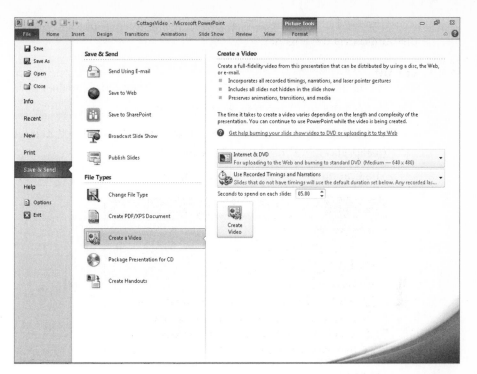

If a presentation does not have slide timings, by default each slide in the video will display for 5 seconds.

4. In the **Create a Video** pane, click **Computer & HD Displays**, and then in the list of size options, click **Internet & DVD**.

5. Click **Use Recorded Timings and Narrations**, and then click **Preview Timings and Narrations**.

    PowerPoint switches to Slide Show view and advances the slides according to their slide timings.

6. Press Esc to return to the Backstage view after you have previewed a few slides.

7. The slide timings are satisfactory, so at the bottom of the right pane, click **Create Video**.

   The Save As dialog box opens with the contents of your Chapter14 practice file folder displayed and Windows Media Video already specified as the file format.

8. In the **Save As** dialog box, name the file **Cottage**, and click **Save**.

   A progress bar on the status bar indicates that the video is being created in the background.

You cannot close the presentation during this process.

9. When the **Creating** progress bar disappears, open Windows Explorer, navigate to your **Chapter14** practice file folder, and double-click **Cottage**.

   The video begins.

10. Click the **Close** button to end the video.

 CLEAN UP Close Windows Explorer, and then save and close the CottageVideo presentation.

Key Points

- For a particular audience, you can create a custom slide show that uses a subset of the slides in a presentation. You can also hide slides and then display them only if appropriate.

- You can assign timings to slides manually, or you can rehearse the presentation and record the slide timings from the rehearsal.

- To run a presentation on a different computer, you can create a presentation package that includes all the required files. PowerPoint does not have to be installed on the other computer if you download the PowerPoint Viewer.

- You can distribute a free-standing presentation by saving it as a video.

Chapter at a Glance

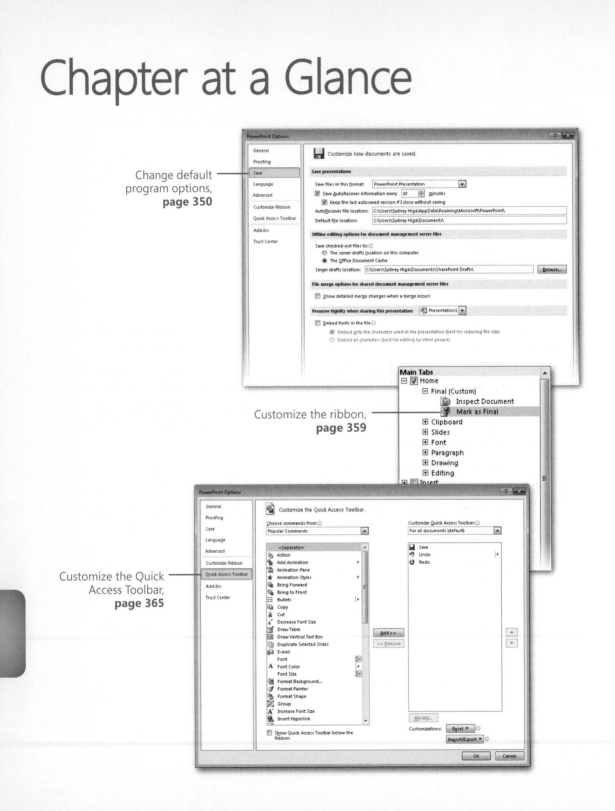

Change default program options, **page 350**

Customize the ribbon, **page 359**

Customize the Quick Access Toolbar, **page 365**

15 Customize PowerPoint

In this chapter, you will learn how to

✔ Change default program options.

✔ Customize the ribbon.

✔ Customize the Quick Access Toolbar.

If you use Microsoft PowerPoint 2010 only occasionally, you might be perfectly happy creating new presentations with the wide range of tools we have already discussed in this book. And you might be comfortable with the default working environment options and behind-the-scenes settings. However, if you create a lot of presentations of various types, you might find yourself wishing that you could streamline the development process or change aspects of the program to make it more suitable for the kinds of presentations you create.

In this chapter, you'll take a tour of the pages of the PowerPoint Options dialog box to understand the ways in which you can customize the program. Then you'll manipulate the ribbon and the Quick Access Toolbar to put the tools you need for your daily work at your fingertips.

> **Practice Files** Before you can complete the exercises in this chapter, you need to copy the book's practice files to your computer. The practice files you'll use to complete the exercises in this chapter are in the Chapter15 practice file folder. A complete list of practice files is provided in "Using the Practice Files" at the beginning of this book.

Changing Default Program Options

In earlier chapters, we mentioned that you can change settings in the PowerPoint Options dialog box to customize the PowerPoint environment in various ways. After you work with PowerPoint for a while, you might want to refine more settings to tailor the program to the way you work. Knowing which settings are where in the PowerPoint Options dialog box makes the customizing process more efficient.

In this exercise, you'll open the PowerPoint Options dialog box and explore several of the available pages.

SET UP You don't need any practice files to complete this exercise. With a blank presentation open and active, follow the steps.

Tip As you work your way through this exercise, don't worry if the settings in your Word Options dialog box are different from ours. Settings can vary depending on changes you might have made while working through the exercises and depending on which programs you have installed.

1. On the **Home** tab, in the **Font** group, point to the **Bold** button.

   PowerPoint displays a ScreenTip.

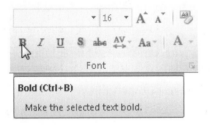

   By default, ScreenTips includes the button name, its keyboard shortcut, and a description of its purpose.

   In a minute, we'll change a setting in the PowerPoint Options dialog box that controls the display of ScreenTips.

2. Display the Backstage view, and click **Options**.

   The PowerPoint Options dialog box opens, displaying the General page.

The General page of the PowerPoint Options dialog box.

If having the Mini Toolbar appear when you select text is more of a hindrance than a help, you can disable that feature by clearing the Show Mini Toolbar On Selection check box. Similarly, you can disable the live preview of styles and formatting by clearing the Enable Live Preview check box.

3. Under **User Interface options**, display the **Color scheme** list, and click **Black**.

4. Display the **ScreenTip style** list, and click **Don't show feature descriptions in ScreenTips**.

5. Under **Personalize your copy of Microsoft Office**, verify that the **User name** and **Initials** are correct, or change them to the way you want them to appear.

6. Click **OK** to close the PowerPoint Options dialog box.

   The program window elements are now black and shades of gray.

7. In the **Font** group, point to the **Bold** button.

The ScreenTip now includes only the button name and its keyboard shortcut.

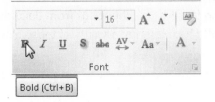

The customized ScreenTip.

8. Open the **PowerPoint Options** dialog box, and in the left pane, click **Proofing**.

This page provides options for adjusting the AutoCorrect settings and for refining the spell-checking and grammar-checking processes.

See Also For information about AutoCorrect and checking spelling, see "Checking Spelling and Choosing the Best Words" in Chapter 3, "Work with Slide Text."

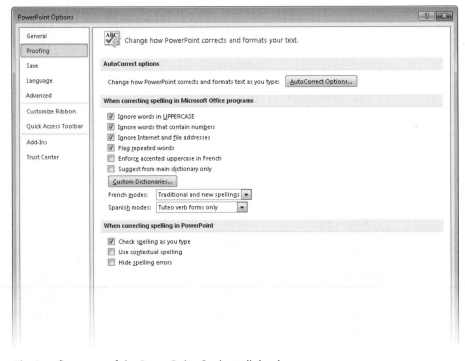

The Proofing page of the PowerPoint Options dialog box.

9. Display the **Save** page.

On this page, you can change the default presentation format; the AutoRecover file save rate and location; the default location to which PowerPoint saves files you create; and the default location for files you check out from document management servers (such as Microsoft SharePoint) and drafts of those files saved while you are working offline.

Tip Although we mention SharePoint in "Collaborating with Other People" in Chapter 12, "Share and Review Presentations," a discussion of SharePoint is beyond the scope of this book.

The Save page of the PowerPoint Options dialog box.

The Save page also has options for specifying whether you want the fonts used within the current presentation to be embedded in the presentation, in the event that someone who opens the presentation doesn't have those fonts on his or her computer.

10. Under **Save presentations**, display the **Save files in this format** list.

   One of the format options is the PowerPoint Presentation 97-2003 format that creates .ppt files compatible with earlier versions of PowerPoint. If you have upgraded to PowerPoint 2010 but your colleagues are still working in an earlier version of the program, you might want to select this option so that they will be able to view and work with any presentation you create.

   Tip If you want to save just one presentation in a format that is compatible with earlier versions of the program, you can click PowerPoint 97-2003 Presentation in the Save As Type list of the Save As dialog box.

11. Click away from the list to close it, and then display the **Language** page.

   If you create presentations for international audiences, you can make additional editing languages available on this page. You can also specify the Display, Help, and ScreenTip languages.

The Language page of the PowerPoint Options dialog box.

12. Display the **Advanced** page.

    This page includes options related to editing presentation content; displaying presentations on-screen; printing, saving, and sharing presentations; and a variety of other options. Although these options are labeled *Advanced*, they are the ones you're most likely to want to adjust to suit the way you work.

The Advanced page of the PowerPoint Options dialog box.

13. Take a few minutes to explore all the options on this page.

14. Skipping over Customize Ribbon and Quick Access Toolbar, which we discuss in later topics in this chapter, click **Add-Ins**.

   This page displays all the active and inactive add-ins installed on your computer. You can add new ones and remove any you no longer need from this page.

The Add-Ins page of the PowerPoint Options dialog box.

See Also For information about add-ins, see the sidebar "Using Add-ins" at the end of this topic.

15. Display the **Trust Center** page.

   This page provides links to information about privacy and security. It also provides access to the Trust Center settings that control the actions PowerPoint takes in response to presentations that are provided by certain people or companies, that are saved in certain locations, or that contain ActiveX controls or macros.

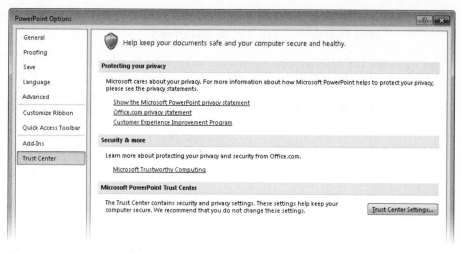

The Trust Center page of the PowerPoint Options dialog box.

16. Under **Microsoft PowerPoint Trust Center**, click **Trust Center Settings**, and then in the left pane of the **Trust Center** dialog box, click **Trusted Locations**.

On this page, you can specify locations from which PowerPoint won't block content.

The Trusted Locations page of the Trust Center dialog box.

17. Explore the other pages of the **Trust Center** dialog box, and then click **Cancel** to return to the **PowerPoint Options** dialog box.

CLEAN UP Reverse any changes you don't want to keep before moving on. Then close the PowerPoint Options dialog box.

Using Add-ins

Add-ins are utilities that add specialized functionality to a program (but aren't full-fledged programs themselves). PowerPoint includes two primary types of add-ins: COM add-ins (which use the Component Object Model) and PowerPoint add-ins.

There are several sources of add-ins:

- You can purchase add-ins from third-party vendors—for example, you can purchase an add-in that allows you to assign keyboard shortcuts to PowerPoint commands that don't already have them.
- You can download free add-ins from the Microsoft Web site or other Web sites.
- When installing a third-party program, you might install an add-in to allow it to interface with Microsoft Office 2010 programs.

Important Be careful when downloading add-ins from Web sites other than those you trust. Add-ins are executable files that can easily be used to spread viruses and otherwise wreak havoc on your computer. For this reason, default settings in the Trust Center intervene when you attempt to download or run add-ins.

To use some add-ins, you must first install them on your computer and then load them into your computer's memory, as follows:

1. At the bottom of the Add-Ins page of the PowerPoint Options dialog box, display the Manage list, click either COM Add-ins or PowerPoint Add-ins, and then click Go.

   An Add-Ins dialog box corresponding to the type of add-in you chose opens.

2. In the dialog box, click Add or Add New.

3. In the Add Add-In dialog box, navigate to the folder where the add-in you want to install is stored, and double-click its name.

   In the Add-Ins dialog box, the new add-in appears in the list of those that are available for use.

4. In the list, select the check box of the new add-in, and then click OK or Load.

   The add-in is now loaded and available for use in PowerPoint.

Customizing the Ribbon

Even if PowerPoint 2010 is the first version of the program you have ever worked with, you will by now be accustomed to working with commands represented as buttons on the ribbon. The ribbon was designed to make all the commonly used commands visible, so that people could more easily discover the full potential of the program. But many people use PowerPoint to perform the same set of tasks all the time, and for them, the visibility of buttons (or even entire groups of buttons) that they never use is just another form of clutter.

See Also For information about minimizing and expanding the ribbon, see "Customizing the Quick Access Toolbar" later in this chapter.

Would you prefer to see fewer commands, not more? Or would you prefer to see more specialized groups of commands? Well, you can. Clicking Customize Ribbon in the left pane of the PowerPoint Options dialog box displays the Customize Ribbon page, which is new in PowerPoint 2010.

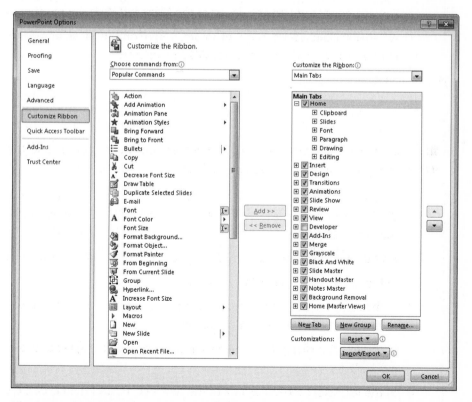

The Customize Ribbon page of the PowerPoint Options dialog box.

On this page, you can customize the ribbon in the following ways:

● If you rarely use a tab, you can turn it off.

● If you use the commands in only a few groups on each tab, you can remove the groups you don't use. (The group is not removed from the program, just from its tab.)

● You can move a predefined group by removing it from one tab and then adding it to another.

● You can duplicate a predefined group by adding it to another tab.

● You can create a custom group on any tab and then add commands to it. (You cannot add commands to a predefined group.)

● For the ultimate in customization, you can create a custom tab. For example, you might want to do this if you use only a few commands from each tab and you find it inefficient to flip between them.

Don't be afraid to experiment with the ribbon to come up with the configuration that best suits the way you work. If at any point you find that your new ribbon is harder to work with rather than easier, you can always reset everything back to the default configuration.

Tip If you have upgraded from PowerPoint 2003 or an earlier version, you might identify a few commands that no longer seem to be available. A few old features have been abandoned, but others that people used only rarely have simply been pushed off to one side. If you sorely miss one of these sidelined features, you can make it a part of your PowerPoint environment by adding it to the ribbon. You can find a list of all the commands that do not appear on the ribbon but are still available in PowerPoint by displaying the Customize Ribbon page of the PowerPoint Options dialog box and then clicking Commands Not In The Ribbon in the Choose Commands From list.

In this exercise, you'll turn off tabs, remove groups, create a custom group, and add a command to the new group. Then you'll create a tab and move predefined groups of buttons to it. Finally, you'll reset the ribbon to its default state.

SET UP You need the ColorNew_start presentation located in your Chapter15 practice file folder to complete this exercise. Open the ColorNew_start presentation, and save it as *ColorNew*. Then follow the steps.

1. Open the **PowerPoint Options** dialog box, and then click **Customize Ribbon**.

   The Customize Ribbon page is displayed.

2. In the right pane, clear the check boxes of the **Insert**, **Design**, **Transitions**, **Animations**, and **Slide Show** tabs. Then click **OK**.

   The ribbon now displays only the File, Home, Review, and View tabs.

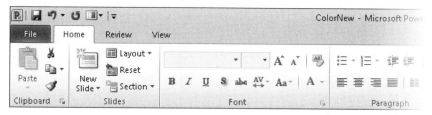

You cannot turn off the File tab.

3. Redisplay the **Customize Ribbon** page of the **PowerPoint Options** dialog box, and in the right pane, select the **Design** check box. Then click the plus sign to display the groups on this tab.

4. Above the left pane, display the **Choose commands from** list, and click **Main Tabs**. Then in the pane below, click the plus sign adjacent to **Design** to display the groups that are predefined for this tab.

5. In the right pane, click the **Page Setup** group, and then click **Remove**.

   The group is removed from the Design tab on the ribbon (the pane on the right), but is still available in the pane on the left. You can add it back to the Design tab, or add it to a different tab, at any time.

6. If the **Home** group is not expanded in the right pane, click the plus sign adjacent to **Home** to displays its groups, and then click the word **Home**.

7. Below the right pane, click **New Group**. When the **New Group (Custom)** group is added to the bottom of the Home group list, click **Rename**, type Final in the **Display name** box, and click **OK**. Then click the **Move Up** button until the **Final** group is at the top of the groups list.

Because of its location in the hierarchy, the new group will appear at the left end of the Home tab.

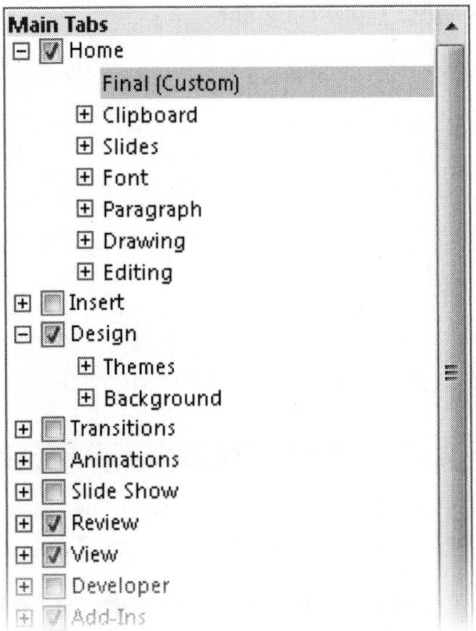

```
Main Tabs
☐ ☑ Home
        Final (Custom)
        ⊞ Clipboard
        ⊞ Slides
        ⊞ Font
        ⊞ Paragraph
        ⊞ Drawing
        ⊞ Editing
⊞ ☐ Insert
☐ ☑ Design
        ⊞ Themes
        ⊞ Background
⊞ ☐ Transitions
⊞ ☐ Animations
⊞ ☐ Slide Show
⊞ ☑ Review
⊞ ☑ View
⊞ ☐ Developer
⊞ ☑ Add-Ins
```

You have created a custom group on the Home tab.

8. Above the pane on the left, display the **Choose commands from** list, and click **File Tab**.

The available commands list changes to include only the commands that are available in the Backstage view, which you display by clicking the File tab.

9. In the available commands list, click **Inspect Document**, and click **Add**. Then repeat this step to add **Mark as Final**.

The two commands are added to the custom group.

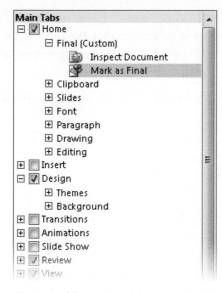

You can add commands to a custom group, but not to a predefined group.

10. In the pane on the right, remove the **Font**, **Paragraph**, and **Drawing** groups from the **Home** tab.

11. Click the word **Home**, and then below the pane, click **New Tab**.

    A new tab is added to the right pane and is selected for display on the ribbon. It has automatically been given one custom group.

12. Remove the custom group from the **New Tab (Custom)**.

13. Click **New Tab (Custom)**, and then click **Rename**. In the **Rename** dialog box, type **Formatting** in the **Display name** box, and click **OK**.

14. Display **Main Tabs** in the pane on the left, and then expand the **Home** and **Design** tabs.

15. With the new **Formatting (Custom)** tab selected in the right pane, add the **Font**, **Paragraph**, and **Drawing** groups from **Home** in the left pane, and then add **Page Setup** from **Design**.

    The right pane now shows the new configuration of the Home, Formatting, and Design tabs.

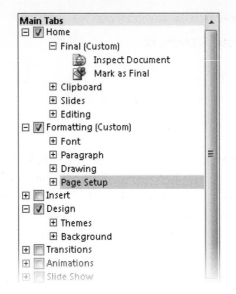

You have moved groups from the Home and Design tabs to a new Formatting tab.

16. In the **PowerPoint Options** dialog box, click **OK**.

    The Home tab displays the new Final group.

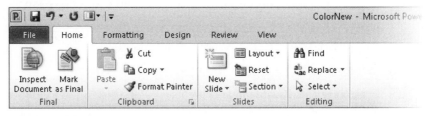

The custom Home tab.

17. With the title of slide **1** selected, click the **Formatting** tab.

    The formatting commands are now collected on the Formatting tab.

The custom Formatting tab.

18. Display the **Customize Ribbon** page of the **PowerPoint Options** dialog box. In the lower-right corner, click **Reset**, and then click **Reset all customizations**. Then in the message box asking you to confirm that you want to delete all ribbon and Quick Access Toolbar customizations, click **Yes**.

19. Click **OK** to close the **PowerPoint Options** dialog box.

The default ribbon configuration is restored.

❌ **CLEAN UP** Close the ColorNew presentation.

Customizing the Quick Access Toolbar

By default, the Save, Undo, and Repeat/Redo buttons appear on the Quick Access Toolbar. If you regularly use a few buttons that are scattered on various tabs of the ribbon and you don't want to switch between tabs to access the buttons or crowd your ribbon with a custom tab, you might want to add these frequently used buttons to the Quick Access Toolbar. They are then always visible in the upper-left corner of the program window.

Clicking Quick Access Toolbar in the left pane of the PowerPoint Options dialog box displays the page where you specify which commands you want to appear on the toolbar.

The Quick Access Toolbar page of the PowerPoint Options dialog box.

On this page, you can customize the Quick Access Toolbar in the following ways:

● You can define a custom Quick Access Toolbar for all presentations, or you can define a custom Quick Access Toolbar for a specific presentation.

● You can add any command from any group of any tab, including contextual tabs, to the toolbar.

● You can display a separator between different types of buttons.

● You can move buttons around on the toolbar until they are in the order you want.

● You can reset everything back to the default Quick Access Toolbar configuration.

If you use only a few buttons, you can add those buttons to the Quick Access Toolbar and then hide the ribbon by double-clicking the active tab or by clicking the Minimize The Ribbon button. Only the Quick Access Toolbar and tab names remain visible. You can temporarily redisplay the ribbon by clicking the tab you want to view. You can permanently redisplay the ribbon by double-clicking any tab or by clicking the Expand The Ribbon button.

As you add buttons to the Quick Access Toolbar, it expands to accommodate them. If you add many buttons, it might become difficult to view the text in the title bar, or all the buttons on the Quick Access Toolbar might not be visible, defeating the purpose of adding them. To resolve this problem, you can move the Quick Access Toolbar below the ribbon by clicking the Customize Quick Access Toolbar button and then clicking Show Below The Ribbon.

In this exercise, you'll add a couple of buttons to the Quick Access Toolbar for all presentations, and then you'll test the buttons.

SET UP You need the BuyersSeminar_start presentation located in your Chapter15 practice file folder to complete this exercise. Open the BuyersSeminar_start presentation, and save it as *BuyersSeminar*. Then follow the steps.

1. Open the **PowerPoint Options** dialog box, and then click **Quick Access Toolbar**.

   A list of available commands appears in the pane on the left, and a list of the commands currently displayed on the Quick Access Toolbar appears in the pane on the right.

   Tip If you want to create a Quick Access Toolbar that is specific to the active presentation, on the right side of the PowerPoint Options dialog box, click the arrow at the right end of the box below Customize Quick Access Toolbar, and then click For <name of presentation>. Then any command you select will be added to that specific toolbar instead of the toolbar for all presentations.

2. At the top of the available commands list on the left, double-click **Separator**.

    You can use separator lines to divide commands into groups, making them easier to find.

3. Scroll down the available commands list, click the **Quick Print** command, and then click **Add**.

4. Repeat step 3 to add the **Text Box** command.

    The two commands have been added to the list of commands that will appear on the Quick Access Toolbar, with a separator between them and the default commands.

    The arrow to the right of the Undo command indicates that clicking this button on the Quick Access Toolbar displays a menu of options.

5. Click **OK** to close the **PowerPoint Options** dialog box.

    The Quick Access Toolbar now includes the default Save, Undo, and Repeat/Redo buttons and the custom Quick Print and Text Box buttons, separated by a line.

    You have added a separator and two buttons to the Quick Access Toolbar.

    To print a presentation with the default settings, you no longer have to click the File tab to display the Backstage view, click Print in the left pane, and then click the Print button. And to create a text box, you no longer need to switch to the Insert tab.

6. If you want to test printing from the Quick Access Toolbar, ensure that your printer is turned on, and then on the Quick Access Toolbar, click the **Quick Print** button.

    Now let's see how easy it is to create a text box when you are working primarily with the commands on a tab other than the Insert tab.

7. Display slide **4**. Then with the **Home** tab active, on the Quick Access Toolbar, click the **Text box** button.

8. On the slide, click below the bulleted list, and type These steps are critical to a successful trip. Then select the text and format it any way you want by using the commands on the active **Home** tab.

   You no longer have to switch tabs to add text box notes to slides.

9. Display the **Quick Access Toolbar** page of the **PowerPoint Options** dialog box, click **Reset**, and then click **Reset only Quick Access Toolbar**.

10. In the **Reset Customizations** message box, click **Yes** to return the Quick Access Toolbar to its default contents. Then click **OK** to close the **PowerPoint Options** dialog box.

✖ **CLEAN UP** Save the BuyersSeminar presentation, and then close it.

Key Points

- The PowerPoint environment is flexible and can be customized to meet your needs.

- Most of the settings that control the working environment are gathered on the pages of the PowerPoint Options dialog box.

- You can customize the ribbon to put precisely the presentation development tools you need at your fingertips.

- You can provide one-click access to any PowerPoint 2010 command by adding a button for it to the Quick Access Toolbar, either for all presentations or for one presentation.

Glossary

action button A ready-made button that you can insert into a presentation and use to define hyperlinks.

adjustment handle A diamond-shaped handle used to adjust the appearance but not the size of most AutoShapes. For example, you can adjust a rounded rectangle to be more or less rounded.

animation In PowerPoint, an effect that you can apply to text or an object to produce an illusion of movement.

attribute Individual items of character formatting, such as style or color, which determine how text looks.

AutoCorrect A feature that automatically detects and corrects typos, misspelled words, grammatical errors, and incorrect capitalization. You can add custom AutoCorrect entries.

background The underlying scheme, including colors, shading, texture, and graphics, that appears behind the text and objects on a slide.

bullet point An item in a list in which each list entry is preceded by a symbol, rather than by a number.

caption Descriptive text associated with a figure, photo, illustration, or screen shot.

case The capitalization (uppercase or lowercase) of a word or phrase. In title case, the first letter of all important words is capitalized. In sentence case, only the first letter of the first word is capitalized.

cell A box formed by the intersection of a row and column in a worksheet or a table, in which you enter information.

cell address The location of a cell, expressed as its column letter and row number, as in A1.

character formatting Formatting you can apply to selected text characters.

chart A diagram that plots the values in a table or worksheet.

chart area A region in a chart that is used to position chart elements, render axes, and plot data.

clip art A piece of ready-made art, often appearing as a bitmap or a combination of drawn shapes.

Clipboard A storage area shared by all Office programs where cut or copied items are stored.

color gradient A gradual progression from one color to another color, or from one shade to another shade of the same color.

color scheme A set of twelve balanced colors that you can apply to slides, notes pages, or audience handouts. A color scheme consists of light and dark background colors, light and dark text colors, six accent colors, and two colors for hyperlinks.

column Either the vertical arrangement of text into one or more side-by-side sections, or the vertical arrangement of cells in a table or worksheet.

column header In an Excel worksheet, a shaded rectangular area at the top of each column that displays a letter. You can click a column header to select an entire column. See also *row header*.

comment An annotation that is associated with text or an object to provide context-specific information or reviewer feedback.

connection points A point on a shape where another drawing object can be connected.

connector A line used to connect two or more shapes and that remains connected to those shapes.

content placeholder See *placeholder*.

contextual tab A tab containing commands that are relevant only when you have selected a particular object type. See also *tab*.

cursor A representation on the screen of the mouse pointer location.

custom slide show A set of slides extracted from a presentation to create a slide show for an audience that doesn't need to see the entire presentation.

cycle diagram A diagram that shows a continuous process.

data marker A customizable symbol or shape that identifies a data point on a chart. A data marker can be formatted with various sizes and colors.

data point An individual value plotted in a chart and represented together with other data points by bars, columns, lines, pie or doughnut slices, dots, and various other shapes referred to as *data markers*. Data markers of the same color constitute a data series.

data series Related data points that are plotted in a chart.

design template A file that contains masters that control the styles used in a presentation, including placeholder sizes and positions; background design, graphics, and color schemes; fonts; and the type and size of bullets.

destination file The file that a linked or embedded object is inserted into. The source file contains the information that is used to create the object. When you change information in a destination file, the information is not updated in the source file.

diagram A drawing that is used to present relationships between abstract ideas and data. For example, an organizational chart or a Venn diagram.

dialog box launcher On the ribbon, a button at the bottom of some groups that opens a dialog box with features related to the group.

dragging A way of moving objects by pointing to them, holding down the mouse button, moving the mouse pointer to the desired location, and releasing the button.

embedded object An object created with one program and embedded into a document created by another program. Embedding the object, rather than simply inserting or pasting it, ensures that the object retains its original format. If you double-click the embedded object, you can edit it with the toolbars and menus from the program used to create it.

encrypting To programmatically disguise content to hide its substance.

file format The structure or organization of data in a file. The file format is usually indicated by the file name extension.

file name extension A set of characters added to the end of a file name that identifies the file type or format.

First Line Indent marker The triangle-shaped control, on the top of the horizontal ruler, that indicates the position of the first line of the paragraph.

font A graphic design applied to a collection of numbers, symbols, and characters. A font describes a certain typeface, along with other qualities such as size, spacing, and pitch.

footer One or more items of information, typically at the bottom of a slide and typically containing elements such as the page number and the date.

gallery Rich, customizable list boxes that can be used to organize items by category, display them in flexible column- and row-based layouts, and represent them with images and text. Depending on the type of gallery, live preview is also supported.

graphic Any image, such as a picture, photograph, drawing, illustration, or shape, that can be placed as an object on a slide.

grayscale The spectrum (range) of shades of black in an image.

group (ribbon) A set of buttons on a tab that all relate to the same type of object or task.

grouping To assemble several objects, such as shapes, into a single unit so that they act as one object. Grouped objects can easily be moved, sized, and formatted.

handle A small circle, square, or set of dots that appears at the corner or on the side of a selected object and facilitates moving, sizing, reshaping, or other functions pertaining to the object.

handout master A template that defines the layout for the printed handout pages distributed to a presentation's audience.

Handout Master view The view from which you can change the overall look of audience handouts.

Hanging Indent marker The triangle-shaped control, on the bottom of the horizontal ruler, that indicates the left edge of the second and subsequent lines of the paragraph.

hierarchy diagram A diagram that illustrates the structure of an organization or entity.

hyperlink The text or graphic that you click to go to a file, a location in a file, or a Web site. Hyperlinks usually appear underlined and in color, but sometimes the only indication is that when you point to them, the pointer changes to a hand.

Hypertext Markup Language (HTML) An application of the Standard Generalized Markup Language (SGML) that uses tags to mark elements in a document to indicate how Web browsers should display these elements to the user and should respond to user actions.

Indent marker One of four controls located on the horizontal ruler that indicate how far text is indented from the left or right margin.

keyboard shortcut Any combination of keystrokes that can be used to perform a task that would otherwise require a mouse or other pointing device.

kiosk mode A display mode in which a single window takes over the whole screen and the desktop is inaccessible.

Left Indent marker The square-shaped control, on the bottom of the horizontal ruler, that indicates how far text is indented from the left margin.

legend A key that identifies the data series plotted in the chart.

line break A manual break that forces the text that follows it to the next line.

linked object An object that is created in a source file to which a link is inserted into a destination file, maintaining a connection between the two files. The linked object in the destination file can be updated when the source file is updated.

Live Preview A feature that temporarily displays the effect of applying a specific format to the selected element.

macro An action or a set of actions you can use to automate tasks. Macros are recorded in the Visual Basic for Applications programming language.

master A slide or page on which you define formatting for all slides or pages in a presentation. Each presentation has a set of masters for slides, as well as masters for speaker notes and audience handouts.

merging In an Excel worksheet, to combine cells to create one cell that spans two or more columns or rows.

Microsoft Office Clipboard See *Clipboard*.

Microsoft PowerPoint Viewer A viewer with which you can display presentations on a computer that does not have PowerPoint installed.

Mini Toolbar A toolbar that is typically displayed after you select text on a slide so that you can quickly format the text.

Normal view A view that displays three panes: Overview, Slide, and Notes.

notes master A template that defines the formatting and content used by speaker notes pages.

Notes Master view The view from which you can change the overall look of speaker notes pages.

Notes Page view The view in which you can add speaker notes that contain objects such as tables, charts, and graphics.

Notes pane The pane in Normal view in which you type notes that you want to accompany a slide. You print these notes as speaker notes pages.

object An item, such as a graphic, video clip, sound file, or worksheet, that can be inserted into a PowerPoint slide and then selected and modified.

Outline tab The tab of the Overview pane that shows all the text of the slides displayed as an outline.

Overview pane The pane that appears in Normal view on the left side of the program window and that contains the Slides and Outline tabs.

Package for CD A feature to help you gather all the components of a presentation and store them to a CD or another type of removable media so that they can be transported to a different computer.

paragraph formatting Formatting that controls the appearance of a paragraph. Examples include indentation, alignment, line spacing, and pagination.

password The string of characters that must be entered to open a password-protected presentation for editing.

path A sequence of folders (directories) that leads to a specific file or folder. A backslash is used to separate each folder in the path. For example, the path to a file called *invoice.txt* might be C:\Documents\July\invoice.txt.

photo album A specific kind of presentation into which you can insert and arrange collections of digital images.

picture A photograph, clip art image, illustration, or another type of image created with a program other than PowerPoint.

picture diagram A diagram that uses pictures to convey information, rather than or in addition to text.

pixel The smallest element used to form the composition of an image on a computer monitor. Computer monitors display images by drawing thousands of pixels arranged in columns and rows.

placeholder A area on a slide designed to contain a specific type of content that you supply.

plot area In a two-dimensional chart, the area bounded by the axes, including all data series. In a three-dimensional chart, the area bounded by the axes, including the data series, category names, tick-mark labels, and axis titles.

point The unit of measure for expressing the size of characters in a font, where 72 points equals 1 inch.

Presenter view A tool with which you can control a presentation on one monitor while the audience sees the presentation's slides in Slide Show view on a delivery monitor or projector screen.

process diagram A diagram that visually represents the ordered set of steps required to complete a task.

property Settings of a file that you can change, such as the file's name and read-only status, as well as attributes that you can't directly change, such as the file's size and creation date.

Quick Access Toolbar A small, customizable toolbar that displays frequently used commands.

Reading view The view in which each slide fills the screen. You can click buttons on the navigation bar to move through or jump to specific slides.

read-only A setting that allows a file to be read or copied, but not changed or saved. If you change a read-only file, you can save your changes only if you give the file a new name.

relationship diagram A diagram that shows convergent, divergent, overlapping, merging, or containment elements.

ribbon A user interface design that organizes commands into logical groups, which appear on separate tabs.

Rich Text Format (RTF) A format for text and graphics interchange that can be used with different output devices, operating environments, and operating systems.

rotating handle A small green handle that you can use to adjust the angle of rotation of a shape.

row header In an Excel worksheet, a shaded rectangular area to the left of each row containing a number. You can click a row header to select an entire row. See also *column header*.

ScreenTip A note that appears on the screen to provide information about a button, tracked change, or comment, or to display a footnote or endnote. ScreenTips also display the text that will appear if you choose to insert a date or AutoText entry.

selecting To specify, or highlight, an object or block of text so that you can manipulate or edit it in some way.

shape An object created by using drawing tools or commands.

sizing handle A small circle, square, or set of dots that appears at the corner or on the side of a selected object. You drag these handles to change the size of the object horizontally, vertically, or proportionally.

slide library A type of SharePoint document library that is optimized for storing and reusing PowerPoint slides.

slide master The set of slides that stores information about a presentation's design template, including font styles, placeholder sizes and positions, background design, and color schemes.

Slide Master view The view from which you make changes to the slide masters.

Slide pane The area in Normal view that shows the currently selected slide as it will appear in the presentation.

Slide Show view The view in which each slide fills the entire screen, the way it will when you deliver an electronic presentation to an audience.

Slide Sorter view The view in which the slides of the presentation are displayed as thumbnails so that you can easily reorganize them.

slide timing The time a slide will be displayed on the screen before PowerPoint moves to the next slide.

Slides tab The tab in the Overview pane that displays thumbnails of all the slides in the presentation.

SmartArt graphic A predefined set of shapes and text used as a basis for creating a diagram.

source file A file containing an object that is inserted in a destination file.

source program The program used to create a linked object or embedded object. To edit the object, you must have the source program installed on your computer.

splitting To separate a single cell into two or more cells.

stack A set of graphics that overlap each other.

status bar A line of information related to the current program. The status bar is usually located at the bottom of a window. Not all windows have a status bar.

subpoint A subordinate item below a bullet point in a list.

tab (ribbon) An organizational element of the ribbon that displays related groups of buttons.

table One or more rows of cells commonly used to display numbers and other items for quick reference and analysis. Items in a table are organized into rows and columns.

tag A text string used in HTML and XML to identify a page element's type, format, or appearance. Many elements have start and end tags that define where the element starts and stops.

template A file that can contain predefined formatting, layout, text, or graphics, and that serves as the basis for new presentations with a similar design or purpose.

text box A movable, resizable container used to give text a different orientation from other text on the slide.

theme A set of unified design elements that combine color, fonts, and graphics to provide a professional look for a presentation.

Thesaurus A feature that looks up alternative words, or *synonyms*, for a word.

thumbnail A small representation of an item, such as an image, a page of content, or a set of formatting, obtained by scaling a snapshot of it. Thumbnails are typically used to provide visual identifiers for related items.

tick-mark A small line of measurement, similar to a division line on a ruler, that intersects an axis in a chart.

title A name you designate for a slide in the title placeholder.

title bar The horizontal bar at the top of a window that contains the name of the window. Most title bars also contain boxes or buttons for closing and resizing the window.

title slide The introductory slide in a presentation.

transition An effect that specifies how the display changes as you move from one slide to another.

View Shortcuts toolbar The toolbar at the right end of the status bar with tools you can use to change the view of the open presentation.

Web browser Software that interprets HTML files, formats them into Web pages, and displays them. A Web browser, such as Internet Explorer, can follow hyperlinks, transfer files, and play sound or video files that are embedded in Web pages.

WordArt object A text object you create with ready-made effects to which you can apply additional formatting options.

x-axis Also called a *category axis*, the axis for grouping data in a chart, usually the horizontal axis.

y-axis Also called a *value axis*, the axis for plotting values in a chart, usually the vertical axis.

z-axis Also called a *series axis*, the optical axis that is perpendicular to the x-axis and y-axis, usually the "floor."

Keyboard Shortcuts

This section presents a comprehensive list of all keyboard shortcuts built into Microsoft PowerPoint 2010. The list has been excerpted from PowerPoint Help and formatted in tables for convenient look up. Some of these shortcuts might not be available for your edition of PowerPoint 2010 or for your keyboard layout.

Keyboard Shortcut Lists from PowerPoint Help

In the following lists, keys you press at the same time are separated by a plus sign (+), and keys you press sequentially are separated by a comma (,).

Microsoft Office General Tasks

Display and Use Windows

Action	Keyboard shortcut
Switch to the next window.	Alt+Tab
Switch to the previous window.	Alt+Shift+Tab
Close the active window.	Ctrl+W or Ctrl+F4
Restore the size of the active window after you maximize it.	Alt+F5
Move to a task pane from another pane in the program window (clockwise direction). You may need to press F6 more than once.	F6
Move to a task pane from another pane in the program window (counterclockwise direction).	Shift+F6
When more than one window is open, switch to the next window.	Ctrl+F6
Switch to the previous window.	Ctrl+Shift+F6
Maximize or restore a selected window.	Ctrl+F10
Copy a picture of the screen to the Clipboard.	Print Screen
Copy a picture of the selected window to the Clipboard.	Alt+Print Screen

Change or Resize the Font

Tip The cursor needs to be inside a text box to use these shortcuts.

Action	Keyboard shortcut
Change the font.	Ctrl+Shift+F
Change the font size.	Ctrl+Shift+P
Increase the font size of the selected text.	Ctrl+Shift+>
Decrease the font size of the selected text.	Ctrl+Shift+<
Change the font.	Ctrl+Shift+F

Move Around in Text or Cells

Action	Keyboard shortcut
Move one character to the left.	Left Arrow
Move one character to the right.	Right Arrow
Move one line up.	Up Arrow
Move one line down.	Down Arrow
Move one word to the left.	Ctrl+Left Arrow
Move one word to the right.	Ctrl+Right Arrow
Move to the end of a line.	End
Move to the beginning of a line.	Home
Move up one paragraph.	Ctrl+Up Arrow
Move down one paragraph.	Ctrl+Down Arrow
Move to the end of a text box.	Ctrl+End
Move to the beginning of a text box.	Ctrl+Home
Move to the next title or body text placeholder. (If it is the last placeholder on the slide, inserts a new slide with the same slide layout as the original slide.)	Ctrl+Enter
Repeat the last Find action.	Shift+F4

Find and Replace

Action	Keyboard shortcut
Open the Find dialog box.	Ctrl+F
Open the Replace dialog box.	Ctrl+H
Repeat the last Find action.	Shift+F4

Move Around and Work in Tables

Action	Keyboard shortcut
Move to the next cell.	Tab
Move to the preceding cell.	Shift+Tab
Move to the next row.	Down Arrow
Move to the preceding row.	Up Arrow
Insert a tab in a cell.	Ctrl+Tab
Start a new paragraph.	Enter
Add a new row at the bottom of the table.	Tab at the end of the last row

Access and Use Task Panes

Action	Keyboard shortcut
Move to a task pane from another pane in the program window. (You may need to press F6 more than once.)	F6
When a task pane is active, select the next or previous option in the task pane, respectively.	Tab, Shift+Tab
Display the full set of commands on the task pane menu.	Ctrl+Down Arrow
Move among choices on a selected submenu; move among certain options in a group of options in a dialog box.	Down Arrow or Up Arrow
Open the selected menu, or perform the action assigned to the selected button.	Spacebar or Enter
Open a shortcut menu; open a drop-down menu for the selected gallery item.	Shift+F10
When a menu or submenu is visible, select the first or last command, respectively, on the menu or submenu.	Home, End
Scroll up or down in the selected gallery list, respectively.	Page Up, Page Down
Move to the top or bottom of the selected gallery list, respectively.	Home, End
Close a task pane.	Ctrl+Spacebar, C
Open the Microsoft Office Clipboard.	Alt+H, F, O

Resize a Task Pane

1. In the task pane, press Ctrl+Spacebar to display a menu of additional commands.

2. Use the Down Arrow key to select the Size command, and then press Enter.

3. Use the Arrow keys to resize the task pane. Use Ctrl+ the Arrow keys to resize one pixel at a time.

Tip When you finish resizing, press Esc.

Use Dialog Boxes

Action	Keyboard shortcut
Move to the next option or option group.	Tab
Move to the previous option or option group.	Shift+Tab
Switch to the next tab in a dialog box. (A tab must already be selected in an open dialog box.)	Down Arrow
Switch to the previous tab in a dialog box. (A tab must already be selected in an open dialog box.)	Up Arrow
Open a selected drop-down list.	Down Arrow, Alt+Down Arrow
Open the list if it is closed and move to an option in the list.	First letter of an option in a drop-down list
Move between options in an open drop-down list, or between options in a group of options.	Up Arrow, Down Arrow
Perform the action assigned to the selected button; select or clear the selected check box.	Spacebar
Select an option; select or clear a check box.	The letter underlined in an option
Perform the action assigned to a default button in a dialog box.	Enter
Close a selected drop-down list; cancel a command and close a dialog box.	Esc

Use Edit Boxes Within Dialog Boxes

An edit box is a blank box in which you type or paste an entry, such as your user name or the path of a folder.

Action	Keyboard shortcut
Move to the beginning of the entry.	Home
Move to the end of the entry.	End
Move one character to the left or right, respectively.	Left Arrow, Right Arrow
Move one word to the left.	Ctrl+Left Arrow
Move one word to the right.	Ctrl+Right Arrow
Select or cancel selection one character to the left.	Shift+Left Arrow
Select or cancel selection one character to the right.	Shift+Right Arrow
Select or cancel selection one word to the left.	Ctrl+Shift+Left Arrow
Select or cancel selection one word to the right.	Ctrl+Shift+Right Arrow
Select from the cursor to the beginning of the entry.	Shift+Home
Select from the cursor to the end of the entry.	Shift+End

Use the Open and Save As Dialog Boxes

Action	Keyboard shortcut
Open the Open dialog box.	Alt+F then O
Open the Save As dialog box.	Alt+F then A
Move between options in an open drop-down list, or between options in a group of options.	Arrow keys
Display a shortcut menu for a selected item, such as a folder or file.	Shift+F10
Move between options or areas in the dialog box.	Tab
Open the file path drop-down menu.	F4 or Alt+I
Refresh the file list.	F5

Navigating the Ribbon

Access Any Command with a Few Keystrokes

1. Press Alt.

   The KeyTips are displayed over each feature that is available in the current view.

2. Press the letter shown in the KeyTip over the feature that you want to use.

3. Depending on which letter you press, you may be shown additional KeyTips. For example, if the Home tab is active and you press N, the Insert tab is displayed, along with the KeyTips for the groups on that tab.

4. Continue pressing letters until you press the letter of the command or control that you want to use. In some cases, you must first press the letter of the group that contains the command. For example, if the Home tab is active, pressing Alt+H, F, S will take you to the Size list box in the Font group.

Tip To cancel the action and hide the KeyTips, press Alt.

Change the Keyboard Focus Without Using the Mouse

Action	Keyboard shortcut
Select the active tab of the ribbon and activate the access keys.	Alt or F10. Press either of these keys again to move back to the presentation and cancel the access keys.
Move left or right to another tab of the ribbon, respectively.	F10 to select the active tab, and then Left Arrow, Right Arrow
Hide or show the ribbon.	Ctrl+F1
Display the shortcut menu for the selected command.	Shift+F10
Move the focus to select each of the following areas of the window: ● Active tab of the ribbon ● Any open task panes ● Your document	F6
Move the focus to each command on the ribbon, forward or backward respectively.	Tab, Shift+Tab
Move down, up, left, or right among the items on the ribbon, respectively.	Down Arrow, Up Arrow, Left Arrow, Right Arrow
Activate the selected command or control on the ribbon.	Spacebar or Enter
Open the selected menu or gallery on the ribbon.	Spacebar or Enter

Action	Keyboard shortcut
Activate a command or control on the ribbon so you can modify a value.	Enter
Finish modifying a value in a control on the ribbon, and move the focus back to the document.	Enter
Get help on the selected command or control on the ribbon. (If no Help topic is associated with the selected command, a general Help topic about the program is shown instead.)	F1

Common Tasks in PowerPoint

Move Between Panes

Action	Keyboard shortcut
Move clockwise among panes in Normal view.	F6
Move counterclockwise among panes in Normal view.	Shift+F6
Switch between Slides and Outline tabs in the Outline and Slides pane in Normal view.	Ctrl+Shift+Tab

Work in an Outline

Action	Keyboard shortcut
Promote a paragraph.	Alt+Shift+Left Arrow
Demote a paragraph.	Alt+Shift+Right Arrow
Move selected paragraphs up.	Alt+Shift+Up Arrow
Move selected paragraphs down.	Alt+Shift+Down Arrow
Show heading level 1.	Alt+Shift+1
Expand text below a heading.	Alt+Shift+Plus Sign
Collapse text below a heading.	Alt+Shift+Minus Sign

Work with Shapes, Pictures, Boxes, Objects, and WordArt

Insert a Shape

1. Press and release Alt, then N, then S, and then H to select Shapes.

2. Use the Arrow keys to move through the categories of shapes, and select the shape that you want.

3. Press Ctrl+Enter to insert the shape that you selected.

Insert a Text Box

1. Press and release Alt, then N, and then X.

2. Press Ctrl+Enter to insert the text box.

Insert An Object

1. Press and release Alt, then N, and then J to select Object.

2. Use the Arrow keys to move through the objects.

3. Press Ctrl+Enter to insert the object that you want.

Insert WordArt

1. Press and release Alt, then N, and then W to select WordArt.

2. Use the Arrow keys to select the WordArt style that you want, and then press Enter.

3. Type the text that you want.

Select a Shape

Tip If your cursor is within text, press Esc.

- To select a single shape, press the Tab key to cycle forward (or Shift+Tab to cycle backward) through the objects until sizing handles appear on the object that you want to select.

- To select multiple items, use the Selection And Visibility task pane.

Group or Ungroup Shapes, Pictures, and WordArt Objects

- To group shapes, pictures, or WordArt objects, select the items that you want to group, and then press Ctrl+G.

- To ungroup a group, select the group, and then press Ctrl+Shift+G.

Show or Hide a Grid or Guides

Action	Keyboard shortcut
Show or hide the grid.	Shift+F9
Show or hide guides.	Alt+F9

Copy the Attributes of a Shape

1. Select the shape with the attributes that you want to copy.

   Tip If you select a shape with text, you copy the look and style of the text in addition to the attributes of the shape.

2. Press Ctrl+Shift+C to copy the object attributes.

3. Press the Tab key or Shift+Tab to select the object that you want to copy the attributes to.

4. Press Ctrl+Shift+V.

Select Text and Objects

Action	Keyboard shortcut
Select one character to the right.	Shift+Right Arrow
Select one character to the left.	Shift+Left Arrow
Select to the end of a word.	Ctrl+Shift+Right Arrow
Select to the beginning of a word.	Ctrl+Shift+Left Arrow
Select one line up (with the cursor at the beginning of a line).	Shift+Up Arrow
Select one line down (with the cursor at the beginning of a line).	Shift+Down Arrow
Select an object (when the text inside the object is selected).	Esc
Select another object (when one object is selected).	Tab or Shift+Tab until the object you want is selected
Select text within an object (with an object selected).	Enter
Select all objects.	Ctrl+A (on the Slides tab)
Select all slides.	Ctrl+A (in Slide Sorter view)
Select all text.	Ctrl+A (on the Outline tab)

Delete and Copy Text and Objects

Action	Keyboard shortcut
Delete one character to the left.	Backspace
Delete one word to the left.	Ctrl+Backspace
Delete one character to the right.	Delete
Delete one word to the right. (The cursor must be between words to do this.)	Ctrl+Delete
Cut selected object or text.	Ctrl+X
Copy selected object or text.	Ctrl+C
Paste cut or copied object or text.	Ctrl+V
Undo the last action.	Ctrl+Z
Redo the last action.	Ctrl+Y

(continued)

Action	Keyboard shortcut
Copy formatting only.	Ctrl+Shift+C
Paste formatting only.	Ctrl+Shift+V
Open the Paste Special dialog box.	Ctrl+Alt+V

Move Around in Text

Action	Keyboard shortcut
Move one character to the left.	Left Arrow
Move one character to the right.	Right Arrow
Move one line up.	Up Arrow
Move one line down.	Down Arrow
Move one word to the left.	Ctrl+Left Arrow
Move one word to the right.	Ctrl+Right Arrow
Move to the end of a line.	End
Move to the beginning of a line.	Home
Move up one paragraph.	Ctrl+Up Arrow
Move down one paragraph.	Ctrl+Down Arrow
Move to the end of a text box.	Ctrl+End
Move to the beginning of a text box.	Ctrl+Home
Move to the next title or body text placeholder. If it is the last placeholder on a slide, this will insert a new slide with the same slide layout as the original slide.	Ctrl+Enter
Move to repeat the last Find action.	Shift+F4

Move Around in and Work on Tables

Action	Keyboard shortcut
Move to the next cell.	Tab
Move to the preceding cell.	Shift+Tab
Move to the next row.	Down Arrow
Move to the preceding row.	Up Arrow
Insert a tab in a cell.	Ctrl+Tab
Start a new paragraph.	Enter
Add a new row at the bottom of the table.	Tab at the end of the last row

Edit a Linked or Embedded Object

1. Press Tab or Shift+Tab to select the object that you want.

2. Press Shift+F10 for the shortcut menu.

3. Press the Down Arrow until Worksheet Object is selected, press the Right Arrow to select Edit, and then press Enter.

Tip The name of the command in the shortcut menu depends on the type of embedded or linked object. For example, an embedded Microsoft Excel worksheet has the command *Worksheet Object*, whereas an embedded Microsoft Visio Drawing has the command *Visio Object*.

Format and Align Characters and Paragraphs

Change or Resize the Font

Action	Keyboard shortcut
Open the Font dialog box to change the font.	Ctrl+Shift+F
Increase the font size.	Ctrl+Shift+>
Decrease the font size.	Ctrl+Shift+<

Apply Character Formats

Action	Keyboard shortcut
Open the Font dialog box to change the formatting of characters.	Ctrl+T
Change the case of letters between sentence, lowercase, or uppercase.	Shift+F3
Apply bold formatting.	Ctrl+B
Apply an underline.	Ctrl+U
Apply italic formatting.	Ctrl+I
Apply subscript formatting (automatic spacing).	Ctrl+Equal Sign
Apply superscript formatting (automatic spacing).	Ctrl+Shift+Plus Sign
Remove manual character formatting, such as subscript and superscript.	Ctrl+Spacebar
Insert a hyperlink.	Ctrl+K

Copy Text Formats

Action	Keyboard shortcut
Copy formats.	Ctrl+Shift+C
Paste formats.	Ctrl+Shift+V

Align Paragraphs

Action	Keyboard shortcut
Center a paragraph.	Ctrl+E
Justify a paragraph.	Ctrl+J
Left-align a paragraph.	Ctrl+L
Right-align a paragraph.	Ctrl+R

Run a Presentation

Slide Show Shortcuts

Action	Keyboard shortcut
Start a presentation from the beginning.	F5
Perform the next animation or advance to the next slide.	N, Enter, Page Down, Right Arrow, Down Arrow, or Spacebar
Perform the previous animation or return to the previous slide.	P, Page Up, Left Arrow, Up Arrow, or Backspace
Go to a specific slide number.	Number+Enter
Display a blank black slide, or return to the presentation from a blank black slide.	B or Period
Display a blank white slide, or return to the presentation from a blank white slide.	W or Comma
Stop or restart an automatic presentation.	S
End a presentation.	Esc or Hyphen
Erase on-screen annotations.	E
Go to the next slide, if the next slide is hidden.	H
Set new timings while rehearsing.	T

Action	Keyboard shortcut
Use original timings while rehearsing.	O
Use mouse-click to advance while rehearsing.	M
Re-record slide narration and timing.	R
Return to the first slide.	Press and hold right and left mouse buttons for 2 seconds
Show or hide the arrow pointer.	A or =
Change the pointer to a pen.	Ctrl+P
Change the pointer to an arrow.	Ctrl+A
Change the pointer to an eraser.	Ctrl+E
Show or hide ink markup.	Ctrl+M
Hide the pointer and navigation button immediately.	Ctrl+H
Hide the pointer and navigation button in 15 seconds.	Ctrl+U
View the All Slides dialog box.	Ctrl+S
View the computer task bar.	Ctrl+T
Display the shortcut menu.	Shift+F10
Go to the first or next hyperlink on a slide.	Tab
Go to the last or previous hyperlink on a slide.	Shift+Tab
Perform the "mouse click" behavior of the selected hyperlink.	Enter while a hyperlink is selected

Media Shortcuts During Presentation

Action	Keyboard shortcut
Stop media playback.	Alt+Q
Toggle between play and pause.	Alt+P
Go to the next bookmark.	Alt+End
Go to the previous bookmark.	Alt+Home
Increase the sound volume.	Alt+Up
Decrease the sound volume.	Alt+Down
Seek forward.	Alt+Shift+Page Down
Seek backward.	Alt+Shift+Page Up
Mute the sound.	Alt+U

Tip You can press F1 during your presentation to see a list of controls.

Use the Selection And Visibility Task Pane

To open the Selection And Visibility task pane, press Alt, then H, then S, then L, and then P.

Action	Keyboard shortcut
Cycle the focus through the different panes.	F6
Display the context menu.	Shift+F10
Move the focus to a single item or group.	Up Arrow or Down Arrow
Move the focus from an item in a group to its parent group.	Left Arrow
Move the focus from a group to the first item in that group.	Right Arrow
Expand a focused group and all its child groups.	* (on numeric keypad only)
Expand a focused group.	+ (on numeric keypad only)
Collapse a focused group.	- (on numeric keypad only)
Move the focus to an item and select it.	Shift+Up Arrow or Shift+Down Arrow
Select a focused item.	Spacebar or Enter
Cancel selection of a focused item.	Shift+Spacebar or Shift+Enter
Move a selected item forward.	Ctrl+Shift+F
Move a selected item backward.	Ctrl+Shift+B
Show or hide a focused item.	Ctrl+Shift+S
Rename a focused item.	F2
Switch the keyboard focus within the Selection And Visibility task pane between tree view and the Show All and Hide All buttons.	Tab or Shift+Tab
Collapse all groups. (The focus must be in the tree view of the Selection And Visibility task pane to use this shortcut.)	Alt+Shift+1
Expand all groups.	Alt+Shift+9

Index

A

C

N

O

T

About the Authors

Joyce Cox

Joyce has 30 years' experience in the development of training materials about technical subjects for non-technical audiences, and is the author of dozens of books about Office and Windows technologies. She is the Vice President of Online Training Solutions, Inc. (OTSI).

As President of and principal author for Online Press, she developed the *Quick Course* series of computer training books for beginning and intermediate adult learners. She was also the first managing editor of Microsoft Press, an editor for Sybex, and an editor for the University of California.

Joan Preppernau

Joan has worked in the training and certification industry for 13 years. As President of OTSI, Joan is responsible for guiding the translation of technical information and requirements into useful, relevant, and measurable training and certification tools.

Joan is a Microsoft Office Master (MOM), a Microsoft Certified Application Specialist (MCAS), a Microsoft Certified Technology Specialist (MCTS), a Microsoft Certified Trainer (MCT), and the author of more than two dozen books about Windows and Office (for Windows and Mac).

The Team

This book would not exist without the support of these hard-working members of the OTSI publishing team:

- Kathleen Atkins
- Jan Bednarczuk
- Jenny Moss Benson
- Rob Carr
- Susie Carr
- Jeanne Craver
- Patty Gardner
- Elizabeth Hansford
- Kathy Krause
- Marlene Lambert
- Patty Masserman
- Brianna Morgan
- Jaime Odell
- Jean Trenary
- Liv Trenary
- Elisabeth Van Every

We are especially thankful to the support staff at home who make it possible for our team members to devote their time and attention to these projects.

Devon Musgrave provided invaluable support on behalf of Microsoft Learning.

Online Training Solutions, Inc. (OTSI)

OTSI specializes in the design, creation, and production of Office and Windows training products for information workers and home computer users. For more information about OTSI, visit:

www.otsi.com

What do you think of this book?

We want to hear from you!

To participate in a brief online survey, please visit:

microsoft.com/learning/booksurvey

Tell us how well this book meets your needs—what works effectively, and what we can do better. Your feedback will help us continually improve our books and learning resources for you.

Thank you in advance for your input!

Stay in touch!

To subscribe to the *Microsoft Press® Book Connection Newsletter*—for news on upcoming books, events, and special offers—please visit:

microsoft.com/learning/books/newsletter